rebellion in the wilderness

george w. coats

THE MURMURING MOTIF IN THE WILDERNESS
TRADITIONS OF THE OLD TESTAMENT

rebellion in the wilderness

NASHVILLE • ABINGDON PRESS • NEW YORK

to sandy

preface

The purpose for publishing this monograph is to present the results of research on the murmuring tradition in the Old Testament to colleagues, students, and others who may have an interest in specialized biblical exegesis. With financial assistance from a grant made available through the Fulbright-Kommission in Bad Godesberg, West Germany, the major portion of research for the monograph was conducted at the Georg-August-Universität in Göttingen, West Germany. I am especially indebted to Professor D. theol. Walther Zimmerli of the university in Göttingen for suggestions and encouragement while the work was in progress and for time freely given in spite of a busy schedule as Rektor of the university. I would also cite in appreciation Prof. Brevard S. Childs of Yale University, New Haven, Connecticut, whose seminars introduced me to the methods of current biblical studies as well as problems in pentateuchal research. Finally, for patiently listening

7

to numerous versions of sentences and passages from the project, and for faithfully typing three drafts, I express my gratitude to my wife. Without her encouragement and help, the project would have been less exciting and more difficult to complete.

GEORGE W. COATS

contents

abbreviations

AJSL	*American Journal of Semitic Language and Literature*
ATANT	*Abhandlungen zur Theologie des Alten und Neuen Testaments*
ATD	*Das Alte Testament Deutsch*
BA	*Biblical Archaeologist*
BASOR	*Bulletin of the American Schools of Oriental Research*
Bib	*Biblica*
BKAT	*Biblischer Kommentar, Altes Testament*
BWANT	*Beiträge zur Wissenschaft vom Alten und Neuen Testament*
BZAW	*Beihefte zur Zeitschrift für die alttestamentliche Wissenschaft*
CBQ	*Catholic Biblical Quarterly*
FRLANT	*Forschungen zur Religion und Literatur des Alten und Neuen Testaments*
Ges.K.	*Gesenius' Hebrew Grammar* (Kautzsch)

HAT	*Handbuch zum Alten Testament*
HKAT	*Handkommentar zum Alten Testament*
HSAT	*Die Heilige Schrift des Alten Testaments*
ICC	*International Critical Commentary*
JAOS	*Journal of the American Oriental Society*
JBL	*Journal of Biblical Literature*
JSS	*Journal of Semitic Studies*
JTS	*Journal of Theological Studies*
KAT	*Kommentar zum Alten Testament*
KHAT	*Kurzer Hand-Commentar zum Alten Testament*
LXX	Septuagint
MSS	Manuscripts
MT	Masoretic Text
OLZ	*Orientalistische Literaturzeitung*
OTL	*Old Testament Library*
Sam.Pent.	Samaritan Pentateuch
SAT	*Die Schriften des Alten Testaments*
SBT	*Studies in Biblical Theology*
TSK	*Theologische Studien und Kritiken*
VT	*Vetus Testamentum*
VT Sup	*Vetus Testamentum Supplements*
Vul	Vulgate
WMANT	*Wissenschaftliche Monographien zum Alten und Neuen Testament*
ZAW	*Zeitschrift für die alttestamentliche Wissenschaft*
ZThK	*Zeitschrift für Theologie und Kirche*
2.m.s.	Second person, masculine, singular
3.f.pl.	Third person, feminine, plural
	(Any combination of these categories may appear.)

introduction

Old Testament descriptions of Israel's relationship with Yahweh during the wilderness wandering range widely between positive and negative poles. Jer. 2:2, for example, depicts the wilderness period as a time of Israel's faithful devotion to Yahweh, devotion comparable to bridal love, while Ezek. 20:10 ff. views the same period as an age of Israel's most grievous rebellion against Yahweh. The relationship between these two apparently conflicting points of view constitutes one of the principal problems now confronting Old Testament scholarship.

Gerhard von Rad observes that the positive category of descriptions is characterized by a confessional style which features an "exclusive concentration upon the action of God." [1] The negative pole he then considers a product of reflection about that action: "The more Israel came to regard Jahweh's leadership through the wilderness as an extremely marvellous event, the more urgent became the question: how did she stand up to the test during the period? The answer becomes more and more negative till it reaches the devastating

---

[1] Gerhard von Rad, *Old Testament Theology*, tr. D. M. G. Stalker (New York: Harper & Row, 1962), I, 281.

13

verdict expressed in Ezek. 20." [2] Particularly in the Hexateuch, according to von Rad, the negative reflection belongs to a later stage of the wilderness traditions.[3] But did the earliest form of those traditions recount nothing of Israel's response to Yahweh's deeds?

Christoph Barth sharpens the issue: "Ist die These haltbar, dass ein frühes Stadium der Traditionsgeschichte den 'negativen' Aspekt der Wüstenzeit überhaupt nicht gekannt habe?" [4] He establishes clearly that pre-exilic texts, some dating from the middle or perhaps the early period of the monarchy, do indeed reflect a negative view of the wilderness wandering.[5] But negative descriptions in pre-exilic texts do not permit a priori the conclusion that all pre-exilic texts fall into that category.[6] Quite the contrary, the issue is focused just at this point: Is there any evidence for a positive description of the period alongside, or perhaps prior to, the rather early appearance of negative aspects? And if so, does the evidence suggest that the positive and negative points of view were mutually complementary strands? [7] Or did the two exist in some sense as independent traditions, or perhaps as contradictory poles?

References to a "positive point of view" in these questions must not be confused with the discussion of a so-called "nomadic ideal." [8] Recent examination of the "nomadic ideal" hypothesis has seriously challenged the validity of the initial

---

[2] *Ibid.*, pp. 282-83.

[3] *Ibid.*, p. 284.

[4] Christoph Barth, "Zur Bedeutung der Wüstentradition," *Volume du Congrès Genève; VT Sup* xv (Leiden: E. J. Brill, 1966), 20.

[5] *Ibid.*, p. 21.

[6] Cf. Barth's conclusion, p. 23: "So scheint es an Zeugnissen für eine radikal 'negative' Betrachtungsweise der Wüstentradition aus vorexilischer und vorprophetischer Zeit doch nicht ganz zu fehlen. Dieser negative Aspekt ist je und je in anderer Weise gesehen worden, aber eine Wüstentradition *ohne* negativen Aspekt hat es m. E. in Israel gar nie gegeben."

[7] So, S. Talmon, "The 'Desert Motif' in the Bible and in Qumran Literature," *Biblical Motifs, Origins and Transformations*, ed. A. Altmann (Cambridge: Harvard University Press, 1966), pp. 47-48.

[8] For a brief survey of the discussion, cf. Talmon, pp. 31 ff.

argument and its subsequent applications.[9] But arguments against a "nomadic ideal" cannot be employed as arguments against a positive description of Israel's relationship with Yahweh during the wilderness wandering. We agree, for example, that Jer. 2:2 and Hos. 2:17 cannot be construed as "the nucleus of a reputed 'desert ideal.' " [10] The imagery in these texts does not arise from an idealized conception of life in the wilderness or nostalgia for a desert society. But it does describe the *relationship* between Yahweh and Israel during the wilderness wandering.[11] And that relationship is basically positive.

Since particularly in the Pentateuch the wilderness traditions are dominated by the negative pole, it seems methodologically sound to begin our study here. Moreover, the negative pole is characterized by a motif which presents the wilderness generation as a people who "murmured" about the circumstances of their life. We shall thus limit the scope of our discussion to an analysis of the murmuring motif in the wilderness traditions of the Old Testament.[12]

Martin Noth defines the murmuring as "ein stereotyp gewordenes Erzählungsmotiv innerhalb des Themas 'Führung in der Wüste,' . . . dessen ständig in ziemlich gleicher Form erfolgendes Auftreten schon zeigt, dass es in den meisten Fällen ein erst nachträglich in die Einzelerzählungen eingegangenes Element darstellt." [13] But if the murmuring is indeed a secondary motif in the various wilderness narratives, what was the nature of those narratives before they were associated with the murmuring? And why would the murmuring have

[9] Paul Riemann, *Desert and Return to Desert in Pre-Exilic Prophets* (unpublished dissertation, Harvard University, 1964), pp. 55 ff.; Talmon, pp. 34 ff.

[10] Talmon, p. 48.

[11] Neither Talmon nor Riemann maintains clear distinctions between these two subjects, and as a consequence, the argument against a "nomadic ideal," which seems quite cogent to me, loses valuable precision.

[12] We thus exclude relevant texts in the New Testament, rabbinic sources, and Qumran literature.

[13] Martin Noth, *Überlieferungsgeschichte des Pentateuch* (Stuttgart: W. Kohlhammer Verlag, 1948), p. 136.

been incorporated with them? Noth suggests: "This motif has its roots in the realization of the miserable conditions of life in the wilderness with its constant privations, above all the shortage of food and water." [14] Frank Schnutenhaus develops a similar position: "Man kam auf dies Motiv bei der Durchdenkung der typischen Wüstensituation." [15] He then argues that the murmuring was cast into a theological schema: "Gottes Rettung—Israels Undank—Gottes Strafe, bzw., meist Rettung." [16] Israel murmurs in spite of God's salvation expressed through the Exodus, and God responds to that murmuring by meeting their needs, mercifully "overlooking" the murmuring itself, or on occasion by exacting punishment against the murmurers.

But the schema oversimplifies the motif. We cannot simply assume that Yahweh's response by meeting Israel's need and his punishment for Israel's murmuring are mutually complementary themes. Indeed, the incongruous picture of Yahweh alternating between aid and punishment suggests that the two themes belong to quite different levels of the wilderness traditions.[17] Would it not be possible, if that were the case, to suggest that Yahweh's gracious response to Israel places Israel, not in a negative light as murmurer, but in a positive light as faithful devotee (cf. Jer. 2:2)? Could it not be the confession of Yahweh's aid which has its roots in the miserable conditions of wilderness life? And if so, must we

---

[14] Martin Noth, *Exodus, a Commentary;* tr. J. S. Bowden. *OTL* (Philadelphia: The Westminster Press, 1962), p. 128. Cf. also Eberhard von Waldow, *Der traditionsgeschichtliche Hintergrund der prophetischen Gerichtsreden; BZAW* LXXXV (Berlin: Alfred Töpelmann, 1963), 33-34; H.-H. Mallau, *Die theologische Bedeutung der Wüste im Alten Testament* (unpublished dissertation, Kiel, 1963), p. 35.

[15] Frank Schnutenhaus, *Die Entstehung der Mosetraditionen* (unpublished dissertation, Heidelberg, 1958), p. 129.

[16] *Ibid.,* pp. 131-32.

[17] Robert Bach, *Die Erwählung Israels in der Wüste* (unpublished dissertation, Bonn, 1951), p. 1, contends that the positive tradition reflected in Hosea, *et al.,* is completely independent of the murmuring—and aid—in the Pentateuch, thus denying that the two themes could represent different levels of tradition. But to eliminate this possibility too quickly begs the question.

see both themes as products of the same roots? Or does the murmuring motif reflect a different origin, with different goals stimulating its formulation? Does it constitute a specific and distinct tradition with a specific and distinct *Sitz-im-Leben*?

Our procedure in offering answers for these questions will be governed by the methods of traditio-historical analysis.[18] Our purpose is not to raise questions about the historical accuracy of the motif; i.e., we shall not ask whether the people actually murmured during the wilderness period. Rather, we shall be concerned to discover how and why successive generations of Israelites remembered their fathers in the wilderness as murmurers. We do not thereby deny the importance of historiography; quite the contrary, we recognize simply that the historical accuracy of sources cannot be determined until the nature of the traditions in those sources has been clarified.

---

[18] References to the wilderness traditions or the Wilderness theme throughout this monograph must be understood in the strict sense set forth by Noth, *Überlieferungsgeschichte*, pp. 48-67, viz., distinguished from the Patriarchal, Exodus, Sinai, and Conquest themes.

PART I
lexical and form-critical analyses

lexical analysis

One of the most characteristic collocations of the murmuring motif is the vocable לון with the preposition עַל. With one exception, Josh. 9:18 ff., this combination is to be found only in the Pentateuch (Exod. 15:24; 16:2, 7, 8; 17:3; Num. 14:2, 27, 29, 36; 16:11; 17:6, 20, and as a substantive, Exod. 16:7, 8, 9, 12; Num. 14:27; 17:20, 25). Of these various occurrences, only Exod. 15:24 and 17:3 are not a part of the P narrative. Exod. 15:24 is commonly assigned to J, while Exod. 17:3 is questionable and for convenience may be assigned to JE. These two texts are especially valuable for our study since they establish that the murmuring motif is not simply the creation of P but was in fact already a part of the tradition which P received.

The etymology of לון is uncertain. Nöldeke suggested that since many of the verbal forms in this complex are written defectively in the Samaritan Pentateuch, they may derive from an original double *'ayin* root, thus לָנַן.[1] This hypothesis is

---

[1] Theodor Nöldeke, *Beiträge zur semitischen Sprachwissenschaft* (Strassburg: Karl J. Trübner, 1904) , p. 42, n. 2. Cf. also W. Gesenius, *Hebräisches und aramäisches Handwörterbuch*, ed. Frants Buhl, *et al.* (14th ed., revised; Leipzig: F. C. W. Vogel, 1921) , p. 345.

weakened by the absence of clear occurrences of the root in either the Old Testament or other ancient sources. But it does raise the possibility that some linguistic connection may exist between our word and the more widely used root רנן since on occasion the consonants *lamed* and *reš* interchange,[2] and in late Hebrew the Pi'el stem of רנן is used in reference to past events of Israel's murmuring.[3] But the evidence to support such a connection is at best tenuous. It seems advisable, therefore, to accept the position of recent lexicographers who consider the verb under discussion to be from a middle weak root.[4] There is apparently no connection between the middle *waw* root and a middle *yod* root, לין, normally translated "to pass the night." We conclude, then, that the root for our word is a middle *waw*, thus לון.

The appearance of this root in extra-biblical sources is rare and questionable. Köhler-Baumgartner suggest some contact with the Arabic word *l(y)m*, to blame. But the final *mem* instead of *nun* renders this hypothesis improbable.[5] S. Herrmann has argued more cogently that the obscure verb in line 10 of the inscription of King Kilamuwa from Sengirli is to be interpreted as a Hithpolel form from our root.[6] He supports his argument by the close parallel between this text and Ps. 59:15-16. But it is not clear that וילינו in vs. 16 of this psalm should be interpreted as murmuring, at least in the same sense which can be attributed to the occurrences of לון cited above. The strongest evidence in favor of such a reading is the LXX translation of the text with γογγύσουσιν, the verb nor-

---

[2] Carl Brockelmann, *Grundriss der vergleichenden Grammatik der semitischen Sprachen* (Berlin: Reuther und Reichard, 1908), pp. 136 ff.

[3] The primary meaning of the verb from this root is "to cry aloud." Cf. Arabic *rnn*. But a more primitive connotation for this verb may be "the twang of a bowstring." Cf. Francis Brown, S. R. Driver, and C. A. Briggs, eds., *A Hebrew and English Lexicon of the Old Testament* (3rd ed.; Oxford: The Clarendon Press, 1957), p. 943.

[4] Ludwig Köhler and W. Baumgartner, *Lexicon in Veteris Testamenti Libros* (Leiden: E. J. Brill, 1953), p. 477; Brown, Driver, and Briggs, p. 534.

[5] But cf. Ugaritic *pʿn* and its Hebrew cognate, פעם.

[6] S. Herrmann, "Bemerkungen zur Inschrift des Königs Kilamuwa von Sengirli," *OLZ* VII (1953), 295-97.

mally used by the LXX for לון. Yet despite this witness, many
lexicographers are unconvinced. Brown, Driver, and Briggs,
for example, prefer to read "to pass the night," thus, לין.[7]
On the basis of the parallel in vss. 6-7, unfortunately without
the word לון, and the parallel in the Kilamuwa inscription,
this translation appears to be inadequate. The context in
both cases demands accord with יהמו in vs. 15, i.e., the sound
of discontented dogs. This might be best rendered by "growl,"
and perhaps here we have some insight into the original
meaning of the word.

This meaning would not be foreign to the murmuring
motif. But the juxtaposition of לון with the preposition על
gives the verb in the murmuring motif a somewhat more
specialized connotation. The verb appears regularly in either
a Niph'al or a Hiph'il stem, construed either as a plural or
singular perfect or imperfect, or as a plural participle. On
occasion, the stem in the MT is changed by either the Samaritan Pentateuch or the Qere to the other stem without apparent
shift in meaning (cf. Exod. 16:2, 7; Num. 14:36; 16:11), suggesting that the connotations of the two stems are indistin-
guishable.[8] To be sure, in one instance (Num. 14:36), the
Hiph'il designates a causative. But the causative does not
change the basic meaning which the verb otherwise carries
in both Niph'al and Hiph'il. The traditional translation of
the verb is "to murmur." This English equivalent is defined
by *The Interpreter's Dictionary of the Bible* as "to express
dissatisfaction or anger by subdued, often inarticulate, and
always resentful complaint." [9] But the combination . . . לון

[7] Cf. also Hans-Joachim Kraus, *Psalmen*, BKAT XV/1 (2nd ed.; Neukirchen, Kreis Moers: Neukirchener Verlag, 1961), 420, *et al*. On the
translation of the verb in the Kilamuwa inscription in the same manner,
cf. Ch. F. Jean and J. Hoftijzer, *Dictionnaire des inscriptions sémitiques
de l'ouest* (Leiden: E. J. Brill, 1965), p. 136.

[8] Brown, Driver, and Briggs confirm the significance of this observation
by drawing no distinction in meaning between the two forms of the
verb. Cf. also Schnutenhaus, p. 130.

[9] *The Interpreter's Dictionary of the Bible*, ed. George A. Buttrick,
et al. (Nashville: Abingdon Press, 1962), III, 457. Cf. also *Webster's
Seventh New Collegiate Dictionary:* "a half-suppressed or muttered [in-
distinct] complaint; grumbling."

על is not adequately defined by "to murmur against." The difficulty, as we shall show in detail below, is that the specification effected by the preposition על moves the action described by the verb from an inarticulate complaint to a well-defined event. The preposition is always present,[10] and in each case it must be interpreted in its hostile sense. The event itself consistently involves a face to face confrontation between the murmurers and the object of the preposition. The precise nature of this hostile event is defined in Num. 14:9 and 17:25 by the roots מרד and מרה (cf. Num. 20:10; Deut. 9:7, 24; Ezek. 20:8, 13, 21; Ps. 78:40, 56). These words refer to the same acts which were initially described by לון and suggest a common connotation of an open act of rebellion.

Several occurrences of the two roots יעד and קהל in relationship to the preposition על carry a meaning which is synonymous to לון and must therefore be considered a part of the murmuring motif (יעד: Num. 14:35; 16:11; 27:3; קהל: Exod. 32:1; Num. 16:3, 19; 17:7; 20:2; Jer. 26:9).[11] In the wilderness traditions, these synonyms are entirely in P. The meaning of יעד is perhaps best indicated by the Qal stem of

[10] The verbal forms of the root always appear in conjunction with this preposition, while the substantives must be interpreted in the same manner. Twice the noun is constructed in direct relation with על (Exod. 16:7; Num. 17:25). On three occasions (Exod. 16:8; Num. 14:27; 17:20), it appears in immediate juxtaposition with an אשר clause which uses a verbal form of the vocable and the preposition. In two further cases (Exod. 16:9, 12), the noun is in a context which previously has used the verb with its preposition (vs. 8). One might in fact suggest that these two verses anticipate a modifying אשר clause such as the ones in Exod. 16:8 and Num. 14:27. But be that as it may, the fact remains that even for the substantives the preposition is germane to the proper construction of the motif.

[11] All three instances of יעד refer to previous events of murmuring which are defined by the verb לון. Three of the instances where קהל occurs with this meaning are in contexts which employ לון in reference to the same act (Num. 16:3, 19; 17:7). One appears in a narrative which has a parallel where לון is used instead of קהל (Num. 20:2 ff., cf. Exod. 17:1 ff.). Exod. 32:1 is problematic. It is widely recognized that the text represents a conflation of various levels as a polemic against Jeroboam's cultic centers. It is therefore likely that the proper continuation of vs. 1 is no longer preserved. Cf. the Excursus below. On Jer. 26:9, cf. below, p. 35.

the Hebrew root, translated by Brown, Driver, and Briggs with the verbs, "to assign, designate, or appoint." This translation can be supported by the third stem of the Arabic root, w'd, "to appoint a time or place," developing from a primary meaning, "to promise or predict," and by the Akkadian verb, ādu, "to decide." The Niph'al is reflexive: "to meet at an appointed place." In the murmuring motif, יעד regularly appears as a Niph'al plural participle. It is used uniformly in reference to previous events of murmuring and gives no impression of adding further information to our understanding of the murmuring motif.

קהל has a similar meaning. The basic denotation, as suggested by the various cognate languages, is "to assemble." It comes into Hebrew in the form of a noun, with the Hebrew verb considered a denominative. This verb appears only in the Niph'al with a reflexive or passive connotation and the Hiph'il as a causative from the same connotation. In the wilderness traditions, קהל introduces two extensive narrative units. In each of these, it is formed as a Niph'al 3. m. pl. waw consecutive imperfect (Num. 16:3; 20:2). Two other occurrences also appear in a narrative context, one as a Niph'al infinitive construct (Num. 17:7), and the other as a Hiph'il 3. m. s. waw consecutive imperfect (Num. 16:19). Thus the Niph'al character of these synonyms, with this one exception, is remarkably consistent. Both connote a gathering of people for a specific purpose, and the use of the preposition על shows that this purpose has a hostile character (cf. Jer. 26:9).

In three texts the verb דבר with the preposition ב must also be considered a part of the murmuring motif (Num. 21:5, 7; Ps. 78:19).¹² Num. 21:5, 7 cannot be assigned with certainty to any of the pentateuchal sources; the unit in which these verses appear, Num. 21:4-9, is instead a secondary addition

---

¹² Job 19:18 and Ps. 50:20 are clearly not a part of the murmuring motif. Num. 12:1, 8, though having a similar setting, involve a peculiar problem concerning Moses' leadership and are not considered a part of the murmuring motif as it is defined here (cf. Appendix III).

to the pentateuchal tradition.[13] Ps. 78:19 also seems to be a part of a unit which is dependent on, rather than prior to or a part of, the form of the tradition in the Pentateuch.

The etymology of this root is also uncertain. Brown, Driver, and Briggs nevertheless offer a useful hypothesis. They define four categories of use for the Hebrew root on the basis of the Arabic root *dbr*. The meaning of the Arabic verb, they suggest, is "to go away." Of the four categories, only the fourth is relevant for our interest. *Dabbara* has the sense of concluding an issue or story. It is particularly noteworthy, in the light of the use of the preposition על with the previous verbs, that the combination, *dabbara 'ala*, means "to plan against." The Pi'el stem of the Hebrew verb, which corresponds with this Arabic form, is usually translated "to speak." In the three texts cited above, the verb is regularly construed as a Pi'el, once as a 3. m. pl. *waw* consecutive imperfect (Ps. 78:19), once as a 3. m. s. *waw* consecutive imperfect (Num. 21:5), and once as a 1. pl. perfect (Num. 21:7). The preposition used with this verb is ב rather than על. We can thus draw no conclusions on the basis of the Arabic combination, *dabbara 'ala*. But the connotation is nevertheless hostile: "to speak against." And it is in this sense that the combination is considered a part of the murmuring motif.

The subject of the murmuring in the wilderness traditions can be the בני ישראל (Exod. 14:11; 16:12; Num. 14:27, 29; 17: 20; cf. also Num. 11:4), כל בני ישראל (Exod. 16:7, 8; Num. 14:2), כל־עדת בני־ישראל (Exod. 16:2, 9; Num. 17:6), [כל־] העדה, הרעה הזאת (Num. 14:27, 35), or כל־העדה (Num. 14:2, 36). The four occurrences which are not ascribed to P regularly have העם (Exod. 15:24; 17:3; Num. 21:5, 7; cf. Num. 11:18). It is thus striking that the subject of the action is consistently the whole people of Israel. The only exception to this observation is in the Korah narrative, Num. 16:11 (cf. also Num. 27:3). The identity of the subject here must be left open for the moment, for it is not clear whether וכל־עדתך refers to a

[13] Martin Noth, "Num. 21 als Glied der 'Hexateuch' Erzählung," *ZAW* LVIII (1940/41), 170 ff.; *Überlieferungsgeschichte*, p. 133.

limited number of the congregation or all of Israel (cf. Num. 16:19).

With לון, יעד, and קהל, the object of the preposition is commonly Moses and Aaron together, either explicitly (Exod. 16:2; Num. 14:2; 16:3; 17:6, 7; 20:2), or in the form of a plural suffix which can only refer to them (Exod. 16:7, 8; Num. 16:19; 17:20). On three occasions the object is only Moses (Exod. 15:24; 17:3, texts attributed to JE, and Num. 14:36), and on one, only Aaron (Num. 16:11). The object of the preposition is thus quite commonly the leaders of the people. In other texts, however, the object is Yahweh himself (Exod. 16:7, 8; Num. 14:27, 29, 35; 16:11; 17:20; 27:3). In each of these texts, there is either some textual confusion where the LXX reads in part a pronoun which refers to Moses and Aaron,[14] a reference to an earlier event involving only human leadership (Num. 14:29, 35; 27:3), or a reinterpretation of an earlier reference to Moses and/or Aaron as a reference to Yahweh (Exod. 16:7, 8; Num. 16:11). These texts, especially Exod. 16:7, 8, and Num. 16:11, suggest that the office of leadership represented by Moses and Aaron is endowed with authority by Yahweh. Out of deference to that authority, the leaders suggest that the action taken by the people is against the office and the authority that stands behind the office rather than the person in the office. This is explicitly stated in Exod. 16:8: "Your murmurings are not against us but against Yahweh." [15]

On the other hand, the object of the preposition ב which accompanies the verb דבר is directly אלהים (Num. 21:5; Ps. 78:19) or יהוה (Num. 21:7). In Num. 21:5, 7, Moses is also considered a part of the object. But there is no indication that the murmuring was actually directed against Moses and only through him against Yahweh. Quite the contrary, Moses

---

[14] In Num. 14:27bβ, the LXX reads περὶ ὑμῶν, while in 17:20bα, the Codex Alexandrinus reads ἀπὸ σοῦ. Cf. also Exod. 16:8aβ, where the LXX has καθ' ἡμῶν.

[15] Cf. also those texts which simply shift an original designation of the object of the murmuring from the human leadership to Yahweh, viz., Num. 14:29, 35; 27:3.

seems to be included here only by virtue of his normal role in the motif. The Kethib form of the verb in question (vs. 5) suggests that the addressee may have originally been singular. The reason for this probably does not lie in Moses' secondary role in this unit but in the stereotyped form of this expression taken over from other texts in the murmuring motif (cf. Exod. 17:3). These observations would suggest that דבר ב־ belongs to a subsequent development in the history of the motif.

To summarize the results of our work thus far: It seems clear that the motif is dominated by the verb לון in conjunction with the preposition על. The verb appears in both Niphʻal and Hiphʻil with no legitimate distinction in meaning between the two forms. The meaning of the verb in the murmuring motif is best indicated by recognition of the hostile nature of the action it describes: "to rebel against." The two verbs יעד and קהל depend on the Niphʻal stem and their construction with the preposition על for the connotation of murmuring; i.e., to gather against someone is synonymous with murmuring against someone. The verb דבר is a part of a subsequent development in the history of the motif. As with the other synonyms, so with דבר the connotation of rebellion depends on a Piʻel form of the verb in conjunction with the preposition ב. The subject of the event is consistently the people of Israel. The object is primarily the human leadership of the community, although a tendency for recognizing divine authority behind the human leadership appears.

form-critical analysis

We shall next consider the formal structure of the murmuring motif in the wilderness traditions. The various texts which do not simply report a previous act of murmuring show that the murmuring is a concrete event which occurs in a concrete setting. The people present themselves before the leaders and ask a question. Thus, in Exod. 17:3: "Why did you bring us up from Egypt to kill us, our children, and our cattle with thirst?" Num. 14:3: "Why did Yahweh bring us to this land to fall by the sword?" Num. 16:3: "Why will you make yourselves princes over the congregation of Yahweh?" Or perhaps a more accurate translation of the imperfect verb here would be: "Why are you now making yourselves princes over the congregation of Yahweh?" Num. 20:4-5: "Why have you brought the congregation of Yahweh to this wilderness to die here, both us and our cattle? [1] And why have you brought us up from Egypt to bring us to this evil place?" And finally, Num. 21:5: "Why have you brought us up from Egypt to die in the wilderness?" [2]

These questions are regularly introduced by an interrogative particle, either למה or מדוע. With the exception of Num.

[1] According to the LXX: ἀποκτεῖναι ἡμᾶς καὶ τὰ κτήνη ἡμῶν.
[2] According to the LXX: ἀποκτεῖναι ἡμᾶς ἐν τῇ ἐρήμῳ.

29

14:3, the particle is followed by a verb in the second person, addressed directly to the object of the murmuring. The verb is usually constructed as a perfect, indicating that the event in question is completed and lies in the past. It is possible, however, for an imperfect form of the verb to be used; in this case, the event would be incomplete. In Num. 14:3, the verb is a participle, with Yahweh as the subject. But it is clear from vs. 2 that Moses and Aaron are nevertheless the object of the murmuring. Since we have seen that the office in which Moses and Aaron stand represents the authority of Yahweh, and since Moses and Aaron are held responsible for the same event elsewhere (cf. Exod. 17:3, *et al.*), this formal change offers no great difficulty. The two leaders are simply addressed with a question about an event which Yahweh has enacted through their office. The purpose of the question is to challenge the interrogated for an explanation of the event described by the principal verb. The implication of the challenge is to accuse the interrogated of irresponsibility.

Num. 17:6 is not in the form of a question, but nevertheless questions the validity of a past event and the role of the leaders in it: "*You* [the pronoun comes before the verb, emphasizing the role of the leaders in the event described by the verb] [3] have killed the people of Yahweh." In a similar manner, Exod. 16:3 challenges the past actions of Moses and Aaron through a כי clause: "For you have brought us to this wilderness to kill this whole congregation with hunger" (cf. Exod. 17:3). Exod. 14:11 can also be included in this group of questions, for even though it has no verbal introduction which employs the verb לון or its various synonyms, it offers a question which has the same setting and form. The people collectively challenge what Moses has done. In this case, however, the question is introduced by a complete interrogative sentence: מה־זאת עשית לנו.

A problem of interpretation arises here. We might assume that this question, instead of challenging a past event by

---

[3] *Gesenius' Hebrew Grammar*, ed. E. Kautzsch (2nd English ed., rev. by A. E. Cowley; Oxford: The Clarendon Press, 1910), # 32b, p. 105; # 135a, p. 437.

means of an accusation, does nothing more than request information. If this were the case, then the information sought by the interrogators would be a statement of what the interrogated had done in the past. Thus the perfect form of the verb עשית would refer to an action which has been completed. But difficulties arise here, for this sentence is followed by a verbal form (infinitive construct) defining exactly what Moses has done. We could hardly suppose that the people ask for information and then provide the answer themselves. It might be possible to suppose that they are asking for some different aspect of the information which they might not as yet have. But there is no basis in the text to permit such a supposition. The question might be considered simply rhetorical, but the answer provided by the interrogators would reduce the effectiveness of such a construction.[4] It seems clear that a different kind of question lies before us here. In order to express the character of this difference, we propose that the translation be more analogous to the questions which commonly appear in the murmuring motif: "Why have you done this to us? Why have you brought [Heb: to bring] us out from Egypt?" In this case, the long interrogative sentence would serve the same function as the interrogative particles למה and מדוע.

The principal verb in question is normally followed by an infinitive construct. The purpose of the infinitive is to define the nature of the result expected from the action described by the principal verb. That result may have already occurred (Num. 20:5) but is often an anticipated event (Exod. 17:3, et al.). It is significant to emphasize here that it is not the result, either real or anticipated, which is challenged by the question, but the action producing the result. Thus, in Exod. 17:3, the point of the challenge does not lie in the fact

[4] Hans J. Boecker, *Redeformen des Rechtslebens im Alten Testament,* *WMANT* XIV (Neukirchen-Vluyn: Neukirchener Verlag, 1964), 26 ff., analyzes this particular form and concludes: "Sie hat mehr rhetorische als fragende Funktion." But it seems far more adequate to the form of the question and its context to recognize a legitimate questioning character.

that thirst poses a threat to the lives of the people and their cattle. This threat is subordinated to the principal event, the Exodus out of Egypt under Moses' leadership. In Exod. 14:11, the infinitive construct serves a different purpose. The event described by this verbal form is not the result of the action in the principal verb but equivalent to that action. It is thus to be described as a more precise definition of the primary event [5] and as such carries an equal burden of the challenge.

We have now seen a question appearing in a consistent structure in the context of the murmuring event, formulated to demand an explanation for past deeds. But does this form of question appear outside the murmuring motif in the wilderness traditions? And if it does, how does it illumine our understanding of the questions cited above? The questions are fortunately abundant: Gen. 3:13; 4:10; 12:18; 20:9; 26:10; 29:25; 31:26; Exod. 1:18; 5:15; Num. 23:11; Josh. 7:7;[6] 22:16; Judg. 2:2; 8:1; 12:1; 15:11; 20:12; I Sam. 24:9; II Sam. 3:24; 12:21; 16:10; 19:42; I Kings 1:6; Job 9:12; Neh. 2:19; 13:11, 17; Jer. 26:9; et al.

We shall choose two examples from this list for initial comparison with the form in the murmuring motif of the wilderness traditions. In Neh. 13:17 ff., the interrogative introduction, מה־הדבר הרע הזה (cf. Exod. 14:11), is followed by a definition of the act under question. The definition, which appears in an אשר clause, contains two participles. The first, עשים, clearly refers to הדבר הרע הזה from the main clause, while the second, מחללים, defines precisely the character of the first. Finally, the whole process is introduced by the verb ריב (cf. also vs. 11). But this unit appears to be truncated, offering no response to a question apparently constructed to demand one.

Josh. 22:16 ff. again employs the same form of question, introduced by the same long interrogative sentence. The question demands an explanation for the act defined by the

---

[5] Ges.K. # 114o, p. 351.

[6] In every other case, the particle בי (vs. 8) introduces a new unit. This would suggest that the form of the question in vs. 7 does not continue into vs. 8.

infinitives construct לשוב and בבנותכם with the force of an accusation.[7] It is followed by a response from the accused (vss. 21 ff.), which appears to be in answer to the question, "Why?" Vs. 34 refers to a witness and guarantee. But the witness does not confirm a previous settlement of the dispute, nor does it attest a new resolution. The word עד in vs. 34*b* refers to the altar in vs. 34*a*. But the altar was not built to show that the dispute was settled.[8] The Israelites are not involved in its construction. Only the Reubenites and the Gadites give the altar a name, and these people were the ones who were first challenged to explain their actions. Moreover, the name given to the altar is missing, and vs. 34 alludes to vs. 27. The witness here has nothing to do with a resolution of the dispute but with an explanation of the event challenged by the question: "Why have you built an altar and rebelled against Yahweh?" "We did not build it for sacrifice but as a witness." Thus the only elements of the form now present in this text are an accusation, constructed as a question, and a response explaining the point on which the defense is based.

Both the verb ריב, which appears with this form (cf. Neh. 13:17 ff.), and the general character of accusation and response suggest that the *Sitz-im-Leben* for the question is legal process.[9] Joachim Begrich laid the foundation for subsequent study of legal forms with his analysis of the *Gerichsrede*.[10] Beginning with an earlier description of *Gerichsreden* by Gunkel,[11] he first defines the structure of legal process. The first

[7] B. Gemser, "The Rib- or Controversy-Pattern in Hebrew Mentality," *Wisdom in Israel and in the Ancient Near East*. M. Noth and D. Winton Thomas, eds., *VT Sup* iii (Leiden: E. J. Brill, 1960), 121 ff.

[8] Against Gemser, p. 121.

[9] Hans Walter Wolff, *Hosea*, BKAT XIV/1 (Neukirchen, Kreis Moers: Neukirchener Verlag, 1961), 39, describes ריב as a term for "den Wechsel der Reden vor Gericht (c. עם 4:1; 12:3) und somit die Prozessführung im ganzen." Cf. also Gemser, p. 122.

[10] Joachim Begrich, *Studien zu Deuterojesaja*, BWANT, 4. Folge, Heft 25 (77) (Stuttgart: W. Kohlhammer Verlag, 1938), 18 ff. For a review of the various contributions to the discussion of *Gerichtsreden*, cf. von Waldow, pp. 1 ff.

[11] Hans Schmidt, *Die grossen Propheten*, mit Einleitungen versehen von H. Gunkel, SAT II/2 (Göttingen: Vandenhoeck & Ruprecht, 1915), lxv.

stage of the structure is an initial quarrel between two parties, either private individuals or groups. This quarrel is composed of an exchange of accusations and counteraccusations. These appear in the form of a question which carries the burden of the case against the opposition and challenges him to some kind of explanation. The point to note here is that this stage is informal. There is no judge present, no witness. The entire process occurs only between the two parties involved. Moreover, if the one succeeds in persuading the other of the validity of his argument, the quarrel is over. It is only in the event that neither can convince the other of the justice of his argument that a transition must be made to official procedure. The transition is usually indicated by some designation of and appeal to a judge or judges who can decide the question. Thus, in I Sam. 24:12 ff., David concludes his quarrel with Saul by saying: "Let Yahweh judge between me and you and avenge me on you. . . . Let Yahweh be the judge and decide between me and you, that he may see and decide my case (ריב) and judge in my favor." It is noteworthy that the same form of question which appears in connection with the murmuring precedes this appeal. And this question bears the burden of David's accusation against Saul: "Why do you listen to the words of the men who say, 'David seeks your harm!'?"

The second stage is the formal process of law.[12] The plaintiff and defendant present themselves at the public square where the judges and witnesses can be chosen from the full citizens of the community. The case is presented, the judges call the appropriate witnesses to inform themselves concerning the case, and the decision is returned. If the defendant's case is strong, he may follow his defense with an accusation of his own (cf. Gen. 31:41-42). In either the defense of the accused or the renewed accusation by the defendant, it is not unusual to find motifs or even formal elements from the first, pre-official stage reappearing. This is readily understandable since

---

[12] Ludwig Köhler, *Deuterojesaja stilkritisch untersucht*, *BZAW* XXXVII (Giessen: A. Töpelmann, 1923), 110-20. Cf. also L. Köhler, *Hebrew Man*, tr. P. Ackroyd (London: SCM Press, 1956), pp. 149 ff.

the goal of the official procedure is to present the quarrel which began in the first stage. One of the most common of these forms is the question now under consideration.

Jer. 26 presents the full scope of this legal process. In a narrative account of Jeremiah's Temple sermon and the re-action to it, the priests, prophets, and people address Jeremiah with an accusation in the form of our question: "Why have you prophesied in the name of Yahweh saying, 'This house shall be like Shiloh, and this city shall be desolate, without inhabitant'?" (vs. 9a). The accusation is then described in vs. 9b by a 3. m. s. Niph'al *waw* consecutive imperfect of the verb קהל, followed by the subject, כל־העם, and the object specified by the preposition אל.[13] It is only after this accusa-tion that official proceedings begin in the New Gate of the Temple before judges. We conclude, therefore, that the *Sitz-im-Leben* of our question is to be found in the preofficial stage of legal process.

Begrich feels that the whole scope of legal process, from the preofficial accusation and response to the official court pro-cedure, contains enough cohesion to be considered a unified form (*Gattungseinheit*).[14] The term *rîb,* he feels, does not describe the total process but serves instead as "die technische Bezeichnung der Verhandlung des Streites vor Gericht."[15] The form which we have seen in our question would thus fall outside the technical character of the *rîb* but still within the formal unity of a *Gerichtsrede*.[16]

[13] Several MSS and versions suggest על.
[14] Begrich, p. 29.
[15] *Ibid.,* p. 30. Ernst Würthwein, "Der Ursprung der prophetischen Gerichtsrede," *ZThK* XLIX (1952), 4, n. 1, sees the primary meaning of the word as presentation of a complaint (*Anklage*) either within or out-side the official process.
[16] Würthwein, pp. 1-16, distinguishes the secular process of law, and thus the secular *Gerichtsrede,* from the setting for an independent cultic *Gerichtsrede.* Von Waldow, p. 20, opposes this hypothesis and suggests to the contrary that the form of the cultic *Gerichtsrede* is rooted in secular legal process, with only the content showing distinct cultic background. The [prophetic] *Gerichtsrede* itself he cannot consider a *Gattung,* but rather a collective category for a whole series of different *Gattungen* from the secular legal world (p. 10).

Boecker apparently agrees with this position but refines the definition by one further step. He recognizes that the question of accusation, which belongs primarily to a "vorge-, richtlichen Auseinandersetzung," may nevertheless be found in the context of a formal suit and in that sense be considered a part of the *rîb;* in fact, he is willing to include the whole *Gerichtsrede,* both the official process and the preofficial quarrel, under this term. But, he concludes, "für unsere Beleg-stellen kann eine Entscheidung offenbleiben, da das Wort hier nicht in seiner strengen Bedeutung steht und einen offi-ziellen Gerichtsakt im Auge hat, sondern mit einer unpräzisen Ausdrucksweise bereits den vorgerichtlichen Akt mit diesem Terminus belegt." [17]

Thus, for our purposes, the character and original setting of the question in the murmuring motif are defined. It is necessary only to note that when the term *rîb* is used in con-nection with this question, we must be careful to distinguish between its narrow sense, thus construing the accusation as a part of the official process of law, and its broader connotations, allowing the possibility that the question may still be stand-ing in its original preofficial state. Or to address the problem from the opposite direction, we must be careful to determine whether the questions which appear in the murmuring motif reflect their original use in the informal setting of a quarrel between two parties and thus only in a broad and imprecise sense are to be considered a part of a *rîb,* or whether they have been introduced into a formal setting of justice in the court and thus appear in the context of a technical *rîb.*

We have observed that the accusation presupposes a re-sponse while the quarrel is still in a preofficial stage. The responses, both in the wilderness traditions and outside, vary in form and content according to the content and setting of the challenge. In the broad scope of the material, two ob-servations can be made:

1) The responses appear consistently in the form of a *Be-gründung,* a motivation or reason for the deed challenged

[17] Boecker, p. 30, n. 1. Cf. also von Waldow, pp. 5-6.

by the question. The character of the response as motivation or reason is most commonly indicated by an introductory כי with a causative connotation (Gen. 20:11; 31:31; Exod. 1:19; II Sam. 19:43) and followed by either a verbal or a nominal clause which explains why the deed was done. Or the definition of the reason may lie simply in a noun marked by a causative *mem* (Josh. 22:24). But even when the response does not bear any distinguishable formal indication of a causative character, it is nevertheless clear that a reason is being offered which corresponds in content to the challenge. Thus Gen. 29:25 poses the question: "Why have you cheated me?" And the response is in vs. 26: "It is not done in our country to give the younger before the first-born." The appeal is to custom; the *Begründung* lies in custom. Or in Gen. 3:13, the question is posed: "What have you done?" (Or better: "Why have you done it?") And the response sets forth the reason: "The serpent deceived me, and I ate."

2) The responses may be appropriately categorized according to the adequacy or inadequacy of the reasons which are offered (Gen. 3:13; 31:31; Judg. 12:2; 15:11; II Sam. 19:42). In some cases, the accusation may be considered so serious or so worthless that no explanation is given (Judg. 2:2; 12:3; 20:13; I Sam. 24:10 ff.). The absence of an explanation presupposes either that any response which might have been given would have been inadequate, or that the interrogated feels his position secure enough to be maintained without response. Moreover, it is apparent that for each inadequate answer an appropriate consequence follows. That consequence is normally an appeal for official judgment (Gen. 31:36 ff.; I Sam. 24:10 ff.). But this need not be the case. If the accuser is Yahweh, he can immediately pronounce judgment (Gen. 3: 13 ff.; Judg. 2:2 ff.). Or if the situation is one of extreme hostility, the accuser (Judg. 12:4) or the accused (Judg. 20:13) may also take justice into his own hands.

A further category of responses must be considered here. In II Sam. 12:22, David's servants are so shocked by his unusual action that they pose this same form of question in order to elicit some explanation. But there can be no doubt that his response will be quite satisfactory. One does not press such a question on a king (or leader?) unless he is in open rebellion (cf. Exod. 5:15; Judg. 12:1 ff., also Judg. 9:6 ff.). On the other hand, if the accused can cite a reason for having so acted which lies in authority arising from Yahweh, there is once again no possibility for pressing the matter. Thus David replies to Abishai's request to defend the king's honor against Shimei: "If Yahweh said to him: 'Curse David!' who shall say: 'Why are you doing so?' " (II Sam. 16:10; cf. Num. 23:11; Josh. 9:18 ff.).

In the wilderness traditions, two factors make the task of categorizing responses to the murmuring difficult: (1) The questions are often followed by elements which seem unrelated in both form and content to the murmuring, thus giving the murmuring a strong appearance of a secondary addition to the text. (2) The responses that do occur vary from case to case according to the content of the murmuring, just as we have seen in the overall review of the form. There are nevertheless two recurring forms here which demand our attention. The first, and perhaps the most puzzling, appears in Num. 14:5 and 16:4. After hearing the question of the people, Moses and Aaron (the question in 16:3 is also directed to Aaron, although vs. 4 has only Moses responding) fall on their faces (ויפל משה ואהרן על-פניהם). This expression is also widespread in the Old Testament (Gen. 17:17; Lev. 9:24; Josh. 7:10; I Sam. 25:23; II Sam. 9:6; I Kings 18:7; Ezek. 1:28; 3:23; 11:13; 43:3; 44:4; and Dan. 8:17. With a slight addition, ארצה, it also appears in Gen. 44:14; Josh. 5:14; 7:6; Judg. 13:20; II Sam. 14:4, 22; Ruth 2:10 [with the insertion of ותשתחו]. II Kings 4:37 uses the same formula with רגליו substituted for פנים). It occurs in the murmuring motif at points which do not appear to be associated with a response to murmuring: Num. 16:22; 17:10; 20:6. In each case, the subjects are clearly presenting themselves before Yahweh. In the various occurrences of this formula outside the wilderness traditions, it is apparent that the person or persons involved are presenting themselves before an individual of greater estate than they. That individual is commonly the deity, either when he appears before the people (Lev. 9:24) or when the people appear before him (Josh. 7:6). But also, a subject would follow the same procedure when he appears before the king (II Sam. 9:6), or a woman before a man (I Sam. 25:23; Ruth 2:10). There is no intrinsic petition or supplication involved in the formula, although such items do appear in connection with it. Rather, it seems to be simply a matter of self-abasement before one of higher rank.

But if this is the case, why should Moses and Aaron respond in such a manner to the murmuring of the people? Again, we may interpret this act as humility before Yahweh rather than the people. To be sure, it happens in the presence of the people (cf. Num. 14:5), but it nevertheless signifies their self-presentation before Yahweh. This is in fact clearly stated in Num. 20:6: "Then Moses and Aaron went from the presence of the congregation to the door of the tent of meeting, and fell on their faces." The significance of the response for the murmuring motif lies in Moses', or Moses' and Aaron's, deference in favor of the authority against whom this murmuring is really directed.

The second form appears in Exod. 16:6b-12 and Num. 16:25 ff. The characteristics of the form (*Erweiswort*) have been carefully defined.[18] It is enough here to point to the fact that Moses responds to the challenge with an announcement that an event will occur in the near future which will prove to the people that Yahweh is the one who stands behind the deed which has been challenged, or better, that he is the authority who stands behind the man who has been challenged (cf. Num. 16:28). In both forms, the burden of the response is placed on the fact that the authority for the event arises from Yahweh.

If, on the other hand, Moses is not able to produce sufficient evidence to satisfy the questioning of the people, then his office of leadership (Num. 14:4), or even his life (vs. 10),

---

[18] Walther Zimmerli, "Das Wort des göttlichen Selbsterweises (Erweiswort), eine prophetische Gattung," *Mélanges Bibliques rédigés en l'honneur de André Robert. Travaux de l'institut catholique de Paris* IV (Paris: Bloud et Gay, 1957), 154-64.

is in danger. This points to the extreme hostility involved in the murmuring. Moreover, since the people murmur against Yahweh as well as his chief representative, they are in effect threatening to depose Yahweh from his position as their deity in the wilderness. If such a challenge is indeed so serious, we may also consider what would happen to the people who originally raised the question when a successful response has been provided. This level of response again varies from case to case according to the degree of hostility involved. It is possible for normal relationships to be resumed by mutual agreement (cf. Josh. 22:16 ff.), or even for the problem to be dismissed without explicit consequences for the challengers (cf. Josh. 9:16 ff.). But when the content of the challenge implies full-scale rebellion, the rebels may be subject to severe punishment or death (Judg. 12:4, where Jephthah, not Ephraim, initiates the battle). The murmuring motif in the wilderness traditions also involves such severe punishment (Num. 14:22-23).

Thus the formal structure associated with the verbs of murmuring comprises at least two principal elements: (1) a question addressed directly to the object of the murmuring which challenges some past deed, and (2) a response from the addressee which provides an explanation for that event. Both of these elements have their setting in the preofficial stage of the *Gerichtsrede*.

We shall next test our observations about the murmuring motif by examining the one occurrence of the combination על . . . לון which appears in neither the Pentateuch nor the wilderness traditions—Josh. 9:18. This verse is a part of a larger narrative unit, vss. 3-21, but only vss. 16-21 demand our attention here.[19] These verses are basically narrative in

---

[19] The literary background of both the larger unit and this smaller section is complex. If vss. 16-21 should be related to the pentateuchal source P, or even to the work of R^P (cf. Wilhelm Rudolph, *Der "Elohist" von Exodus bis Josua,* BZAW LXVIII [Berlin: Alfred Töpelmann, 1938], 202 ff.), we might posit some literary connection between this reference to murmuring and the P form of the murmuring motif in the wilderness traditions. But evidence to support an identification of the P source in this unit is weak. Noth argues instead that this unit reflects an

style but involve at least an element of dialogue in vss. 19-20.
The verb לון is in the narrative introduction (vs. 18*b*), constructed as a *waw* consecutive 3. m. pl. Niph'al imperfect. It
appears in context with the preposition על, which obviously
is used here in its hostile sense. The subject of the verb is "all
the congregation" (כל־העדה), while the object of the preposition is "the leaders" (הנשיאים). Though no question is
associated with the verb, its significance is neverthless indicated by vss. 19-20. Here we have a direct address from the
leaders, addressed to all the congregation. This construction
recalls the subject and object from vs. 18 and is apparently
formulated as a conscious response to the verb לון in that verse.
Thus it is clear that in this context, just as in the wilderness
traditions, לון has the character of eliciting a direct response
from the object of the preposition which so closely accompanies
it.

But can this character be more explicitly determined? The
reply of the leaders in vss. 19aβ*b*-20 provides some insight in
this direction. The verb, a 1. pl. Niph'al perfect from שבע,
refers to the completed act originally narrated in vss. 15*b* and
18*a*. The reference is in fact formulated in exactly the same
words as those in vs. 18*a*, with the obvious exceptions involved
in the shift from narrative style to direct address. But the address is not introduced with the normal sentence order of
verb-subject. Instead, the pronoun אנחנו appears as the subject
before the verb. The antecedent of the pronoun cannot be
mistaken, since vss. 15*b* and 18*a* say unequivocally that the
leaders were responsible for the oath; indeed, the juxtaposition of the leaders (נשיאי העדה) with the Israelites (בני ישראל)
in vs. 18*a* indicates that the leaders alone bore responsibility
for the oath. But what significance lies in the change of the
normal word order? The general explanation for this change

ancient tradition from the premonarchial period of Israelite history
(Martin Noth, *Das Buch Josua*, *HAT* VII [Tübingen: J. C. B. Mohr,
(Paul Siebeck), 1953], 54). If this is indeed the case, then Josh. 9:18 represents a witness to the use of the verb לון which is independent of any
of the pentateuchal sources. At least we may conclude that it is tied to
local traditions about Gilgal rather than the wilderness traditions.

is that the pronoun places strong emphasis on the subject,[20] and nothing more than this is necessary here (cf. Num. 17:6). Thus the leaders appear to be explaining an earlier event to the people: "*We* swore to them in the name of Yahweh, the God of Israel." We may therefore conclude that the combination על . . . לון in this context also demands that the object of the murmuring give an explanation of something which he has done in the past.

But in order for the verb לון to elicit a definite response from the leaders which can be formed as a direct address, must we not presuppose that the event of murmuring itself involved at least some kind of statement from the congregation addressed directly to the leaders? This would apparently be required by the setting in vs. 19 which has the leaders in a position to speak before the congregation. And what better form of direct address could be imagined for calling forth such an explanation of one's activity than a question! But what sort of question might be presupposed here? On the basis of our analysis of the murmuring motif in the wilderness traditions, we might anticipate a question formed with either למה or מדוע (cf. Jer. 26:9). But does the response that follows permit such a hypothesis? Vs. 20a is governed by cohortative verbs: "Let us so act and preserve them alive." [21] Vs. 20b is formulated as a negative final clause (ולא־יהיה) [22] and thus is an explanation for the exhortation to preserve the Gibeonites. If the congregation should act otherwise, the wrath (קצף) which would be the consequence of breaking an oath sworn in the name of Yahweh would rise against them.

But why would such an exhortation as this be necessary? The text provides no clear answer, but the probability is that the congregation, contrary to the direction of their leaders, had set out to kill the Gibeonites. This hypothesis would be supported in the total narrative unit both by the

[20] Cf. above, p. 30, n. 18.
[21] The infinitive absolute is to be understood as a continuation of the finite verb; it would thus carry a cohortative connotation. Cf. Brockelmann, p. 47.
[22] Ges.K., # 109g, p. 323.

fact that the text reports explicitly that they did *not* kill the people (vs. 18*a*), and by the notation that this stay of execution occurs only after they had arrived in Gibeon (vs. 17*a*). Indeed, the murmuring immediately follows the note that the Israelites could not kill the Gibeonites and seems to be motivated by this fact. But if the motivation for the murmuring is to be seen here, the question implied in the murmuring might well concern the leaders' opposition to executing the Gibeonites. We could then suggest that the answer in vss. 19-20 was given to the question: "Why have you not allowed us to kill the Gibeonites according to the instruction of Yahweh?" And the *reason* offered in answer to this question lies in the oath given in the name of Yahweh (vs. 1*a*). Since nothing more is heard of the murmuring, we may presume that this explanation was considered adequate.

It seems clear, then, that the form which is associated with the verb לון in Josh. 9:18 ff. is identical to the one appearing consistently in the murmuring motif of the wilderness traditions. The whole people of Israel murmur against their leaders, and the leaders respond with an explanation for the necessity of preserving the Gibeonites. Since this correspondence apparently does not rest on any literary or traditio-historical relationships with the murmuring motif in the Pentateuch, we may confirm our conclusions above that the formal structure is not a creation for the wilderness traditions alone but is in fact a form of speech which appears in a pre-official quarrel.

traditio-historical analysis

We shall now proceed to a more detailed exegesis and traditio-historical analysis of the murmuring motif in the wilderness traditions. The principle of organization has been chosen arbitrarily according to the form and content of the various units: the spring narratives (Chap. 3); the food narratives (Chap. 4); the remaining narratives (Chap. 5); and the non-narrative texts (Chap. 6).

the spring narratives

Exodus 15:22-27

This unit is clearly framed in vss. 22a and 27 by formulas from the P itinerary. Noth feels that vs. 22aβ, the notice of Israel's arrival in the Wilderness of Shur, should be detached from the itinerary and included in the principal body of the unit.[1] But the itinerary formula normally includes both a statement of departure and a statement of arrival (cf. 16:1; 17:1; 19:2; *et al.*). This, coupled with the parallel form of the verbs in vs. 22a,[2] and the redundancy between vss. 22aβ and 22b, suggests that vs. 22a should be considered a unified piece of framework for the unit. To be sure, the P formula for indicating the arrival of the people ordinarily uses חנה or בוא (cf. 15:27; 16:1; 17:1; 19:2; *et al.*), while the verb which appears here is יצא. And the name מדבר־שור does not appear elsewhere in P (but cf. Num. 33:8-9). These difficulties are especially noteworthy since in vs. 27 the P itinerary fails to note the departure of the people from this site. But they do

---

[1] Noth, *Exodus*, p. 127.

[2] In 22aβ, the Sam.Pent. reads ויוצאהו in the place of the MT ויסעו. The LXX supports this change with a causative καὶ ἤγαγεν αὐτούς. Since vs. 22aα begins with a Hiph'il and accusative, the parallel in vs. 22aβ may also be considered causative.

not seem to be sufficient basis for excluding vs. 22*a*β from the itinerary.[3] In all probability a firm resolution of the question is impossible. For our purposes, however, we shall assume that the P framework appears in vss. 22*a* and 27, with vs. 22*b* representing the beginning of the unit.

A further break appears between vss. 22*b* and 23, for vs. 22*b* points to a crisis produced when no water could be found (cf. 17:1 ff.), while vs. 23 suggests that the water which had after all been found was not palatable. But there is no indication of a transition from the one crisis to the other. Gressmann saw this problem and concluded: "Wenn 23 direkte Fortsetzung wäre, müsste es heissen: 'Da kamen sie nach Mara (und fanden dort Wasser), aber das Wasser war nicht zu trinken.' "[4] It could be argued that vs. 22*b*α is a part of a spring narrative from P. This is suggested by Num. 33:8, where a similar expression about the same event occurs in an itinerary list. Yet it seems likely that Num. 33:8 is not a part of P but a late creation dependent on the final form of the Pentateuch.[5] The only remaining indication of a second fragmentary source in vs. 22*b* would be the change in the type of crisis. But the question which must be raised here is whether such a change offers sufficient basis for positing a second source. It seems more likely that the change indicates nothing more than a combination of a fragment from a spring tradition with a completely different narrative in a preliterary level. Thus we shall concur with Noth that in spite of the uneven transition this half verse belongs to the following section.[6]

Vs. 23 is the basis for a naming aetiology. Since the aetiology is concluded with an עַל־כֵּן clause which contains the aetiological formula and is built only on the basis of vs. 23*a*, this verse appears to be complete as it stands. Yet vss. 24 and 25*a* depend on this verse and cannot be separated from it as a differ-

[3] Against Noth, *Exodus*, p. 127.
[4] Hugo Gressmann, *Mose und seine Zeit*, *FRLANT* XVIII (Göttingen: Vandenhoeck & Ruprecht, 1913) , 121, n. 1.
[5] Noth, *Überlieferungsgeschichte*, p. 238.
[6] Noth, *Exodus*, p. 127.

ent literary unit. Once again we shall simply note the uneven character of the unit and attribute all of vss. 22b-25a to one literary source. That source is in all probability J.[7]

Vs. 26 is doubtlessly from the deuteronomistic redactor of the unit. The only question here is whether vs. 25b is to be considered a part of the same redaction or a continuation of the J section in vs. 25a. The style is so sharply different from vs. 25a that the latter possibility must be denied. But it is also noticeably different from vs. 26. A firm resolution for the question is again elusive. Yet Noth's conclusion seems to be relatively well founded: "As in this half-verse too only very general expressions are used, . . . we may decide in favour of the first alternative." [8] We therefore have the following literary structure: J, (22b), 23-25a; P, 22a, 27; Dtr., 25b-26.

Our next step is to determine the type of material in this unit. We have already noted that the P framework constitutes a notation of the itinerary in Israel's move through the wilderness; it is not necessary to comment further on this. The material in the deuteronomistic section is also distinctive. Vs. 25b, according to Noth, is "meant to do no more than create a foundation [assumption] for the deuteronomistic warning in vs. 26." [9] But what is the nature of that "warning"? "If vs. 25b belongs with vs. 26, Yahweh must already be meant as the subject in vs. 25b." [10] Vs. 26a, however, refers to Yahweh in the third person, both by mentioning the divine name and by referring to that name with third person suffixes. It is thus not clear that Yahweh is the speaker here. The same phenomenon is to be found in Deut. 11:13. The protasis, though using a first person suffix and pronoun initially, nevertheless refers to Yahweh by name and third person suffix. But the apodosis in both cases has Yahweh as the speaker. The change of subject seen here undoubtedly reflects the speech of a leader in the community announcing divine conditions or

---

[7] *Ibid.*, p. 127.

[8] *Ibid.*, pp. 127-28. Cf. also Bruno Baentsch, *Exodus-Leviticus-Numeri*, *HKAT* I/2 (Göttingen: Vandenhoeck & Ruprecht, 1903), 142-43.

[9] Noth, *Exodus*, p. 129.

[10] *Ibid.*, p. 129.

laws, with the consequence for obedience (or disobedience) to those conditions set in a first person address from Yahweh.[11]

The material in the J section is somewhat more complex. Vs. 23 is an aetiology, concluding with a typical aetiological formula על־כן קרא־שמה מרה. But what is the relationship between the aetiology and the context in which it appears? There is no formal necessity for vs. 22b in the aetiology. The aetiology itself provides the only foundation which is required (vs. 23a). The identification of the subject of the verbs lies outside vs. 23, but this is not an important factor in the aetiology. It is not even necessary to suggest that the aetiology depends on its continuation in vss. 24-25. As we have suggested above, it stands alone, complete in itself: "They came to Marah, but were not able to drink the water from Marah because it was bitter. Therefore, they called its name Marah." This verse would, then, form the substance of an aetiological saga which sought to explain the name of the locality with which it was connected.

On the other hand, vss. 24-25 do not stand alone. They depend on the aetiology to set the scene in a crisis concerning bitter water. But the name of the locality is no longer the important element. Here the subject of the verbs stands in the foreground and the goal seems to be to show how Yahweh resolved the crisis by giving his servant Moses the means for sweetening the water. The material here may therefore be designated a legendary expansion of the aetiological saga. It is, moreover, important to emphasize that the Israelites and Moses enter the tradition only *after* the aetiology is complete. The local tradition had no essential contact in its primary form with the specification of the subject. It is thus clear that the murmuring motif could not be associated with the primary form of the aetiological saga but is centered instead in the legendary expansion.

We must now consider the character of the murmuring

[11] H. Strack, *Die Bücher Genesis, Exodus, Leviticus, und Numeri. Kurzgefasster Kommentar zu den heiligen Schriften Alten und Neuen Testamentes* (München: C. H. Beck'sche Verlagsbuchhandlung, 1894), I, 214-15.

motif itself. Vs. 24 offers a typical introduction to the murmuring with a 3. m. pl. (or singular, according to the Sam.
Pent.) Niph'al imperfect form of לון, and העם as the subject.
As we might expect, the direct address of the people which
constitutes the murmuring is in the form of a question. But
this question is not introduced with למה or מדוע. The particle
is simply מה. We have noted above that this particle can introduce a question which serves as a substitute for the normal
particle: מה־זאת עשית לנו. But that question does not appear
here. Nor can the particle be interpreted in this case in the
same sense as למה. The verb which follows is not in the second
person perfect construction which would normally be found.
Instead, it is a first person plural imperfect Qal form of שתה.
There is no reference to a previous act of Moses, no demand
for an explanation, no response which might offer an explanation. The question as it stands simply does not appear in the
form of an accusation. Quite the contrary, its principal function seems to be a request for information: "What shall we
drink?"

What is the nature of the rebellion contained in this question? And how does it relate to the formal structure of the
accusation which, as we have argued, is to be associated with
the murmuring motif? It is possible that this particular request disguises a demand. The people obviously want not
only information but the water itself (cf. 17:2). Moreover,
it would be reasonable to assume that such a demand was
presented in a negative attitude, and thus legitimately described in terms of the combination על . . . לון. But if this
should be the case, what significance could be placed in the
deviation from the formal structure of the accusation? Would
the demand be simply an implied threat, a stylistic variation
of the same form? This must be denied since this question in
no sense accuses a second party of irresponsible action. Does
it mean that a different form, and as a consequence, a different type of negative motif is introduced by the murmuring?
If this is the case, our understanding of its character must
come from a source other than the question, for the question
in itself connotes no hostile overtones. The only remaining

alternative is the supposition that the motif introduced by
על . . . לון in vs. 24 does not have the same character as the
one described above.

The response to the question in vs. 25a would support this
hypothesis. Instead of addressing the people with a reply to
their question, Moses addresses Yahweh with a cry (צעק).
This address could well be a part of the murmuring motif
(cf. Exod. 5:15). Yet the verb צעק is pregnant with connotations of petition (cf. Gen. 27:34; 41:55; Exod. 5:8; Num.
12:13; Deut. 22:24, 27; Judg. 4:3; 7:23; II Kings 4:1; 6:26;
8:3, 5; Isa. 46:7; Pss. 34:18; 88:2; et al.). If this connotation
is to be seen here, the cry to Yahweh would involve nothing
more than a request for help in meeting the crisis. Yahweh's
response is in accord with this interpretation, for he simply
gives Moses the means for sweetening the water. There is
no evidence to suggest that this event is used to defend Moses;
there is no sign that the people's question is interpreted as
rebellion; there is no indication that the sweetened water will
actually be punishment for rebellion. To the contrary, the
whole section of response to the murmuring seems to be dominated by the gift of Yahweh's gracious aid. And this, like the
question, has no intrinsic negative connotation. The only
contact in this unit with the murmuring motif, and thus with
a negative view of the people's request for water, lies in the
narrative introduction. It seems appropriate, then, to suggest
that we have here not just the one motif of rebellion against
the leaders of the people but an interweaving of two motifs.
The second appears to be devoid of all negative elements,
having as its content the quite positive request for something
to drink and Yahweh's gracious response to that request.

There is no evidence that the original form of the tradition
might have recounted an accusation and response in accord
with the introductory לון, and thus no basis to assert that the
positive motif displaced an earlier account of Israel's murmuring. It would appear probable, then, that the על . . . לון
combination has been employed in contradiction to its primary meaning. Moreover, the positive motif constitutes the
basic expansion of the aetiological saga. Whether it had a

life which was independent of this local setting cannot be determined.[12] At least it would be clear that the specific instruction to throw a piece of wood into the water to make it palatable would not be independent of the local tradition of Marah. If this reconstruction is correct, then the use of the murmuring introduction would appear to be a subsequent development in the expanded tradition of Marah. Unfortunately, the reconstruction must remain tentative. With the exception of the reference to Marah as the name of a station in the itinerary list in Num. 33:8-9, the name never appears again in the Old Testament.

The deuteronomistic section reflects a background in legal process. The principal meaning of the governing verb נסה is to decide between two opposing alternatives without prejudice in favor of the one over the other (cf. Judg. 3:1, 4; 6:39; I Kings 10:1; Eccl. 2:1; 7:23; et al.). The legal character of the unit is also suggested by reference to laws (חק ומשפט). But the play on the verb נסה suggests a closer relationship with the tradition of Massah than Marah.[13] If this is the case, it is noteworthy that Yahweh, not Israel, is the subject of the verb נסה (cf. Exod. 17:2).[14] But since this unit is chiefly concerned with the tradition of the spring at Marah, we cannot pursue the question further here. It is sufficient to note that this addition contributes nothing to our analysis of the Marah tradition or the role of the murmuring in it.

Exodus 17:1-7

Vs. 1abα is once again the P itinerary notation and marks the beginning of the narrative unit with a well-defined introductory formula. The narrative itself begins in vs. 1bβ with a circumstantial nominal clause and continues in normal

[12] Cf. Noth, *Exodus*, p. 129.
[13] Noth, *Exodus*, p. 129.
[14] Gressmann, p. 148; P. Heinisch, *Das Buch Exodus, HSAT* I/2 (Bonn: Peter Hanstein Verlagsbuchhandlung, 1934), 128; Georg Beer, *Exodus, HAT* III (Tübingen: J. C. B. Mohr [Paul Siebeck], 1939), 86; *et al.* In a different vein, cf. Otto Eissfeldt, *Hexateuch-Synopse* (Leipzig: J. C. Hinrichs Verlag, 1922), p. 44.

fashion into vs. 2. The first apparent break in the narrative occurs between vss. 2 and 3. Noth feels "that there are clear doublets in vss. 1bβ-2 and vs. 3; vs. 3 is an obvious new beginning connected with geographical details which had come immediately before ('there' [שׁם]) and which must have described a definite place at which the Israelites arrived." [15] A connection with geographical details which might be posited as the antecedent for שׁם is weak evidence for the conclusion that vs. 3 is an "obvious" new beginning, for those details could have been immediately before vs. 2 and still served as a point of reference for the adverb in vs. 3.[16] The burden of this observation must be carried instead by the assertion that vss. 1bβ-2 and vs. 3 are clear doublets. That some disunity exists here can be admitted. But the move from this observation to an identification of sources is difficult. Noth is aware of this problem and observes that apart from this single element of disunity, "we have no criteria for distributing the transmitted material between the two versions which can be detected in vss. 1bβ-2 and vs. 3. . . . It is plausible to suppose that in the combination of two versions, E once again appears alongside J, but there are no positive indications of this." [17] He then concludes that since the divine name "Yahweh" appears in vss. 1bβ-2, this must be J, while vs. 3 remains as E.

But the problems here are complex. First, we must consider carefully whether vs. 3 can be so simply isolated from its context, or whether vs. 4 may be considered its natural continuation. If the latter should be the case, we would have difficulty in attributing the whole to E, since vs. 4 also con-

[15] Noth, *Exodus*, p. 138. Cf. also Beer, p. 91.
[16] Noth, *Exodus*, p. 138, concludes that these details must have been similar to the "ones which should precede vss. 1bβ-2." Both would have been displaced, according to his reconstruction, by the P itinerary. But if details must be posited for both vss. 1bβ-2 and vs. 3, why not conclude that the same set of details served in both instances? The only reason would be the supposition that the two sections were not originally connected. The details would therefore not serve as evidence to prove that they were in fact not connected.
[17] Noth, *Exodus*, p. 139. Cf. also Gressmann, pp. 145-46, n. 1.

tains the divine name "Yahweh." The question cannot be resolved on literary grounds. We shall show below that vs. 4 constitutes the response of Moses to the murmuring. But if vss. 1$b\beta$-2 form a doublet of vs. 3 and thus a parallel form of the murmuring, vs. 4 could be considered the continuation of either. Second, and more important, it is at least doubtful that vss. 1$b\beta$-2 and vs. 3 can be designated *clear* doublets. This problem will be considered in detail below. For the moment, it is sufficient to note that vss. 1$b\beta$-2 serve as the foundation for the aetiological play on the place name, Meribah, while vs. 3 introduces the murmuring motif with a typical narrative formulation. This does not establish that the two are not doublets. But it at least casts doubt on a conclusion that vs. 3 must be a part of the E narrative because it is a "clear" doublet of the J narrative in vss. 1$b\beta$-2. The duality here may well be the same kind of interweaving between two or more traditions on a preliterary level which was suggested above (cf. also Num. 20:3).[18]

The same complexity in the literary unity continues from this point to the end of the unit. If two parallel literary sources are to be recognized and each reflects the murmuring, then the larger section should probably be attributed to J, leaving only the fragment in vs. 3 for E. But if the complexity is not a matter of literary unity but an expansion in the tradition at a preliterary level, then the literary form of the Meribah tradition in this text should probably be attributed entirely to J. The play on the name Massah in vs. 2$b\beta$ and the explanation of the name in vs. 7 seem certainly to be secondary additions. Since outside this text Massah appears only in Deuteronomy and deuteronomistic sections (Exod. 15:25b; Ps. 95:8; Deut. 6:16; 9:22; 33:8), we may presume for the moment that this is also a deuteronomistic addition.[19] Vs. 7 is distinguished sharply from the following unit by the shift

---

[18] Cf. the methodological discussion by Claus Westermann, "Arten der Erzählung in der Genesis," *Forschung am Alten Testament* (München: Chr. Kaiser Verlag, 1964), pp. 9 ff.

[19] Noth, *Exodus*, p. 139, attributes the Massah traditions in this unit to a "later hand."

in the narrative from the spring tradition of Meribah to the battle with the Amalekites.

The type of material which appears in this unit is somewhat more difficult to determine than that which appears in 15:22 ff. We have already noted that vs. 1aba is another of the itinerary formulas. We have also noted that this unit has an aetiological element just as the Marah traditions did (cf. vs. 7). But the original form of the aetiology has already been lost through legendary expansions in the aetiology itself. It is probable, for example, that the original aetiology was concerned only with an explanation of the name by reference to legal cases resolved there. Von Rad notes that this name, along with Massah, implies

that legal cases were investigated and decided by ordeal there. . . . The same thing is implied in the name "Spring of Judgment" עין משפט, which was a current name of Kadesh or for one of its oases (Gen. 14:7). Kadesh was therefore a well-known sanctuary where divine justice was administered and cases in dispute decided.[20]

But here the play on the name has been expanded to include the Israelites. Whether the deity which was originally worshiped there was Yahweh cannot be clearly determined. But it is at least likely that Yahweh, along with his people, was introduced at a later period of development in the tradition.[21] Thus the only conclusion possible about the type of material here is that one or more legendary motifs have been combined with a basic aetiological saga, obscuring the original form of the saga. The purpose of the combination would once again be to give the legendary material a precise setting by associating it with a local tradition.

The principal goal of our exegesis is to determine where the murmuring motif appears and what it seems to express. But in the light of our literary analysis, our immediate problem is to determine the relationship between vss. 1bβ-2 and vs. 3. Or, more precisely, we must determine what relationship vss. 1bβ-2 have to the murmuring motif and the rest of the unit.

[20] von Rad, p. 12.
[21] Ibid., p. 12.

We shall therefore begin our analysis with these verses. Vs. 2*a* is the foundation for the aetiology as it now stands, using the verb ריב with the preposition עם to designate Moses as the object and the noun העם to specify the subject. Since the combination, ריב . . . עם, is a technical term for legal process,[22] this verse is also tied closely to the legal character of the local aetiology.

But we have noted above that the term ריב can be used in a broad sense to include the preofficial quarrel that forms the basis of the murmuring. If this act of "striving" with Moses is to be interpreted as an accusation which challenges the past deeds of Moses, we could expect the direct address which accompanies it to be in the form of a question addressed directly to Moses. The address is indeed directed to Moses. But it is not a question. It is a demand; the verb is a 2. m. s.[23] Qal imperative. This suggests that the *rib* which the people have with Moses is not an informal accusation-response (cf. vs. 3) but instead a (formal?) claim.[24] The water is desperately needed, and the leader's responsibility demands that he meet the need.

Since the imperative does not accuse the addressee of irresponsible action, vs. 2 must be considered distinct from, and not parallel to or a doublet of, vs. 3. It is possible, nevertheless, to interpret the claim in a basically negative fashion and thus as a supporting part of the murmuring motif: "Give us water [or we will rebel]!" (cf. Ps. 78:18). But such an interpretation depends on the assumption that the term ריב in vs. 2*a*α is necessarily negative. Beyond this assumption, no negative connotations can be found. Is it not possible, then, that these verses represent the same kind of positive tradition concerning Israel's request (demand) for Yahweh's aid that we suggested for Exod. 15:24?

[22] Wolff, p. 39.

[23] Since the object of the verb in vs. 2*a*α is singular and the verb in vs. 2*a*β, תנו, is clearly addressed to that object, we shall read a singular imperative, תנה, with 21 MSS and the Sam.Pent.

[24] Cf. von Waldow, p. 36. The term *rib* is not obviously appropriate for this kind of legal claim, for the root is never again used with a sentence controlled by an imperative.

But what is the significance of the response in vs. 2b? The juxtaposition of מה־תריבון עמדי with מה־תנסון את־יהוה can be misleading. Since it is probable that the verb נסה and all reference to Massah appear as secondary additions to the unit, מה־תריבון עמדי must be interpreted without reference to Israel's testing Yahweh. A similar expression is found in Exod. 14:15. Yahweh responds to Moses' petition for help with the same formulation: מה־תצעק אלי.[25] And this is followed by a favorable response to the petition; i.e., the aid requested by Moses is granted. The same results appear in Exod. 17:5. Yahweh has responded to the demand with instructions for finding water (vs. 5) in a place which originally had none (cf. vs. 1bβ). The tradition is complete without negative connotations and bears striking similarities with our reconstruction of the positive level of tradition associated with Marah.[26] At least we may conclude that it does not belong to the murmuring motif.

But still we face the problem of the role of the *rib* in this

[25] Von Waldow, p. 36, observes that this expression belongs to the legal sphere of Israel's life, the response a defendant might give to his accuser. But there is no suggestion in Exod. 14:15 that Yahweh responds in a mood of self-defense.

[26] Von Waldow, pp. 34 ff., sees Israel's *rib* with Moses as a basic violation of covenantal relationship with Yahweh. But his argument overlooks two important distinctions: (1) The *rib* is not necessarily equated with the murmuring. Cf. Noth, *Überlieferungsgeschichte*, p. 135, n. 348; "Zur ursprünglichen Form der Geschichte gehört dieses Element [murmuring] vielleicht nicht; denn der Name Meriba führt nicht ungezwungen auf den Gedanken vom Murren des Volkes, da das Verbum ריב kein recht geeigneter Ausdruck dafür ist." Thus the shift from a *rib* with Moses to a supposed *rib* against Yahweh by citing the reference to murmuring in Exod. 16:8 (cf. p. 35, n. 9) appears methodologically unsound. (2) The *rib* at Meribah is not to be equated with testing Yahweh at Massah. Thus to suggest that Israel's *rib* at Meribah violates the covenant by posing an illegitimate test to see whether Yahweh was really among the people (p. 35) defines the nature of the *rib* by importing evidence from the Massah traditions (cf. vs. 7bβ). The earliest level of the Meribah tradition in this unit never construes Yahweh as the object of the *rib*. And the content of the *rib* with Moses does not permit a definition of its character by comparing it with the warning against a *rib* with one's creator in Isa. 45:9-13 (cf. von Waldow, p. 37). The *rib* in this tradition questions neither Moses' nor Yahweh's behavior, but simply presents a claim: "Give us water that we may drink."

tradition. In every occurrence of the name Meribah, with the single exception of Ps. 95:8, the prefix מ is to be found. But in none of those occurrences which might be called aetiological is any effort made to explain how the water might have become associated with the name. Even in Exod. 17, the text which shows how the water suddenly appeared in a place which originally had none, the aetiology is not directly concerned with the spring. Its presence is simply the consequence of the *rib* (cf. Deut. 33:8). It seems clear, then, that the local tradition is not concerned to give an aetiological explanation of the spring. The narrative of the spring out of a rock would thus represent a subsequent development which has been added to a local aetiology.

Moreover, there is some evidence to suggest that the motif of a spring produced from a rock was not primarily tied to Meribah. This is shown by a series of credo-like affirmations which relate Yahweh's aid in the face of crises (Deut. 8:14 ff.; Pss. 78:12 ff.; 105:37 ff.; Isa. 48:21; Neh. 9:9 ff.; cf. also Pss. 107:35; 114:8). These texts refer to the miracle of water being produced from the rock as we find it in the Meribah narratives in Exod. 17 and Num. 20. (The two obvious differences are: (1) It is Yahweh himself rather than Yahweh through Moses who performs the miracle, and (2) the people seem to fall into the background.) And these texts do not mention Meribah. Furthermore, there can be no doubt from these texts that the motif of water out of the rock is a positive one. Yahweh provides for the needs of the Israelites as the needs arise. Thus it seems clear that the Meribah tradition exhibits a secondary growth which introduces the motif of Yahweh's gracious aid in the wilderness into the context of a local tradition. To be sure, the *rib* which the people have with Moses points to some connection between the local aetiology and the narrative of the spring out of the rock in a locality which has no water. This connection may be explained as a secondary link between the two traditions, a link which gives the motif of water out of a rock a setting which it originally did not have. The term *rib* itself is a part of the link and thus not properly employed for either the request (demand) for the water or the murmuring.[27] Indeed, it seems to be tied more closely to the name, Meribah, and the legal character of the local tradition than to either of the principal themes in the expanded tradition.

The murmuring is first introduced in vs. 3. Vs. 3aα defines the nature of the crisis as the lack of water (cf. vs. 1bβ), while vs. 3aβ introduces the murmuring motif proper. The rebels are the people (העם), and the object of their rebellion is Moses. But in contradistinction to vs. 2 and Exod. 15:24, this event of murmuring is associated with a direct address in the form of an accusation. The introductory particle is למה; the verb is a 2. m. s. perfect form of עלה. Moses is challenged by this accusation to explain why he brought the people up from Egypt to die of thirst.

The significance of this challenge must be carefully defined. One might suppose that since the setting for the rebellion is a tradition about a spring and a crisis involving the threat of death from thirst is a part of the tradition, the focus of the rebellion would be on Moses' failure to provide water. But this is not the case. To be sure, the murmuring in vs. 3 is *introduced* with the notation that the people were thirsty. But in the question of accusation, the problem of thirst plays at best a minor role, appearing only in a dependent infinitive construct clause. It is not impossible for such a clause to carry the emphasis of the sentence. But when it does, the infinitive is normally placed before the governing verb (cf. Gen. 42:9).[28] The infinitive in vs. 3 seems to do nothing more than state the attendant circumstance of the primary action, in effect, the result of the action.[29] If, on the other hand, the threat of thirst were in fact the subject of the rebellion, the accusation could just as easily have been constructed: "Why have you brought us to a place without water to kill us with thirst?" But quite the contrary, the subject of the principal clause is the Exodus: "Why have you brought us up out of Egypt to kill us, our sons, and our cattle with

---

[27] Cf. above, p. 57, n. 24; p. 58, n. 26.
[28] Ges.K., # 114g, p. 348.
[29] Cf. above, p. 31.

thirst?" The problem of death by thirst is thus only the result of the fact that Moses had seized the authority (or had been given the authority by Yahweh) to bring the people out of Egypt. Indeed, the reference to thirst provides nothing more than the setting for the murmuring in a context of "no water." It can, then, be most adequately interpreted as a link between the murmuring motif and the tradition of a spring at Meribah.

But this does not complete the motif. Vs. 4 is, according to the narrative introduction, Moses' appeal to Yahweh (צעק). The appeal is in the form of a question. But the question is not an accusation against Yahweh. Rather, Moses is simply asking for help in handling a particular situation (cf. I Sam. 28:15). The situation is defined by vs. 4b as a grave crisis which poses a threat to Moses' life (וסקלני). That crisis can be nothing other than the rebellion (vs. 3; cf. Num. 14:10).

If, therefore, vs. 4 represents a request for help in responding to the murmuring, we must also consider whether Yahweh's response corresponds to the demand of the rebels. If it were intended to be an effort to establish Moses' authority in bringing the people out of Egypt, we might expect to find some indication of this. It could take the form of an *Erweiswort,* proving that Moses had had the authority to bring the people out by producing water out of the rock (cf. Exod. 16:6 ff.). Or the text could have bypassed the need to establish the authority of Moses by expressing sharp punishment for the rebellion (cf. Num. 16:25 ff.). But there is no word in the response about the problem of Moses' authority in the Exodus; there is no indication of punishment. To be sure, Yahweh instructs Moses to take some of the elders to witness the event (cf. vs. 6b: לעיני זקני ישראל). But there is no indication that they are there to witness evidence which will successfully establish Moses' authority vis-à-vis the accusation of the people. Rather, the elders seem to be the representatives of the people who are present to witness the execution of a miracle which will fulfill their need for water.[30]

---

[30] Cf. below, p. 77.

It seems probable, therefore, that the response in vss. 5-6 is not directly a part of the murmuring motif.

But if it is not a part of the murmuring, how does it fit into the complex of traditions in this unit? The most obvious recourse in answering this question is to suggest that here Yahweh is responding, not to a rebellion of the people, but to their positive request for water. It would appear to me, then, that the complexity in this unit, which drives Noth to conclude that two different, though undefined literary sources can be detected, is in fact to be explained on the basis of growth in the preliterary form of the tradition. This growth apparently involved an interweaving of two opposing motifs. We must conclude, moreover, that the murmuring motif has been introduced into and presupposes the positive motif, for the primary form of the local aetiology was expanded with the introduction of a legend about Israel's request for water, the substance of the positive motif. And this form of the tradition provides the setting for the murmuring in a situation of "no water."

Before we turn to the parallel Meribah narrative in Num. 20:1-13, we must consider still another negative element in this unit. This element is centered in the references to Massah, both in vs. 2bβ and vs. 7aβ. There can be little doubt that the name Massah refers to a locality which was quite distinct from Meribah. This can be seen chiefly from the various references to both place names which unmistakably hold them to be two different and independent places (Deut. 6:16; 9:22; Num. 20:13; esp. Ezek. 47:19; 48:28. But cf. Ps. 95:8-9). And even Deut. 33:8, a text which refers to both places in the same context, offers no evidence that the one was identified with the other.[31] Moreover, it is clear from the introduction in vs. 2, וירב העם עם־משה, and suggested by the uninterrupted juxtaposition of the name and its explanation in vs. 7, that Massah was not the original subject of the unit. It seems to be clear, then, that all references to

---

[31] Noth, *Exodus*, p. 139. But in a different line, cf. Eissfeldt, p. 43. Ps. 95:8 will be given detailed attention below, pp. 68-69.

Massah in vs. 7, as well as the preparation for the aetiology through the use of the verb נסה in vs. 2bβ, represent secondary additions to the text.

Our problem lies, then, in determining the significance of the appearance of Massah in the Meribah spring traditions. The name does not appear again in the Pentateuch, but by virtue of its association with Meribah and the possible allusion to Massah through the verb נסה in Exod. 15:25b, again in the context of a spring tradition, it seems certain that a fragment of another spring tradition lies before us. As it is reflected here and in Deut. 6:16; 9:22; and Ps. 95:8, the Israelites have subjected Yahweh to some sort of testing. Deut. 6:16; 9:22; and Ps. 95:8 reveal clearly that this event is held in a negative light. In the form of an apodictic commandment (Deut. 6:16) or an exhortation (Ps. 95:8), the testing at Massah is cited as an event which subsequent generations must not duplicate. Deut. 9:22 refers to the same event as one which provoked Yahweh to wrath.

Yet we have not reached the significance of the event. We have suggested that the verb נסה does not necessarily connote anything more than an unprejudiced testing of alternatives in order to see which is preferable. Thus it is noteworthy that Exod. 17:7bβ, the quotation immediately following the remark that Israel tested Yahweh, is formulated in terms of alternatives: "Is Yahweh in our midst or not?" (cf. also Ps. 78:18 ff.). But if this is an unprejudiced question, then on what basis is the negative interpretation of the event built? The principal difference between the testing as it is reflected in the Massah tradition and the testing which occurs, for example, in Judg. 3:4 is the fact that in the Massah tradition the testing is applied to *Yahweh* rather than a human or inanimate object. Thus Deut. 6:16 and Ps. 95:8 are not so much concerned with the fact that the Israelites *tested* Yahweh, but with the fact that the object of the testing was *Yahweh*.

The importance of this concern for Israelite piety is shown especially by Isa. 7:12. The prophet invites Ahaz to seek a sign from Yahweh which will show him that the crisis now facing Judah will shortly disappear under Yahweh's protective hand. Ahaz answers: "I will not ask, and I will not test Yahweh!" (ולא־אנסה את־יהוה). This response must be interpreted as a reflection of popular piety. Such testing would reveal a tragic lack of faith in the midst of a grave crisis. To be sure, the verb is used with reference to Gideon's trial (Judg. 6:39), but it appears only in the second sign, the first being much more similar to the sign which Isaiah had apparently expected Ahaz to seek. But even at this point, Yahweh is not the object of the verb. And this point notwithstanding, Gideon nevertheless must ask Yahweh's patience in view of his testing. Thus we may conclude that the significance of testing Yahweh lies in the question of faith. It is doubtlessly for this reason that Deuteronomy exhorts the subsequent generation to avoid the practice.

Since we have suggested that the basis for the concern about testing Yahweh comes out of popular piety extant in Israel as early as the time of Ahaz but given expression especially in Deuteronomy, we may now confirm our earlier observations that this addition to the Meribah tradition represents a deuteronomistic interpretation of the event at the spring, an interpretation which holds the event in a negative light. At least it would be clear that the "later hand" responsible for its presence here stands in the same pious tradition that is also found in Deuteronomy.

But the question of the nature of the tradition associated with Massah has not yet been completely resolved. In view of the fact that נסה itself has no negative connotations, we must now consider whether the view of Massah, which holds Israel to be the subject of the event and the event itself to be a negative example for future generations, represents the primary level of the tradition. We noticed in reference to the use of נסה in Exod. 15:25b that Yahweh rather than Israel was the subject, and that by means of "testing" Israel, he gave them his law and ordinance (חק ומשפט). According to vs. 26, if the Israelites would only obey these laws, the laws would work for the good of the people. Thus the connotation of the verb here is not negative. But the place name itself is not mentioned, and any suggestion about the original form of the Massah tradition based on this text alone would be only conjecture.

The same pattern which places Yahweh as the subject of the verb is also to be found in Deut. 33:8. The critical problems in the text of the so-called Blessing of Moses, Deut. 33:1-29, have received adequate attention[32] and need not detain us. Of more importance for our concern is the question of relationship between the Levitical tradition in the blessing of Levi and Massah: [33] Was the event of Levi's ordination the original event of testing at Massah, or have the two traditions come together at a subsequent stage of development? We are not so much concerned with the problem of whether the ordination of Levi was originally attached to Massah. Our question is focused on the Massah tradition: Does the Massah tradition reflect an earlier stage than the one which supports the Levitical ordination? And here we can be relatively certain that Levitical ordination does not constitute the oldest level of traditions associated with Massah. Yet it is probable that the form of testing in the Levitical ordination is at least older than the form of the Massah tradition which appears so predominantly in the Deuteronomist. And earlier stages of the tradition than the one reflected in the blessing of Levi cannot be defined on the basis of evidence in the Old Testament. Thus we must ask: What does this text reveal about the pattern of the Massah tradition? Vs. 8 shows Yahweh as the subject of the verb, Levi as the object of the testing, and the results in a *positive* light. By means of the testing, Levi was given authority for preservation and transmission of sacred traditions.

There is a significant parallel to the blessing of Levi in

[32] Frank M. Cross and David N. Freedman, "The Blessing of Moses," *JBL* LXVII (1948), 191 ff.; A. H. J. Gunneweg, *Leviten und Priester, Hauptlinien der Traditionsbildung und Geschichte des israelitisch-jüdischen Kultpersonals,* FRLANT LXXXIX (Göttingen: Vandenhoeck & Ruprecht, 1965), 39.

[33] That the references to Massah and Meribah in this text are intended as place names seems to be clear. Cf. Gunneweg, pp. 42-43, against S. Lehming, "Massa und Meriba," *ZAW* LXXIII (1961), 71-77.

Exod. 32:25-29. This brief unit is commonly recognized as a secondary addition to the complex of traditions in the Golden Calf narrative.[34] Moses calls all who support Yahweh to his side. The Levites answer the call and as a result receive the commission to execute a portion of the people. The consequence of the execution is the consecration of the Levites to Yahweh, clearly a reference to their ordination.[35] There are at least two points of parallel. The most obvious is the ordination. But it is also clear that in both texts Levi no longer represents a secular tribe; in both cases he is contrasted to near kinsmen who are not Levitic.

The problem here lies in the nature of the event which constitutes the ordination, i.e., the testing. In Exod. 32, the execution of the people suggests that the Levites have set themselves in opposition to a rebellion of the people (cf. the Excursus on Exod. 32 below). But is this a rebellion which is distinct from the Golden Calf incident? Or does the execution presuppose the connection of this bit of Levitical tradition with the larger context of Exod. 32? It is clear that vs. 25 provides a connection with the context, but its character is difficult to determine. Vs. 27 commissions the Levites to slay a portion of the people, not just the immediate kinsmen of the Levites, but the friends and neighbors (רעהו וקרבו). But vs. 29, the verse which carries the kernel of the ordination tradition, refers only to the immediate kin (בבנו ובאחיו).[36] Deut. 33:9 corresponds exactly. The Levites are called to reject only immediate kin. But does this rejection imply that the Levites slew their kin as a punishment for a rebellion which they, the kinsmen, initiated? The expression לא ראיתיו is a legal formula of disinheritance.[37] Vs. 9aβ would follow in the same vein: "His brother he disowns, and his son he does not know." The significance of the

[34] Cf. the Excursus below; also Noth, *Exodus*, p. 250; S. Lehming, "Versuch zu Ex. XXXII," *VT* X (1960), 42 ff.; Gunneweg, p. 29.

[35] Noth, *Exodus*, pp. 230-31.

[36] Gunneweg, pp. 31-32.

[37] Gerhard von Rad, *Das fünfte Buch Mose: Deuteronomium, ATD* VIII (Göttingen: Vandenhoeck & Ruprecht, 1964), 148.

fact that Levi disowned his father and his mother (vs. 9aα) is clear. He would not receive the inheritance due him as one of the sons of Israel. And this corresponds exactly with the tradition that Levi, unlike the other sons of Israel, did not have an inheritance. Moreover, it seems clear that when an individual became a Levite, he had to renounce the rights of his inheritance. Thus, in Judg. 17:7, the "Levite" left his Judahite family in Bethlehem "to dwell [גור—without in-heritance?] wherever he should find [a place]." The testing to which each Levite was subjected, then, would appear to be the demand to renounce family and the accompanying in-heritance. But if this is the case, then the demand to *kill* family *and* friends in Exod. 32:27 would represent a general-izing tendency peculiar to that unit and a means for connect-ing the Levitic rejection of family with the apostasy over the calf.[38] This leaves the entire tradition in Deut. 33:8-11 in a positive frame (cf. the designation of Levi as חסידך). At this point in the history of the Massah tradition, then, there is no trace of rebellion on the part of the people. Quite the con-trary, Yahweh tests his servant and finds him worthy of the priesthood.

It is surprising to find that this view of the event at Massah is connected with a parallel reference to Meribah. As in Massah, so with Meribah the subject of the verb is Yahweh, and Levi is the object. This recalls the primary level of local tradition associated with Meribah and supports our view of a positive form of the Massah tradition. But does the parallel mean that Meribah and Massah were already connected at this point in the history of their traditions? And would it then suggest that Massah is not necessarily a foreign element in Exod. 17? This does not necessarily follow, for if the thesis is correct that both Massah and Meribah represent spring traditions, and perhaps even traditions located in the area of Kadesh, and that both are associated with legal process, we would have sufficient grounds for setting them in parallel

---

[38] Cf. the similar analysis by Gunneweg, pp. 32-33.

in this poem. But there is no evidence here to suggest that the two were in fact identical.

We can develop our understanding of this complex of spring traditions one step further. Ps. 81:8 also refers to Meribah with Yahweh as the subject of the verb and Israel the object. The event is described in parallel construction with a sentence which strongly suggests a positive attitude: "In distress you called and I delivered you. I answered you in the secret place of thunder. I tested you at the waters of Meribah." But the verb which defines the event here is בחן. Thus the positive view of the event is maintained even though the concern for an aetiological play on the root ריב has been dropped.[39]

Ps. 95:8-9 reverses this pattern, making Israel the subject of the verb and Yahweh the object.[40] The synonymous parallelism illumines the nature of the reversal:

> 8. Do not harden your hearts, as at Meribah,
>   As on the day of Massah in the wilderness
> 9. When your fathers tested me,
>   When they tried me even though they had seen my work.

In vs. 8 both Meribah and Massah are governed as parallel members by the introductory אל־תקשו, suggesting that only one event is ascribed to both places. But the character of this introductory verb is made more explicit in vs. 9 by two verbs, joined to vs. 8 through an אשר clause. It is unlikely that the first verb refers to one of the sites while the second refers to the other since the אשר connects both verbs in the same way to both sites. The only conclusion that seems possible is that they both refer to a common event introduced by תקשו. If this is the case, it would mean that the two places are here identified with each other and mark this form of the tradition as a late development which corresponds to the addition of

---

[39] Aarre Lauha, *Die Geschichtsmotive in den alttestamentlichen Psalmen* (Helsinki: Druckerei der finnischen Literaturgesellschaft, 1945), p. 78.

[40] Like Ps. 81:8, Ps. 95:8-9 reflects a stage in the tradition which is no longer concerned with an aetiology.

Massah to the narrative in Exod. 17:2, 7. The fact that the prefix מי is omitted from the name מריבה nowhere else in the Old Testament except here would strengthen this conclusion.

But what relationship does this use of נסה have to the murmuring motif? This problem is clarified by reference to the introductory verb קשה in context with the noun לב. The expression "to harden one's heart" suggests an attitude of disobedience and apostasy. In Exod. 7:3-4, Yahweh warns Moses that he will harden Pharaoh's heart (אקשה את-לב); the result will be that Pharaoh will not obey (לא-ישמע) Moses' command to let the people go (cf. also Deut. 2:30; Jer. 7:26; 19:15; Ezek. 2:4; 3:7). The parallel and more common construction of the vocable קשה, either as a verb or a noun, with ערף (cf. II Chr. 36:13) opens an even broader background for understanding the expression in Ps. 95. It is noteworthy that the construction of קשה with ערף occurs several times in contexts which reflect deuteronomistic style (Deut. 9:6, 13; 10:16; 31:27; II Kings 17:14; Jer. 17:23). Moreover, a relatively high concentration of the terms appears in deuteronomistic sections of the story of the Golden Calf, describing in particular an apostate Israel (Exod. 32:9; 33:3, 5; 34:9; cf. also Deut. 9:13). It seems to be clear, then, that this expression has a generalizing and spiritualizing connotation. The citation from Yahweh in Ps. 95:10 supports this conclusion: "They are a people who err in heart, and they do not know my ways."

However, it is not clear from these examples that this expression can be used to refer to events which constitute the murmuring motif. Deut. 9:6, 13 combine the two in the same context, although the two are curiously distinct. II Chr. 30:7 uses the expression for a distinct tradition which recalls the faithlessness (מעל) of the fathers. But it is not clear whether the "fathers" refer to the wilderness generation or a subsequent generation. Indeed, we must be cautious here, for II Kings 17:14 shows quite clearly that the fathers who are indicted in terms of this particular expression represent the generation *after* the wilderness period. It is also clear here that the *sin* is not rebellion, i.e., challenging the authority of the leaders, but apostasy, i.e., worship of idols (cf. Jer. 7:26; 17:23). Thus we cannot assume that every reference to the sin of the "fathers" or to hardening the neck or heart is a part of the murmuring motif in the wilderness traditions.

On the other hand, there can be no doubt that this expression has been taken into the recitation of events which compose the murmuring motif (cf. Deut. 31:27). We might note in this connection the interesting juxtaposition in Neh. 9:17 of disobedience, vs. 17aα, and rebellion, vs. 17aβ, with this expression falling between the two. But it is significant that this text is late; indeed, the expression never occurs in relationship to the wilderness traditions in a text which is certainly earlier than Deuteronomy. This distribution, along with our previous study of Massah, leaves us no alternative to the conclusion that this level of the spring traditions is deuteronomistic in character.

To summarize: Both the Meribah and the Marah traditions as they appear in J exhibit three principal levels. The first is the local aetiology, based on nothing more than a word play. The second level introduces a tradition about Yahweh's miraculous aid in the crises of wilderness life. For both Marah and Meribah, the miraculous aid seems to have had no primary role to play in the aetiological explanation of the place name; in fact, the tradition about a spring out of a rock may not have been originally connected with any particular locality. The third level is the murmuring motif, the first indication in the traditions of a negative interpretation. In the case of Meribah, the negative interpretation is dependent on Yahweh's gracious aid rather than the aetiological tradition. The content of the murmuring is not shown in the Marah tradition, but for the Meribah tradition it is based on an accusation about Moses' responsibility in the Exodus, with the crisis over the lack of water offering only the immediate setting. These levels were in all probability already combined before the tradition reached literary form. Moreover, there is firm basis for suggesting that an even later process of leveling traditional characteristics, probably associated with the Deuteronomist in its earliest stages, has joined Meribah with a tradition about the spring at Massah and interpreted them both as traditions which show Israel's lack of faith in Yahweh.

Numbers 20:1-13

Our next task is to examine the parallel version of the Meribah tradition in Num. 20:1-13. We have noted that the Exodus account of Meribah is basically J. This is particularly important since the tradition already reveals three levels of development in distinct form there. On the other hand, the narrative which now lies before us is predominantly P. The itinerary notation in vs. 1aα cannot be mistaken. But here, as in the previous units, the itinerary is not a part of the narrative which follows. Even for the P source, the itinerary seems to form an artificial framework.[41] Vs. 1b is an element of information essentially attached to the place name and thus to be considered a part of the itinerary rather than the principal unit (on vs. 1aβ, cf. below). The narrative itself begins in vs. 2.

There can be no doubt that the unit here is parallel to the tradition in Exod. 17:1-7, for exactly the same outline is to be found in both cases: (1) The setting involves the lack of water. (2) The people "strive" with Moses. (3) They also murmur against their leaders. (The P form uses קהל instead of לון and directs the murmuring against both Moses and Aaron.) (4) Moses appeals to Yahweh. (5) Yahweh gives instructions for finding water. (6) Moses carries out the instructions before witnesses by striking a rock. (7) The narrative is concluded with an aetiological explanation of the place name.

Yet despite the close parallel, there are only a few points of verbatim agreement with the Exodus account that might suggest literary dependence on the J form of the tradition. The most extensive among these is the notice in vs. 3a that the people presented a *rib* to Moses (וירב העם עם־משה ויאמרו—)

---

[41] Martin Noth, *Das vierte Buch Mose: Numeri, ATD* VII (Göttingen: Vandenhoeck & Ruprecht, 1966), 127-28.

cf. Exod. 17:2*a*α and ויאמרו in vs. 2*a*β). This parallel is especially conspicuous since the Numbers account of the Meribah tradition uses the term העם to refer to the Israelites in only one other case, vs. 1*a*β, and this is a fragment which many scholars assign to an older source, if not specifically to J.[42] Moreover, P seems to take great pains to include Aaron as an equal participant in the problems faced by the leadership of the congregation (cf. vs. 2*b*). But here, as in Exod. 17:2*a*, the object of the preposition is only Moses.

A few other fragments which follow the form of the tradition in J may be seen in the development of the narrative. The first part of the murmuring question from Exod. 17:3*b* appears in vs. 5*a*α (especially if one accepts the insertion of τοῦτο from the LXX). This correspondence is even more apparent in light of the *scriptio defectiva* in vs. 5*a*α (העליתנו); only the pointing harmonizes a consonantal form of the verb which agrees with the singular subject in Exod. 17:3 with the plural subject of this text (cf. also the Codex Vaticanus and Old Latin). The setting of the story from Exod. 17:1*b*β appears only slightly rearranged in Num. 20:5*a*β, but in P it hardly serves as a setting. The narrative introduction to Yahweh's response is addressed only to Moses in both Exod. 17:5*a*α and Num. 20:7, but the P version nevertheless brings Aaron into the account. Beyond these points, there is no evidence of contact in the literary structure of the two narratives.

How, then, are we to evaluate the points of agreement between the two units? Noth concludes that they are to be considered doublets or secondary additions in the P text.[43] But is this a problem in the literary history of P or a question

---

[42] Noth, *Numeri*, pp. 127-28 (cf. also *Überlieferungsgeschichte*, p. 34); G. B. Gray, *Numbers*, *ICC* (Edinburgh: T and T Clark, 1903), p. 260. H. Holzinger, *Numeri*, *KHAT* IV (Tübingen: J. C. B. Mohr [Paul Siebeck], 1903), 84, and Strack, p. 422, simply distinguish vs. 1*a*β from P without assigning it to a source.

[43] Noth, *Numeri*, p. 127. But for a different position, cf. Gerhard von Rad, *Die Priesterschrift im Hexateuch*, *BWANT*, Folge 4, Heft 13 [63] (Stuttgart: W. Kohlhammer Verlag, 1934), 117-18.

in the history of the tradition and sources which lie behind
P? The two principal problem areas are in vss. 2b-3a and
vss. 4-5. We shall show below that vs. 4 does indeed carry the
peculiar emphasis of P. But the second question in vs. 5 cannot be considered its doublet. Quite the contrary, it carries
the proper emphasis of the murmuring motif and must therefore be considered a given part of the tradition which P has
inherited. Moreover, vs. 2b also shows characteristics of P.
And the redundancy between this half verse and vs. 3a poses
the same problem confronted in Exod. 17:1bβ-3. Yet vs. 3a
cannot be discounted as a fragment from the J account in
Exodus which has been secondarily added to the P account,
for as in the J narrative, so here it forms the foundation for
the aetiology. This problem area, then, must also be considered a part of the tradition employed by P. With the exception of vs. 1aβ, then, the entire unit may be attributed to P.

The P account corresponds to its Exodus parallel by making Moses rather than Yahweh the object of the "striving."
But contrary to the Exodus account, there is no imperative
directed to Moses concerning the demand for water. Instead,
both the reference to the murmuring in vs. 2b and the reference to the *rîb* in vs. 3a are followed by an address of the
people in vss. 3b ff. without indication of distinct differences
or connotations.

The address itself constitutes the murmuring. It is significant in the light of our argument concerning the murmuring in Exod. 17:1bβ-2 and 3 that the second person verbs
in the address are consistently plural. This presupposes that
the address is the continuation, not of vs. 3a, where only
Moses is the addressee, but of vs. 2a, where both Moses and
Aaron are the objects of the murmuring. To be sure, vs. 3b
does not have a second person plural verb. But this half-verse
is also a part of the murmuring, as is shown without doubt
by Num. 14:2 (cf. also Josh. 7:7, where the לו clause is also
associated with a *waw* conjunction, but appears *after* the
question) . This form of a wish connected with the accusation
in vss. 4-5 only heightens the note of despair reflected in the

accusation (cf. Exod. 16:3a).[44] But if vss. 3b ff. are a part of the murmuring motif, then vs. 3a as it now stands is isolated from its context. In fact, the only role which may be attributed to it in the entire narrative is the foundation for the aetiology in vs. 13. Thus it seems clear that along with vs. 3a, the problem of relationship between the rib and the murmuring has been incorporated into P from a received tradition. P offers no further evidence to illumine the problem. But the fact that P makes no further use of the phrase in vs. 3a in a context which dwells heavily on the murmuring supports the hypothesis suggested above, for it shows that for P the rib has no intrinsic connection with the murmuring. We could not therefore consider Num. 20:2b and 3a doublets.

Despite the similarity between the J parallel and this unit, especially in the foundation for the aetiology in vs. 3a, the aetiology itself (vs. 13) deviates from its J counterpart: Yahweh is now the object. This construction is in sharp contrast to vs. 3a and underlines the fact that in the earlier form of the tradition Yahweh is never used as the object of the verb ריב. As with the verb נסה, so now we must ask whether ריב with Yahweh as the object is in itself a negative concept which, in the same sense as Exod. 17:2bβ, can be considered a part of the murmuring motif. Jer. 12:1 suggests that it is not impossible for a prophet to have a rib with Yahweh. But it is significant that this rib appears in the context of the confessions of Jeremiah. It is quite plausible to suggest that even for a prophet such activity was undertaken at great risk (cf. Jer. 2:29; Job 33:13; Judg. 21:22). It is, moreover,

[44] Any suggestion about what particular event might have involved the "brethren perishing before Yahweh" must remain at best tenuous. Perhaps it refers to the death of the people associated with Korah (cf. גוע in Num. 17:27, 28). But the point to be considered here is whether it refers to an event in the past which, because of the expression בגוע אחינו לפני יהוה, might also be cited as a part of the murmuring motif. If it does, and this seems likely whether the event is to be identified with Korah or some other, then P presupposes not only a form of the Meribah tradition which is also found in J, but also a connected account of the wilderness traditions which already is organized around some kind of chronological principle. Whether that principle is the murmuring motif itself will be considered below, p. 220, n. 71.

of more than passing importance that in Jer. 12:1 the preposition which accompanies ריב is אל. In contrast, the preposition which governs the object in Num. 20:13 is את. This contrast, plus the fact that the use of את here is a deviation from the combination ריב . . . עם in Exod. 17:2 and Num. 20:3, puts special emphasis on this construction. It is thus significant that Isa. 45:9 reads: "Woe to the one who strives with (רב את־) his maker." (Cf. also Job 9:3 and 40:2, although the preposition here is עם.) Moreover, the fact that in no other case is the deity the object of this verb suggests that we can interpret it here in only one way. This expression, just as מה־תנסון את־יהוה in Exod. 17:2b, must be taken in a negative light. P has thus extended the impact of the murmuring motif even into the aetiological level of the tradition.

The aetiology has a further addition over its parallel in Exod. 17:7. It has been suggested that vs. 13b, perhaps an allusion to the fragment in vs. 1aβ, was intended to be an aetiological reference to Kadesh.[45] That all these spring traditions are tied to localities in the Kadesh area seems to be rather certain. But why should an aetiological play on Kadesh enter the Meribah tradition in P when no reference to it has previously been encountered? The answer to this question lies in the peculiar role of the vocable קדש in this narrative. There is only one other occurrence of this word before vs. 13b; a Hiph'il infinitive construct of the verb from this root appears in vs. 12aβ, associated with the vexing problem of Moses' and Aaron's sin. We shall consider the problem in detail below; for now, we may note simply that vs. 12 accuses Moses and Aaron of failing to sanctify Yahweh through unbelief (לא האמנתם). The unbelief was apparent to all the people and probably refers to an event which was associated in some manner with the miracle of the spring out of the rock (cf. Num. 27:14; Deut. 32:51). In vs. 13, however, the vocable קדש does not refer to something which Moses and Aaron have failed to do but to something which Yahweh has in fact

[45] Noth, *Numeri*, p. 129, concludes that vs. 13b is a later redactional addition to the P material built on vs. 1aβ. Cf. also Gressmann, pp. 150-51.

done for himself (thus, the reflexive sense of the Niph'al). And this is not done *before* the people (לעיני), but *among* them (thus, בם). We may presume the antecedent of the *mem* suffix to be the בני־ישראל in vs. 13a since this is the nearest plural noun and nothing demands a decisive break between the two verse halves. In this case Yahweh's action would be considered his response to the striving of the Israelites. Both vs. 13a and vs. 13b, therefore, have been incorporated into the murmuring motif.

The results of these observations suggest that P shows a process of leveling distinctive characteristics of the Meribah tradition under the one common character of murmuring, a process which has obscured both the first and the second levels which were still distinct in the J form of the tradition. But what is the character of the murmuring here? The single question from Exod. 17:3 which carries the content of the murmuring has been expanded in this narrative into two questions. One of the questions (vs. 5) maintains the emphasis on the Exodus which was seen in Exod. 17. But the infertility of the land plays a much more prominent role. Vs. 5a refers to the wilderness only as המקום הרע הזה, while vs. 5bα defines the character of the place in terms of infertility. But the note about the lack of water in vs. 5bβ still stands virtually as an anticlimax to the emphasis given by the list of plants. The question in vs. 4 is distinctive. It challenges the act of bringing the people to the wilderness, an act which, according to the complaint of the people, will result in the death of the people and their cattle. But the cause of death is not noted. Thus it seems that even here the setting which apparently gives rise to the murmuring has no essential role in the murmuring itself. This question, then, serves to broaden the character of the murmuring in vs. 5 and its parallel in Exod. 17:3. As such, it does not represent a secondary addition to the P form of the tradition, but an indication of P's characteristic manner for handling the murmuring motif.

In response to the murmuring, Moses and Aaron defer to the authority of Yahweh. The instructions which follow give us our next problem. The instructions here are strikingly similar to the ones in the J form of the tradition. Moses alone is commanded to take the staff and a group of witnesses to a rock. To be sure, the witnesses are not a representative group from the elders but the whole congregation. But even in Exod. 17:5, the narrative assumes that the whole congregation is involved since by means of this miracle Moses is to provide water for the whole people (cf. Exod. 17:6aβ). It is possible that the rest of the people may have gathered at the rock after the miracle was over. But what would be the point of that? If the event were too holy for the whole people to witness, then P would not likely drop this facet of the tradition and allow all the people to be there. Moreover, there is no hint in Exod. 17:6 that some length of time elapsed before the remaining people came to the spring to drink. It is possible, too, that the water was carried back for the people. But no mention is made of this, and such a hypothesis would only complicate a tradition which is already very complex. It is much more likely that P preserves the original form of the tradition and that the whole people were in fact witnesses to the event.

But what, then, is the significance of the reference to the elders in Exod. 17:5-6? One is reminded here of the role which the elders play in the J manna narrative in Num. 11:16 ff. In both places, the people are apparently taken to witness the miraculous event (Num. 11:18); but in both places, the tradition is confounded and we find only a representative portion of the elders selected (Num. 11:16). In the manna narrative, however, it is quite clear that a foreign element has intruded into the narrative. This problem will be considered in further detail below. This does not prove, however, that the reference to the elders here is a foreign element in the tradition. It only provides us with a suggestion that the original form of the tradition concerning the miraculous spring from the rock probably involved the whole people rather than selected representatives.

These factors seem to reflect a form of the tradition of Yahweh's aid in the wilderness which is positive in character.

But if the background of this text is a positive tradition, a tradition which would contradict P's emphasis on the murmuring motif, it is quickly given P's own stamp. In vs. 8aα Moses alone is requested to take the staff; the tradition here assumes a form of the miracle which would be effected through the staff (cf. Exod. 17:5-6). But in vs. 8aα Aaron is included as a part of the addressee, and the text notes that the two will be required to *speak* to the rock (ודברתם). Vs. 9 again assumes that the command concerns only Moses; indeed, the MT in vs. 8b returns to the use of a singular verb in its address.[46] Vs. 9a shows that the staff is to be the instrument of the miracle, while vs. 9b suggests that the instructions are being executed according to the form in which they were given. There is no indication of anything amiss here, and we must assume that the background of this lies in the positive tradition of Yahweh's aid.

But the problem of P's form of the tradition arises again in vs. 10. Here both Moses and Aaron are once more the subject of the action. They gather the people at the rock and address them with a participle from the verb מרה. This root is commonly used in later texts to refer to the events which compose the murmuring motif (Deut. 1:26, 43; 9:7, 23, 24; Ezek. 20:8, 13, 24; Pss. 78:8, 17, 40, 56; 106:7, 33, 43; Neh. 9:17, 26), and there can be little doubt that this is intended to be a part of the murmuring motif here.[47] Moreover, this address shows another process of leveling. P has dropped all reference to the Exodus as the basis for the rebellion even though it was present in P in vs. 5. In its place, he now suggests that the substance of the rebellion lies totally in the request for water.

---

[46] The LXX makes the verb plural in vs. 8bα, but this seems to be nothing more than a harmonization with the context.

[47] We cannot agree with Gray, p. 263, that this participle does not refer to the people since the people "had murmured but not rebelled." Nor is it necessary to suppose that vs. 10b (שמעו־נא המרים) is actually addressed to Moses and Aaron (p. 263). To be sure, the two are also called rebels (Num. 20:24; 27:14; cf. also Deut. 32:51 with the verb מעל). But this is hardly enough evidence to demand a major reconstruction of the text that is not supported by any of the MSS or versions. Cf. also the reconstruction suggested by Baentsch, p. 569, and Gressmann, p. 150, n. 2.

This may point to two different P sources here. But it seems more probable that the change reflects a problem in the history of the tradition. We suggest, then, that even though P receives the emphasis on the Exodus from his source, he no longer understands the distinctive impact of that emphasis for the rebellion motif (cf. especially vs. 4). This characteristic of P will be pursued further as the development of the rebellion motif becomes clear.

Vs. 11 further heightens the complexity of this unit. Since it begins with Moses alone as the subject who raises the staff to strike the rock, we may again have a reflection of the positive tradition. But this text is conspicuous in its variation from Exod. 17:6 in that it notes that Moses strikes the rock *twice*. The emphasis on the word פעמים, again a peculiarity of P, especially stands out in contrast to the command in vs. 8a to *speak* to the rock. This is immediately followed by an address from Yahweh to both Moses and Aaron. Both of them have shown their lack of faith in Yahweh, and as a result they will not be allowed to bring the people into the promised land. The first problem to meet us here is why P should incorporate a tradition into his version of Meribah which concerns a capital sin of Israel's leaders. The reason is clear. One of the strongest, if not the strongest, of all traditions about both Moses and Aaron is that they were not a part of the generation that finally entered the promised land. In their place (or perhaps in the place of Moses), Joshua was the leader. This development would provide a traditio-historical foundation for the disturbing fact that they died before they reached the land.[48] Thus the accounts of Aaron's death (Num. 20:24) and of Moses' death (Num. 27:14; Deut. 32:51) allude to Moses' and Aaron's sin. And with three notable exceptions (Deut. 1:37; 3:26; Ps. 106:32), the sin is not mentioned elsewhere in the Old Testament.

Those three exceptions must now occupy our attention. All three exhibit the common tendency to extricate Moses (Aaron falls out of consideration here) from the notion that

[48] Cf. Gressmann, pp. 152-53; Noth, *Numeri*, p. 129.

he was being punished for a sin he might have committed at Meribah. This is done by interpreting his punishment as a vicarious death on behalf of the sins of the people. Thus, Deut. 1:37: "Also Yahweh was angry with me on your account (בגללכם)." Deut. 3:26: "And Yahweh was furious with me because of you (למענכם)." And finally, Ps. 106:32: "They angered him (thus, the LXX and Syriac) at the waters of Meribah, and it went badly for Moses on their account (בעבורם)." Moreover, it seems clear that vs. 33a of Ps. 106 reflects the same tradition. The fathers were responsible for making his spirit bitter, as is shown by the third person plural Hiph'il verb which can refer only to the fathers. Vs. 33b can then be nothing other than a response to the action of the fathers: "And he spoke rashly with his lips."

What was the event which has been interpreted by tradition as such a gross offense? Ps. 106:33b presupposes that Moses had said something and that the character of his statement was rash or thoughtless (ויבטא בשפתיו). This is far from explicit, but it must be an allusion to the sin. But what relationship would a sin of speech have with Num. 20? It seems first that the command to speak, a peculiarity in P which stands out sharply from its context as a plural verb in the midst of other verbs which the MT leaves singular, must lie at the basis of P's construction of this development in the tradition. Moreover, the emphasis on the fact that Moses actually struck the rock twice is also a peculiarity of P. The juxtaposition of the two is too conspicuous to be anything other than a conscious formulation. If the sin also includes a rash statement on the part of Moses, then the statement must be vs. 10b, for that is the only citation immediately associated with the miracle. We have already suggested that at least the introduction of this statement is to be associated with the overall interpretation of Meribah in P as a tradition of rebellion. The participle המרים can refer only to the people. But the remaining part of the address is related at least in content to the event of bringing a spring out of the rock: "Shall we bring water out of this rock for you?"

This question corresponds to our expectations for the rash

words from Ps. 106:32 in at least three ways: First, it shows
that both Moses and Aaron are held responsible for striking
the rock (נוציא). It thus provides a clear relationship with
the event which obviously forms the basis for the sin. Second,
it presupposes the rebellion of the people. It is introduced by
a reference to the people as rebels, while the content of the
question presupposes P's view of what the rebellion was. And
third, it suggests that it is because of the people's rebellion
that Moses speaks and strikes the rock. Thus the vicarious
nature of the sin can also be seen in this text; i.e., it is the
rebellion of the people that was really responsible for Moses'
sin. We may conclude, therefore, that both the question and
event constitute the sin. The ironical inconsistency that Aaron
plays no role in striking the rock, yet is held responsible for
the lack of faith, is softened by the plural verb in vs. 10.
Yet it is important to note here that it is only Moses who
speaks and strikes the rock. This points to an even closer
relationship to Ps. 106:32-33 and raises the question about
the relationship between the two examples of the tradition. If
the rough inclusion of Aaron may be attributed to P, we
might conclude that Deut. 1:37; 3:26; and Ps. 106:32-33
exhibit the primary form of the tradition, concerned only with
the death of Moses. If this is the case, and it seems probable
to me, it would have important consequences for our understanding of the rebellion motif, for it would mean that P is
drawing on a tradition which already holds the events at
Meribah, perhaps including the request for water, to be
rebellion.

In summary, the P version of Meribah is dominated by two
levels of development. The first is a form of the tradition
which levels all previous distinctive characteristics of development under the one stamp of the murmuring motif. This level
is marked especially by the role of the people's *rib* with Moses
in vs. 3a which loses all other significance in the narrative
except its function as the basis for the aetiology in vs. 13.
Some reflections of a positive form of the tradition may still
be seen in vss. 8-9, but vs. 13 shows once again that the tradition
has been made uniformly a part of the murmuring motif. The

murmuring motif itself is much the same as that which was reflected in J. To be sure, it adds several factors, such as, e.g., Aaron as an object of the murmuring and the accusation concerning the fact that Moses had brought them into a barren wilderness. This addition is perhaps due to P's failure to understand the significance which lies in the murmuring. But the emphasis on the Exodus can still be seen. The second level is an adaptation of this broad version of the murmuring motif to form the basis for an explanation of the fact that Moses and Aaron were not allowed to go into the land. This adaptation is related to an interpretation of the punishment as a vicarious substitution for the deserved punishment of the people, a tradition which in P presupposes the problem of the people's rebellion. But the rebellion at this point no longer concerns the Exodus, but now is dominated completely by the request for water. Moreover, this tradition, even in P, has only a rough and indefinite relationship with Aaron. Behind it can be seen a tradition which spoke of Moses alone.

the food narratives

Exodus 16:1-35

The source problem in this chapter is even more difficult to resolve than in the previous sections. Vs. 1 is obviously a part of the same P itinerary framework which we have seen previously. The first literary unit in vss. 2-3 is also P, even though there is no indication of a connection with, or even a conscious transition from, the itinerary. We are thus left with the impression that the itinerary is an artificial construction which has been used as a framework for various sources, including P (cf. Num. 20:1).

Vss. 2-3 are marked as P by the full designation for the people, כל־עדת בני־ישראל, and by the reference to both Moses and Aaron. In contrast, vs. 4 offers an address by Yahweh to Moses alone, with the designation of the people as העם. Vss. 4-5, with the exception of vs. 4bβ, are a literary unity which first announces the coming of the manna and lays the foundation for the stipulation concerning the Sabbath. Vs. 4bβ stands out in these two verses because of its use of נסה and תורה. The catchword נסה connects this fragment with the addition which was noted above in Exod. 17:2bβ, 7, and suggests that this quarter-verse should be labeled a deuterono-

83

mistic gloss.[1] The remaining part of the verses should in all probability be considered a part of J.

Vss. 6-7 return to a reference to both Moses and Aaron as well as the full designation for the people (cf. LXX: πρὸς πᾶσαν συναγωγὴν υἱῶν Ἰσραὴλ). These characteristics connect this section with the P narrative in vss. 2-3. Vs. 8 is corrupt. The verse is composed of two infinitive clauses, each governed by the preposition ב. But there seems to be no essential contact between them and certainly no relationship to a complete sentence; quite the contrary, both clauses seem to be left hanging as incomplete fragments. Since they are incomplete, we might suppose that they are meaningless scraps. But they do have a relationship in content to their context. Vs. 8aβb is virtually a doublet of vs. 7aβb, while vs. 8aα is remarkably similar to both vss. 6-7 and especially vs. 12. We shall therefore consider them glosses intended to explain the rather obscure references in vss. 6-7.

Vss. 9-10 are clearly a continuation of vs. 7 and thus a part of the P narrative. Once again we have a full designation for the people as well as a reference to both Moses and Aaron. But the decisive indication that these verses should be considered a part of the P narrative is the reference to the כבוד יהוה (cf. Exod. 14:4). Vss. 11-13 are not so clear. The address is only to Moses, and the designation of the people is shortened to בני ישראל. Moreover, the content of the address in vs. 12 is quite similar to the address which has already been delivered to them in vss. 6-7, even to the extent of including a repetition of the self-revelation formula (cf. vs. 6b). Yet even though the connection with the foregoing P narrative is far from smooth, there is no firm reason for denying it to P. Vs. 13 follows naturally as an account of the execution of the event announced in vs. 12.

Vs. 14a presents the next problem. This half-verse is apparently a doublet of vs. 13b. But part of the problem which prevents a firm conclusion here lies in the interpretation of the שכבת הטל. If the dew and the manna are distinct entities,

---

[1] Noth, *Überlieferungsgeschichte*, p. 32, n. 109.

THE FOOD NARRATIVES 85

the two half-verses would not be doublets; vs. 14a would
report that after the dew disappeared, the manna was visible
on the ground. This might be implied also by Num. 11:9,
where the appearance of the dew is described by a Qal infinitive construct with the preposition ב while the appearance
of the manna is described by a 3. m. s. Qal imperfect. To
be sure, both verbs are from the root ירד. But they nevertheless
give the impression of distinct events. Yet the antecedent of
the suffix attached to the preposition in vs. 9b (עליו) is not
the dew but the camp, also the object of the preposition
על in vs. 9a. The verse shows nothing more than that the two
were in some way closely related. On the other hand, if Exod.
16:13a and 13b are in parallel construction, as they appear to
be, then the שכבת הטל in vs. 13b would be the manna itself.
This conclusion would suggest that vs. 14a is a new report
of the same event, the appearance of the manna. Moreover,
from vs. 14 to the end of the chapter, the quail play no role,
although in vs. 13 they are equally as important as the manna.
Thus, in contrast to the P account which reports the double
miracle of manna and quail, we now have a new account
concerned only with the manna.[2]

We can thus consider the possibility that vss. 14 ff. form a
continuation of the J source in vss. 4-5. Support for a connection between the two sections would be derived from the
fact that neither mention Aaron, the favorite son of P. Yet
we must weigh the evidence carefully. Vss. 14-15 offer a sort
of popular etymology for the name "manna." Vss. 16-18
could indeed be considered a continuation of vss. 4-5 since
vs. 16 mentions the fact that Yahweh has previously issued a
commandment concerning the manna, a commandment which
in fact appears in vs. 4. This connection is supported by the
fact that the verb which described the action in the commandment is in both cases a Qal plural form of לקט. But
several words appear here which, according to Driver's classic

---

[2] Eissfeldt, p. 37, correctly rejects Holzinger's supposition that the
quail represent a secondary item in the text.

list,[3] are characteristic of P: לאכלה (vs. 15), נלגלת (vs. 16), נפש in the sense of a person (vs. 16), and ערף (vs. 18). The question now is whether an argument from vocabulary is sufficient to deny the section to J.

But the unit is not yet completed. Vss. 19-20 introduce a new element of content into the narrative: The manna is not to be kept until morning. Even though the people have been careful to follow all instructions precisely to this point (cf. vs. 17), they do not do so here. That this deviation leads to no further consequences might suggest that the text is incomplete. But it is nevertheless an essential part of the unit, preparing the reader for the significance of the manna kept overnight for the Sabbath (vs. 24).

In vs. 22 the people are able to gather a double portion of manna in preparation for the Sabbath and respond, apparently in surprise, by going immediately to tell Moses. Noth points out that this surprising event was nevertheless announced in vs. 5.[4] But since that announcement is directed only to Moses, and there is no indication that the information was passed on to the people at that moment, there would be no difficulty here. Vs. 23 makes a further reference to a previous command about the Sabbath (cf. vs. 5). Both this verse and vs. 16 may well be considered the first announcement to the people of the instructions received earlier. Vss. 27-28 can be considered another deuteronomistic gloss; they report that contrary to the direction of Yahweh, the people went out on the Sabbath to gather manna anyway. But this is not prohibited specifically until vs. 29, while the notation in vs. 30 contradicts this gloss by saying that the people stayed in their places on the Sabbath after all. The possibility is thus raised that vs. 29 is the normal continuation of vs. 26. As it now stands, vs. 29 is a part of a speech by Yahweh (cf. vs. 28).

---

[3] S. R. Driver, *An Introduction to the Literature of the Old Testament* (Meridian Library Edition; New York: Meridian Books, The World Publishing Co., 1960), p. 131. Cf. also Beer, p. 87; Baentsch, p. 151. On the other hand, Eissfeldt, pp. 37-38, feels that everything in this section which might be considered P can be resolved as a later reworking in the style of P or as not necessarily a P characteristic.

[4] Noth, *Exodus*, pp. 131-32.

But the speech mentions Yahweh by name. Vss. 25-26, on the other hand, are an address by Moses concerning the Sabbath. Vs. 29 could better be interpreted as a part of Moses' speech since it also concerns the Sabbath. And vss. 29-30 are clearly a part of the J narrative.

Vs. 31 is another explanation of the name manna and thus a doublet of vss. 14-15 (cf. LXX in vs. 31). Vs. 32 is a doublet of vs. 33 and apparently to be assigned to J. If vs. 32 is indeed J, then vs. 31 would appear in a J context, and we might well conclude that it too is a part of the J narrative. This position would lend weight to the identification of vss. 14 ff. as P. The final decision concerning this section is difficult at best, while a firm conclusion is impossible. Perhaps the best solution would be to suggest that if the section in vss. 14-26 is after all P, it presupposes an introduction similar to vss. 4-5, a continuation similar to vss. 29 ff., and is quite distinct from the other P tradition about both quail and manna. We could then suppose that the introduction of this tradition was displaced by the use of vss. 4-5, and that the remaining part of the tradition was inserted here because of the catchword שכבת הטל in vs. 13b.

Would this, then, be grounds for speaking of a second P source in this narrative? [5] With caution, this conclusion must be rejected since it is impossible to define a second complete P source in the Pentateuch, and it would solve no problems to speak of a second P source in one or two chapters. The better course would be to suggest that once again P (or the source he uses) has brought together two rather well-defined and distinct traditions. Vss. 33-34 can also be assigned to P, along with the conclusion of the unit in vs. 35a. Vs. 35b is a doublet of vs. 35a and thus a part of J. Vs. 36 is obviously a gloss that falls out of our consideration. The end of the unit is clearly marked by the new P itinerary in 17:1. We thus have the following literary structure: J, 4abα, 5, 29-32, 35b; P, 1, 2-3, 6-7 (8), 9-13, 14-26, 33-35a; Dtr., 4bβ, 27-28.

It is most striking, in comparison with the units which we

have already examined, that this narrative is not bound to a local aetiology or any other means for designating a precise localization. This is in sharp contrast to the parallel narrative in Num. 11, for there the tradition is associated with an aetiology for Kibroth-hatta'avah. We shall consider the significance of the aetiology in detail when we examine Num. 11. For now, it is enough to note simply that this narrative is composed only of legendary motifs which are centered generally in the Wilderness of Sin, a location which can be roughly associated with the southern desert.

A second striking feature about this unit is that the murmuring motif appears only in the P form of the tradition which deals with the bread *and* meat. Both the J source and the tradition in P which is concerned *only* with the manna are completely free of all connotations of rebellion. Our task now is to determine what the character and relationship of the two opposing traditions might be. The murmuring motif begins in vss. 2-3 with a 3. m. pl. Niph'al *waw* consecutive imperfect of לון: "All the congregation of the Israelites murmured against Moses and Aaron in the wilderness." The quotation which follows constitutes the murmuring. The expression מי יתן is parallel to and serves the same function as the optative particle לו in Num. 14:2 and 20:3. In each case, a death wish is expressed. That this wish is opposed to the normal attitude of the Israelite, which anticipates a long and full life, only accents the serious nature of the rebellion. But it is not simply a wish that death would now remove them from the problems of life in the wilderness. In all three cases, the wish expresses a feeling that an *earlier* death would have been better than what they now face, not because the death would have removed them from the current crisis, but because such a death would have *prevented the events which led to the crisis*. In Exod. 16:3, the circumstances described in connection with that wish are particularly surprising: "Would that we had died by the hand of Yahweh in the land of Egypt when we were sitting by the pots of flesh, when we were eating bread to the full." This wish not only heightens the despair which the people express in their plight (cf. Num. 20:3); it in fact expresses a desire that the Exodus had never occurred. Thus it corresponds closely with the content of the rebellion noted above, i.e., a desire to return to the state of life which they had before the Exodus.

A second observation about this wish must also be made. Noth suggests that the view of life in Egypt expressed in the wish may be set "in rather too rosy a light. For the slave labour in Egypt would hardly as a rule have eaten boiled 'flesh' by the 'fleshpots.' " [6] But it may well be that instead of offering a reflection of life in Egypt which might be considered accurate or judged inaccurate, we have here a conscious connection between the accusation raised about the Exodus and the coming miracle of meat and bread (cf. vss. 8, 12, 13).

Since the people are in the wilderness, threatened with hunger (cf. vs. 3bβ), it seems to be clear that the memory of food left in Egypt forms the *immediate* motivation for the murmuring. But the reference to an unrealistic picture of life in Egypt seems to put the emphasis by virtue of its exaggeration on the fact that the people had been taken out of Egypt. This is supported by vs. 3b. The form of an accusation in a question does not appear here. But the כי clause serves the same function. The verb is a 2. m. pl. Hiph'il *perfect* form of יצא. Its function is to challenge the act which it describes. The Exodus is not mentioned explicitly, but the use of the verb יצא instead of בוא shows that it is intended (cf. the technical use of the verb יצא for the Exodus in the formula ויוציאנו יהוה ממצרים in Deut. 6:21, *et al.*). Moreover, the construction of this verse is strikingly similar to that which follows the interrogative particles in Exod. 17:3 and Num. 20:4, 5. That the verse is in fact the same part of the murmuring motif can hardly be doubted when one compares the complete sentences: "For you have brought us out into this wilderness to kill this whole congregation with hunger." "Why have you brought us up from Egypt to kill us and our children and our

---

[6] Noth, *Exodus*, p. 133. Cf. also P. Heinisch, *Das Buch Numeri, HSAT* II/1 (Bonn: Peter Hanstein Verlagsbuchhandlung, 1936), 48, on Num. 11:5.

cattle [cf. LXX] with thirst?" Once again, we are forced to conclude that the substance of the rebellion is not the lack of food, for the principal verb has nothing to do with this problem. It would have been just as easy to read: "For you have not provided meat and bread for us in this wilderness." Or even: "For you have brought us into this wilderness to kill this whole congregation with hunger" (cf. Num. 20:4). But quite the contrary, the substance of the rebellion clearly lies in the problem of the Exodus. The cause for the complaint is not simply a matter of remembering food that might have been left behind in Egypt, but the fact that they left Egypt at all. The food seems to do nothing more than provide the setting.[7]

Vss. 6-7 are the response of Moses and Aaron to the murmuring. Vs. 6*b* further supports the thesis that the substance of the rebellion is centered in the Exodus rather than the problem of hunger. In the form of an *Erweiswort*,[8] a future event is announced. That which is to be proven by this event, i.e., the כי clause which follows the designation of time, is similar to the self-revelation formula which so often accompanies this form (cf. vs. 12*b*). This formula in its strict construction would appear in the context of a first person address by Yahweh: כי אני יהוה. But this text is more loosely constructed. Neither אני nor אנכי appears; instead, the sentence must be translated as a third person statement: "In the evening, you will know that Yahweh has brought you out from the land of Egypt." The association of the name of Yahweh with the event of the Exodus in this manner is not unusual. But it seems to be more than co-

---

[7] Noth, *Exodus*, p. 128, concludes that "this motif has its roots in the realization of the miserable conditions of life in the wilderness with its constant privations, above all the shortage of food and water." This does not seem to be the case. Instead, the shortage of food and water would be the "rootage" for the motif of Yahweh's gracious aid. Its only connection with the murmuring, providing a setting, would not give any insight into the basic nature and origin of the motif.

[8] Zimmerli, pp. 154 ff. Cf. also *Erkenntnis Gottes nach dem Buche Ezechiel; eine theologische Studie, ATANT* XXVII (Zürich: Zwingli-Verlag, 1954), 49 ff.

incidence that this particular form of the revelation of
Yahweh's name should be used as a' response to the murmuring. Its intent is not to show that Moses and Aaron, or
Yahweh, can provide food, but that Yahweh instigated and
directed the Exodus. And in this sense, it provides an appropriate response to the accusation about the Exodus.

But what is the event which lies at the basis of the
Erweiswort? This is not immediately clear. Vss. 6-7 give
a specification of the time for the event (ערב . . . ובקר), while
vs. 7a suggests that it will be associated with the appearance
of the כבוד יהוה. On the other hand, the fragment in vs. 8
defines the event as the gift of meat and bread. For the
author of the gloss, the question is clear. But since this verse
is at best difficult, its contribution to the resolution of the
problem is limited. In vs. 9 Yahweh instructs Moses and
Aaron to gather the people for presentation before him.
These instructions are announced to the people in vs. 10aα.
We must assume that they were immediately gathered together, for as soon as Aaron finishes his announcement (ויהי
כדבר), the people turn toward the wilderness in order to
see the appearance of the כבוד יהוה in a cloud. This event
is, however, not to be identified with the reference to the
כבוד יהוה in vs. 7, for here there can be no contact with
the specification of time in vss. 6-7. We might expect this
sudden appearance of the כבוד יהוה to involve an announcement of punishment for the rebels, for the setting presents the people who have just rebelled against Moses and
Aaron, and thus against Yahweh, before Yahweh himself. But
Yahweh's address has no element of punishment at all. Instead, he addresses Moses with an announcement of the coming miracle of meat and bread. Moreover, the miracle will
occur . . . בין הערבים . . . ובבקר. It is now clear that the event
which was announced as the appearance of the כבוד יהוה in
vss. 6-7 is in fact the miracle of meat and bread. And this
event serves as the foundation for the revelation concerning
Yahweh (vs. 6; cf. vs. 12).

There is a noticeable duality in this tradition, emphasized
by the repetition of the self-revelation formula in vs. 12.

But we cannot resolve the problem posed by that duality by recourse to two literary sources. The distinctions between the duplicate forms which rise to the surface under closer examination show that they cannot be considered doublets but should probably be explained as different levels in the same literary source. The striking fact about the duplicate form of Yahweh's self-revelation is that the reference to the Exodus is not repeated. To be sure, one could argue that the simple form כי אני יהוה אלהיכם calls to memory, in fact establishes, Yahweh's role in the Exodus. But the mere fact that vs. 6 drops the first person pronoun and includes the expansion of the form, הוציא אתכם מארץ מצרים, only emphasizes its construction as a conscious response to the murmuring.

But what is the significance of the formula which does not mention the Exodus? It, too, is constructed as a response to the murmuring, as the noun תלונת in vs. 12$a\alpha$ clearly shows. But the simple revelation of the name instead of the effort to show Yahweh's role in the Exodus (cf. vs. 6) suggests that in this instance the response may not have been primarily oriented toward the challenge of the Exodus. Would this mean, then, that the motif of meat and bread once had a life of its own without reference to the murmuring motif? There are at least two indications of this. First, we have assumed that the need for meat and bread formed the immediate motivation for the murmuring. But here the appearance of meat and bread is Yahweh's response to the rebellion. And second, it would be rather incongruous if Yahweh should attempt to resolve the rebellion by submitting to the demands of the rebels. The difficulty here might be more reasonably explained by assuming that the people had petitioned Yahweh for meat and bread, and that by means of this form Yahweh responds favorably to the petition (cf. Ps. 105:40).[9] This assumption would also explain why the form is duplicated and the ex-

___

[9] Zimmerli, *Erkenntnis Gottes*, p. 21, uses the verb *"erhören"* with reference to the response to the murmuring.

plicit reference to the appearance of the meat and bread in vss. 6-7 is omitted in favor of the reference to the Exodus; i.e., the murmuring motif has been secondarily incorporated into the more positive narrative of the people's petition for Yahweh's aid.

This brings us to vs. 13. Here the miracle of the meat and bread is unmistakably identified with the appearance of the quail and manna. Yet the text has until this point maintained a curious restraint in making explicit connections between the two. The reason for the restraint may lie in the fact that the naming aetiology for the manna comes only in vs. 15. But this would not explain why the quail are not mentioned by name. Is it possible that the tradition preserves the name as an element which was not associated with a response to murmuring? The parallel narrative in Num. 11 shows that this hypothesis would not apply to the quail. But the quail are dropped from consideration at vs. 15. And the narrative about the manna makes no further reference to the murmuring. Furthermore, Num. 11 holds the two separate as it develops the tradition of the quail, and there is no indication there of a connection between the manna and the murmuring. This suggests that the quail and the manna were originally two separate motifs[10] and that the *manna* was consistently maintained as a positive item (cf. Deut. 8:3). Whether the tradition of the quail also had a positive background cannot be determined from this text. We shall return to this question below. Whether the combined traditions also had a positive form cannot be determined with certainty.

A further problem now arises. How significant is it that no punishment or even reconciliation appears in this unit? We have suggested in the second chapter that punishment is not an essential formal element in the motif; the response may involve various kinds of relationships between the leaders and the rebels. We have not noted punishment in any of the previous texts, with the possible exception of the late tra-

---

[10] von Rad, *Priesterschrift*, p. 55; Gressmann, pp. 124 ff.

dition concerning Moses' vicarious death on behalf of the
rebels. Although one could argue that the motif is incomplete
in those texts as well, the fact that it seems to be dependent
on an earlier positive form of the tradition would suggest
that if the punishment were necessary, it could have been
added. The only conclusion that we may draw, then, is that
even though the element of punishment can appear in the
formal structure of the motif, it is not necessarily incomplete without it. Here the response is appropriate to the rebellion. The gift of meat and bread is used to establish
Yahweh's role in the Exodus and thus his position vis-à-vis the
rebellion. We are, perhaps, left with an expectation for
some further response. But we have no just cause to assume
that a punishment must have been involved.

Noth suggests that the source which begins in vs. 4 must
have had a complaint preceding it.[11] This suggestion would
imply that the J source, too, presupposes some dissatisfaction,
if not rebellion, regarding the state of life in the wilderness.
But this hypothesis is based on the presupposition that every
gift of Yahweh's aid is in response to Israel's murmuring[12]
and does not take into consideration an independent tradition of Yahweh's gracious aid. It is much more logical and,
according to the tradition which we have seen in previous
texts, likely that an event of aid in the face of need such
as we see in vss. 4-5 is in response to a petition. This hypothesis would avoid the necessity for saying that the only negative element in this source, be it rebellion or just dissatisfaction with the state of life, was centered in an original form
of the text which we no longer have. And it would mean that
the question of a connection between this form of the manna
tradition and the murmuring motif must be resolved only
on the basis of what this form of J itself gives.

Vss. 4-5 represent only an announcement of the coming
manna to Moses, along with accompanying instructions for
gathering it daily as well as preparing it for the Sabbath.

---

[11] Noth, *Exodus*, p. 133. Cf. also Gressmann, p. 126.
[12] Noth, *Exodus*, p. 129.

The only other unit of tradition which can certainly be reckoned to J is vss. 29-31, again involving instruction for gathering the manna in preparation for the Sabbath. And here the word השבת is used (vs. 29).[13] The only indication of action on the part of the people is positive; i.e., they followed the instructions and did not go out to gather the manna on the Sabbath (vs. 30). Thus we may conclude that as the J section now stands, it has a quite positive view of the manna. Yahweh gave it as a necessity for life in the wilderness, and it was accepted as a sign of his presence. That no stigma is to be connected with the manna or the event is shown by the instruction in vs. 32, also quite probably a part of J. A *gomer* of manna is to be kept in order to show all future generations, not how Israel rebelled and thus remind them not to act in the same manner, but simply "the bread which I [Yahweh] fed you in the wilderness when I led you out from the land of Egypt."

Vss. 14-26 and 33-34 are probably a part of P, as we have proposed, but they are nevertheless parallel to the manna tradition in J, as shown by the close parallel in vs. 32 and vss. 33-34. This unit of tradition is also concerned with instructions about gathering manna daily and preparing it for the Sabbath. The general impression is that the people followed the instructions carefully (vs. 17a). It is only in vs. 20 that some deviation is reported. A portion of the Israelites refused to follow the instructions about keeping the manna until morning. But no serious consequences are reported (cf. vs. 20b). Instead, one has the impression that the disobedience is an artificial device designed to prepare the reader for the significance of the manna kept overnight for the Sabbath (vs. 24). This hypothesis would be strongly supported by vs. 21, a notation that the command to gather the manna was executed in *proper* fashion. But even if this is the case, the use of such a device to emphasize the nature of the manna would indicate a tendency to cast at least a

[13] Noth, *Exodus*, p. 136, observes that this is probably the earliest occurrence of the word in the Old Testament.

portion of the people (אנשים ממנו) in a role of disobedience. To be sure, this is not the kind or degree of disobedience which is represented in the murmuring, but it is nevertheless a negative element.[14] Thus we must consider the section a unified tradition which reveals a negative interpretation of a part of the people. But there is nevertheless no indication of a negative interpretation of the manna. And just as in J, this is confirmed for P by instructions in vss. 33-34 that a jar of manna be kept as a witness for future generations.

In summary: This narrative is dominated by the murmuring motif. The setting is the demand for meat and bread, but the reflection of the food in Egypt shows that the substance of the rebellion is in fact the problem of the Exodus. The role of the Exodus is particularly clear in the response given by Moses to the rebellion. But the use of an *Erweiswort* in the response, plus a duplicate of the *Erweiswort* in a subsequent verse, raises the question of whether an original form of the tradition which was in response to a petition has here been adapted for the murmuring. If this were the case, then the request for meat and bread would be associated with the tradition of Yahweh's gracious aid in the wilderness. It seems probable that the *manna* tradition, to be identified with the bread in this narrative, was an independent positive element. Whether the quail was also a part of the tradition about Yahweh's aid must be considered below.

Numbers 11:4-34

Noth argues that the units in this narrative cannot be satisfactorily divided into parts of the various pentateuchal sources.[15] But the text is nevertheless not a literary unity.

---

[14] Vs. 21 may be from a different tradition about the manna since it notes that the manna would melt in the sun. This is noticeably contrary to the spoiled manna filled with worms. And yet the situations are also quite different. In the one, the manna which has been gathered and stored overnight spoils. But in the other, the manna which has not yet been gathered melts in the sun.

[15] Noth, *Überlieferungsgeschichte*, p. 34, n. 119; *Numeri*, pp. 74-75.

There are fragments of traditions incorporated into the narrative that are foreign and disruptive. First, the description of the manna in vss. 7-9 is parenthetical and violates the smooth flow of the narrative from vs. 6 to vs. 10.[16] Especially if one accepts the Syriac addition to vs. 7a, the description of the manna here is quite similar to Exod. 16:31 (J), while the instructions for gathering the manna follow the same course as the ones noted in that text. The two texts are not identical (cf. e.g., Num. 11:8b and Exod. 16:31bβ). But Num. 11:7-9 has stylistic features which suggest that it too is a part of J. This specification must remain tentative. But it does seem to be clear that the unit is foreign to the principal narrative. We might suppose, then, that it was inserted here because of the catchword המן in vs. 6b.[17]

Noth also suggests that vs. 12bβ should be considered a foreign element since it departs completely from the imagery used in the first part of the verse. It apparently was intended to connect the reference to "carrying" in vs. 12bα to the Conquest theme.[18]

Moreover, the tradition of the seventy elders is widely recognized as a later addition to this text.[19] As it now stands, the section in vss. 14-17 breaks into Moses' complaint about not being able to provide meat for the people and Yahweh's response concerning the quail.[20] There is no suggestion here that the spirit of Moses is to be divided among the elders because of the complaint about rights of leadership. There is no indication that the elders are appointed to

[16] *Ibid.*, p. 77. Cf. also J. Wellhausen, *Die Composition des Hexateuchs und der historischen Bücher des Alten Testaments* (4th ed., Berlin: Walter de Gruyter, 1963), p. 100.

[17] Noth, *Numeri*, pp. 76-77. Cf. also Gressmann, p. 138.

[18] Noth, *Numeri*, p. 78.

[19] Wellhausen, p. 99; Eissfeldt, p. 39; Gressmann, p. 125, n. 2; Gray, p. 109; Noth, *Numeri*, pp. 75, 78; *et al.*

[20] Noth, *Numeri*, p. 78, observes that vss. 14-15 presuppose Moses' speech to Yahweh in vss. 11-13, especially the reference to the people as a burden (vs. 11bα), but that the division of labor among several "shoulders" points to a literary growth in the tradition. Vss. 16-17 introduce the seventy elders as a preparation for and expansion of vss. 24b-30.

act as witnesses of the miracle (cf. Num. 20; Exod. 17). Their
task is to share the burden of responsibility for the people
with Moses. But how could seventy elders help Moses find
meat? The burden is more likely a matter of community ad-
ministration (cf. Exod. 18:18 ff.).[21] If the Syriac form of vs.
18aα should be accepted,[22] vss. 16-17 would stand out completely as an independent address to Moses. One might then
suppose that the motif of the elders has been inserted here because of the similarity between vs. 14 and Exod. 18:18.

Vs. 18 picks up the motif of meat from vss. 13 ff. and runs
without break through vs. 23. But in vs. 24 the motif of the
seventy elders appears once again. This verse is apparently
a continuation of vss. 16-17; but the motif is confused in vs.
25b, and the principal interest shifts to ecstatic prophecy.
Eissfeldt attributes vss. 7-9, along with the tradition of the
seventy elders, to E.[23] Noth, on the other hand, suggests
some closer contact between the tradition of the seventy
elders and the quail narrative and concludes that the former
should be considered a part of the same literary source
found in the latter, i.e., J.[24] Since the motif of the seventy
elders is so loosely connected with the narrative of the quail,
the locus which carries our point of interest, we shall not
pursue it further here. Only in vs. 31 is the account of the
quail resumed. And this verse is apparently a continuation
of vs. 23. Thus vss. 7-9, 16-17, and 24-30, along with the
quarter-verse 12bβ, must be bracketed in this chapter as
fragments from other traditions which have not been completely integrated into the principal unit.

The remaining verses seem to be J's version of the tradition
of the quail. But the unity of these verses is also uncertain.
It seems clear that no trace of P is to be found here.[25] And
efforts to isolate E or a second J source have produced little

[21] Noth, *Numeri*, p. 78.
[22] Syriac presupposes: ויאמר משה אל העם.
[23] Eissfeldt, p. 39. Cf. also Gressmann, p. 125, n. 2.
[24] Noth, *Überlieferungsgeschichte*, p. 141, *Numeri*, p. 75.
[25] Cf. Gray, p. 98, for a discussion of this problem.

convincing evidence.[26] But still the lack of unity is problematic. Noth's conclusion recognizes both the disunity and
the difficulty in isolating multiple sources: "Die Einheitlichkeit von Num. 11 ist kein literarkritisches, sondern ein
überlieferungsgeschlichtliches Problem." [27]

There are notable differences between this version and the
P narrative in Exod. 16. Chief among these is that Exod. 16
concentrates on the manna and views both manna and quail
as synchronous events, while this text concentrates on the
quail and presupposes that the manna had long been the
staple diet of the Israelites. This fact supports our thesis
that the two motifs were originally independent and suggests that the P version may be a gathering of similar traditions into one unit.

Heinisch uses this difference to argue that the two narratives are not parallel.[28] But if one eliminates the secondary
material in Num. 11 and compares the remaining narrative
with Exod. 16:2-13, the argument does not seem to be so
obvious. To be sure, there are differences between the two
narratives, even above the one previously cited. The verb
בכה dominates the Numbers account without reference to
the verb לון, the question of the bread does not come into
consideration, Moses presents his own personal accusation
to Yahweh, the quail are seen as punishment, and a report of
the appearance and gathering of the quail is related. Yet the
outline of the two is similar enough to suggest that at least
the accounts of the *quail* are parallel: (1) The people remember the varied foods which they had in Egypt. (2)
Moses hears their reminiscences. (3) The case is in some
manner presented to Yahweh. (4) Yahweh responds with the
gift of quail. (5) This process is associated with the murmuring motif. Unless we are to assume that two different

---

[26] Gressmann, p. 125, n. 2; Eissfeldt, pp. 39 ff.; Gray, pp. 98-99; *et al.*
The problem here, as in Exod. 16, is impossible to solve; even Gray admits
the uncertain and tentative nature of the results in trying to isolate two
sources.

[27] Noth, *Überlieferungsgeschichte*, p. 34, n. 119. Gray, p. 101, has a
similar conclusion.

[28] Heinisch, *Numeri*, pp. 51-52.

traditions of the quail existed without contact but nevertheless narrated their material in the same manner, we must
conclude that we have parallel accounts of the same tradition. The differences in form and content could then be
explained as the peculiar emphases of the two sources and
the combination of the P quail narrative with the manna tradition.

Once again, the aetiological saga can be distinguished as a
different type of material from the legendary narrative motifs
composing the main body of the unit. The basis of the
aetiology in vs. 4*a* is built on the vocable אוה and concerns
an unidentified group of people within the Israelites
(האספסף אשר בקרבו).[29] The principal narrative, however,
is built around all the Israelites (בני ישראל) and the vocable
בכה. We shall begin our analysis with the narrative and return to the question of its relationship with the aetiology.

Our first task is to determine the character and extent of
the murmuring motif in the narrative. We are at a disad-
vantage here in comparison to the previous units since we
have none of the verbs which we have considered a part of
the murmuring motif to mark a point of departure. Yet we
are not completely at a loss, for it seems clear that vss. 4*b*-6,
governed by the verb בכה, play a role which is parallel to
Exod. 16:2-3. And that section was introduced by לון. The
root בכה appears in all the cognate languages and in each
means nothing more than "to weep." According to Brown,
Driver, and Briggs, the word can carry varying degrees of
meaning, from weeping for joy (Gen. 43:30) to weeping
in intense grief (I Sam. 1:10). The most common connotation is weeping in lamentation or mourning (Lam. 1:2).
This can easily move into weeping in repentance (II Kings
22:19) or supplication for one's state (II Kings 20:3). If
one can weep for himself, he can also weep for someone else
(Jer. 22:10). Indeed, his weeping can be not only for himself or another person, but also for a simple petition (Judg.

[29] Gray, p. 102, and Heinisch, *Numeri*, pp. 48-49 suggest that this
word may refer to a group of non-Israelites who had attached themselves
to the people as they came out of Egypt (cf. Exod. 12:38).

20:23, 26; Esth. 8:3). This character of petition is shown
conclusively by the juxtaposition of בכה with לה (א) שׁ (I
Sam. 1:10, 17), תחנה and תפלה (Ps. 6:9 ff.). But in none of
the connotations of the word can an interpretation which
would put it into the context of rebellion be seen.

This observation is confirmed by the text which now lies
before us. To be sure, the whole people are involved in the
weeping. But the quotation associated with the weeping is
not addressed to any specific person. Vs. 10 shows clearly
that the people were not gathered together but were weeping independently, each man with his family at the door of his
tent. In fact, this verse gives the impression that Moses just
happened to overhear the statement of their complaint. That
statement does appear in the form of a question (vs. 4bβ),
but the question is not an accusation directed to a particular
person. Rather, it is indefinite: מי יאכלנו בשׂר. This question
might be considered, instead of an accusation, a question of
unfaith; i.e., it could imply that no one, not even Yahweh,
could provide meat to eat (cf. Ps. 78:19-20). But this would
not be derived from the text. An indefinite formulation, particularly when the verb is an imperfect, commonly expresses
a *wish* (e.g., II Sam. 23:15).[30] This use, coupled with the
connotation of the verb בכה which was noted above, strongly
suggests that this part of the quail tradition must be considered an indefinite petition, i.e., a petition which is not addressed to a particular person.

The petition is for meat, and here as in Exod. 16, the desire for meat is motivated by a memory of meat which was
available in Egypt. That vs. 5b is a list of foods from Egypt
which cannot be considered meat suggests that the foods were
included here only to amplify the reference to Egypt. In
Exod. 16, the memory of food in Egypt seemed to anticipate
an accusation about the Exodus. But here there is no accusation. Nor is it possible to suppose that an accusation
has simply dropped out of the tradition. In this context, it
would have no meaning since no one is directly addressed.

[30] Ges.K., # 151a, p. 476.

The reference to Egypt is nothing more than a statement of reason for the people's desire for meat. Yet one must consider the possibility that the allusion to Egypt reflects the accusation about the Exodus.

Vs. 10*a* is relatively straightforward but vs. 10*b* presents new problems for a study of the traditions in this unit. In vs. 10*a*, it is Moses alone who hears the people crying at their tents, but in vs. 10*b*, it is Yahweh whose anger rises. The connection between the two is not clear.[31] Is Yahweh angry because the people are crying for meat? And if so, does it mean that at this point the crying is to be interpreted as murmuring? Or is the cause of the anger something else, some different attitude or event which may be obscured here because of difficulties in the text? Moreover, the antecedent of רע in vs. 10*b*β is not clear. Does the word refer to the crying of the people or to Yahweh's anger? The latter would be implied by vss. 11-15 (cf. esp. the *Tiqqune Sopherim* in vs. 15*b*β: ברעתך). Moses' address to Yahweh is in the form of a complaint. But significantly, the first question in the complaint corresponds formally to the question which we have labeled an accusation (cf. Jer. 14:19; Ps. 88:15). We noted above that the accusation could be used with lesser degrees of intensity, even before the king (cf. II Sam. 12:21), without implying disrespect. But even then, it would be used only in extreme circumstances. In this case, it would be a means for demanding an explanation from Yahweh. That it is a serious question which corresponds to the serious nature previously seen in the questions of accusation is clear: Moses asserts that if Yahweh is not willing to explain his action, i.e., if Yahweh rejects the demand, then Moses is willing, in fact prefers, to die.

The event challenged here (vs. 11) is described by a 2. m. s. Hiph'il perfect form of the verb רעע and must be interpreted as the same event which was described by the adjective רע in vs. 10*b*β. There is no reason to doubt that Yahweh's evil

---

[31] Noth, *Numeri*, p. 77, eliminates the problem by labeling vs. 10*b*α a later addition. But it seems clear that the complaint in vss. 11 ff. depends on this quarter verse.

deed is in fact his act of anger in vs. 10*b*α since the verb is
addressed to Yahweh. There is no literary or traditio-historical
break between these two quarter-verses, and no indication that
the one is to be left without continuation in the other. Moreover, the last word in vs. 11*a*α, לעבדך, shows that the anger is
directed, not at the people's crying, but at Moses. The form
of the question further defines the act which is at first only
introducted with the verb רעע. Vs. 11*b* points to the burden
of responsibility for the people which Moses must carry. But
these are Yahweh's people, not his.

As a consequence of these difficulties, Gray concludes that
the complaint is out of place. It would be better ordered, he
argues, in conjunction with Exod. 33:1-3 where Yahweh announces that he will not accompany the people on their
journey.[32] But in order to argue in this manner, one must
exclude vs. 13 from the unit. This is not necessary; in fact, vs.
13 shows that the unit fits well in the chapter where it is
found. This verse presupposes that Moses has mediated the
petition for meat to Yahweh, but that for some unknown
reason Yahweh has left the full responsibility for finding the
meat on Moses. And this he has done in a mood of anger.
Vss. 21 ff. might suggest that the reason for the anger lies in
Moses' unbelief in response to instructions for finding the
meat (cf. esp. vs. 23). This incredulity may still be reflected
in the question in vs. 13: מאין לי בשר. In any case, it is clear
that Moses feels that he *alone* has the responsibility for finding the meat. Thus it may be more than coincidence that
Moses uses the figure of a wet nurse to describe his relationship with the people.[33]

Vs. 13 is also significant from the point of a traditio-historical analysis of this narrative, for it gives us a slightly
different form of the crying and the direct quotation which
is associated with it. In contrast to the text in vss. 4*b*-6, the
crying is now done in the presence of Moses. The preposition
על is used to indicate this, but it does not seem to carry the

---

[32] Gray, p. 107.
[33] On the masculine form, האמן, cf. Noth, *Numeri*, p. 77.

same hostile sense which it does for the other verbs of the murmuring motif. Instead it connotes simply proximity. This preposition is often used with בכה, but the only text which offers a close parallel to vs. 13 is Judg. 14:16-17. And here it is clear that the weeping indicates an intense presentation of a petition. Brown, Driver, and Briggs suggest that the verb in this text connotes being a burden or annoyance. This is indeed the case. Samson's wife presses her petition until she attains her goal, and the verb הציקתהו indicates that this becomes a burden for Samson to bear. But it is significant that the connotation of pressure must be indicated by another verb. And that pressure was still presented in the form of a petition.

In our text the same observations hold. The crying, in whatever degree it might have become a burden, is nevertheless in the form of a petition. But in this case, the petition is no longer indefinite. The accompanying quotation is addressed directly to Moses and is governed by a singular imperative. In fact, the form of the petition is identical to the one which we encountered above in Exod. 17:2. Moreover, it is striking that this petition, as that one, is not associated in any way with an appeal to Egypt. Thus it seems quite clear that the first stages of the tradition of the quail lie in the realm of a positive petition for aid in the wilderness (cf. Ps. 105:40). This view of the tradition is strengthened by the figure which describes Israel as a suckling child (vs. 12aβ). A sharp contrast to a rebellious character, this picture casts Israel in absolute dependency on either Moses or Yahweh for survival in the wilderness.[34]

Vs. 18 represents the response of Yahweh. Whether it is to Moses' accusation is not clear; it may be simply a response to the crying of the people (כי בכיתם באזני יהוה). In conjunction with the instructions for receiving the meat, we have

---

[34] Noth, *Numeri*, p. 77, observes that the relationship between Yahweh and Israel implied by the analogy of a wet nurse and suckling child is quite unusual. But the implications of using feminine terms to describe the relationship are softened first by the fact that the noun has a masculine form, and second by the explicit reference in the analogy to Moses. In fact, Moses complains that he *alone* holds this position.

yet a third quotation of the people's petition. This one is remarkably similar to the one which appears in vss. 4b-6. The same kind of indefinite question with an imperfect verb is employed, and it is related to an allusion to the state of life in Egypt. The purpose of the allusion is more uncertain here than it was in vss. 4b-6, but we may assume that the same conclusions would obtain. And once again, it appears that the crying is not directed specifically to Yahweh but simply overheard. The response of Yahweh must be interpreted as positive. He has favorably received the wish, and as a result, the people will be given meat to eat.

Vss. 19-20 are clearly dependent on vs. 18. But does vs. 18 necessarily demand continuation in vss. 19-20? Or does the natural continuation lie in nothing more than an account of the execution of the miracle (vss. 31 ff.)? We shall approach this question by asking whether the miracle of the quail is to be seen as an event which, in contradistinction to the manna, occurred only on one day or at the most a few days, or whether it may be viewed as an event which recurs over an extended period of time. The instructions in vs. 18, התקדשו למחר ואכלתם בשר, seem to imply that the former was the case. The Hithpa'el of קדש indicates that the people are to prepare to witness a holy event, while the designation of the time, מחר, suggests that the event will be only on the one day. This suggestion is substantiated by the use of similar formulas in Josh. 3:5 and 7:13 which call the people to prepare for an event on the following day. It is significant that each of these texts refers to events which are to happen on only one day (Exod. 9:5, 18; 32:5; Num. 16:16). The formula may be stylized and indicate nothing more than the preparation for an event which begins on a certain day. If this were the case, we would be forced to suppose that the state of sanctification attained in preparing for the event was maintained over a longer period of time. This is somewhat difficult to imagine. But it may be the case here since the account of the event itself (vss. 31 ff.) shows that the people worked at least two days gathering the meat. But even if this should be the case, the character of the event would nevertheless be different from the steady recurrence of the manna throughout the period of the wilderness wandering; this is an event which occurs at a specific time, be it one day or several.

It is clear, however, that the development of the narrative depends on an extension of the gift of quail over a period of a month until the desired flesh becomes nauseous. Our next problem is whether this form of the miracle must necessarily be seen as punishment for the murmuring. And here again a dual character in the tradition is apparent, as shown most clearly by the fourth quotation of the people's crying (vs. 20bβ), and the second in this context (cf. vs. 18aβ). Vs. 20b is a causative clause, indicating the reason for maintaining that the gift of the quail was in fact a punishment. The verb בכה is followed here by the preposition לפניו and can mean nothing more than weeping in the presence of someone, in this case, Yahweh. But no longer does the quotation involve a petition for food. It is now in the form of a question introduced by למה, and the question raises the problem of the Exodus. The question might be considered an abbreviated form of the wish for better food, employing only an allusion to Egypt. We could presume that since an allusion to Egypt has previously been used in this chapter (vs. 5), an allusion which reflects a lament over the loss of food, this one also laments the loss of food. But there is nothing in the quotation itself which is concerned with the problem of food. Instead, it questions the advisability of having left Egypt: "Why did we come out of Egypt?" And the verb יצא leaves no doubt that the problem has shifted from simply remembering the food in Egypt to the Exodus itself.

The content of this unit thus corresponds to the content which we have observed consistently in the murmuring motif. Only a *first person* plural Qal perfect form of the verb, rather than a second person form, prevents our saying without doubt that the crying is to be considered a part of the murmuring. This difference could be explained by the fact that the verb בכה does not describe an event which is specifically directed against either Moses or Yahweh and thus does not give a setting in which the action of either can be directly challenged;

i.e., the verb does not seem to be primarily a part of the motif.

But the context in which this quotation appears removes even this doubt and shows that in this unit the verb is used to support the murmuring. Vs. 20bβ, composed of the introductory verb בכה and this question, is set in relationship with vs. 20bα and its governing verb מאס. This verb, clearly indicating an event which is in keeping with the rebellion motif, construes Yahweh as the direct object: "Because you have rejected Yahweh who is in your midst and you have cried before him saying, 'Why have we come out of Egypt?' . . ." The relationship of the *waw* consecutive imperfect ותבכו with מאסתם in the יען כי- clause can be labeled as a more exact definition of the event which is governed by יען כי-. Thus the sentence which contains the verb בכה defines how Israel rejected Yahweh (cf. I Kings 13:21-22, where the *waw* consecutive imperfect defines how the prophet disobeyed Yahweh) and shows that at this point the crying is conceived as rebellion directed against Yahweh. It therefore seems clear that the quotation, rather than presupposing the previous requests for food built on the memory of food in Egypt, and thus appearing as a truncated part of a series of quotations on the same plane, is the climax of an intensification. The previous quotations have referred to Egypt in anticipation of the final question. This conclusion has the advantage of resolving the discordant feature in this text which assumes that the Israelites had a quantity and quality of food in Egypt which would not likely have been available to a slave people, for the allusions to Egypt in these quotations simply give the murmuring motif a setting in the tradition of miraculous food in the wilderness.

A statement of Yahweh's response to this rebellion follows: The meat which they wanted will be theirs, but in a greater amount than they ever expected. That this response is to be considered punishment for the rebellion cannot be doubted. The יען כי- formation shows that the abundance of quail is the result of their rebellion. And the abundance, rather than implying blessing in a land without food, results in discomfort for the people and abhorrence for the very item they desired.

But what kind of punishment is this, especially for so serious an act as the rejection of Yahweh? We must still entertain the possibility that the gift of quail for a month was originally a positive note of Yahweh's gracious aid.[35]

Vss. 21-23 presuppose the announcement that the meat would be available for a month. But it is striking that there is no concern in this section for the fact that so much meat is to be interpreted as punishment. Moses reflects only incredulity that so much meat could be found in the wilderness. It would be possible, of course, to suggest that Moses was more impressed with the immediate problem of finding that much meat in order to fulfill Yahweh's threat (promise?) than with the ramifications of the people's rebellion against Yahweh or the consequences of this punishment for his people. But this seems somewhat incongruous (cf. Num. 14:13 ff.). We might propose, then, that this part of the tradition reflects more of the positive motif than the negative; i.e., the original intent of the gift of quail over a period of a month was after all a gracious response to the needs posed by life in the wilderness. The tradition may have reported the gift at this point in a magnified form by extending the duration of the gift. But the intent in that case seems probably to have been only a heightening of the confession.

There is a further indication of the positive character in this motif. Vss. 19-20 announce an event which will come in the future. But if the event is to be effective, we must assume either that the people were not aware of the implication of this event as punishment or that they were forced to eat the meat. Both seem unlikely and suggest once again that the extension *ad nauseam* is an artificial construction. The reason for such a construction would apparently be an effort to interpret a given part of the positive tradition in terms of the murmuring. Thus we would have an explanation for the fact that the punishment is not more serious; the concern is not to provide punishment suitable to the rebellion but to interpret the anomaly of abundant meat as a response to the

[35] Gressmann, p. 141.

rebellion. But what does this imply about the role of punishment in this motif? We shall return to this question below.

The narrative is continued in vss. 31 ff. without a break. Vss. 31-32 convey a kind of uncommitted attitude toward the relationship between Yahweh and the people which causes one to wonder whether this account of the execution of the miracle does not lie in the realm of the positive motif alone. It is only in vs. 33 that a negative connotation appears again, and the sudden shift in attitude here is particularly noticeable. The people seem to be eating without concern that the food is to be their punishment.

But a larger problem also appears here. Vs. 33 reports a new punishment in connection with the quail which apparently contradicts the first. In the first, the punishment was to be nothing more serious than disgust for the thing which they thought they wanted. And this would be effected by extending the miracle *ad nauseam*. But here the quail seem to be the cause of a plague, and the plague strikes while the people are still eating the meat. Moreover, the indication of time for the plague points to a catastrophe at the beginning of the miracle,[36] a fact which would undercut the extension of the event over the period of a month. The most common means for resolving this problem is to conclude that despite the difficulty in finding two sources elsewhere, this must be a reflection of two different forms of the tradition, i.e., two sources.[37] But this would not resolve the difficulty; at best, it only moves the problem back one step since we would still be forced to consider what the relationship between the two forms of the single tradition might be. But why posit a second source at all? We have already seen a tendency toward a duality in the tradition. And this tendency we have attributed to a problem in the history of the tradition itself. Would it not be more likely that the resolution of this difficulty lies on the same plane? The crux of the problem, then, would not

[36] Cf. Gray, p. 118; Noth, *Numeri*, p. 81.

[37] Gray, p. 101, weakens the argument here by admitting that even though he feels this problem is to be resolved in terms of two sources, "it is impossible to carry the analysis through [the chapter] in detail."

be the identification of sources to which these two forms of punishment might belong, but the relationship which might exist between them.

It seems to be clear that both reflect a negative interpretation of the quail miracle. If one must be considered a primary part of the negative motif and the other secondary, it would be difficult to believe that vss. 19-20 would be secondary, for they provide the insight necessary to define the murmuring motif in the rest of the unit. We could suggest, then, that vs. 33, though certainly reflecting the murmuring motif, is not a primary part of it. But how are we to define that relationship? The answer lies in the contact between vs. 33 and the aetiology in vss. 4a and 34.

The aetiology, as we noted above, is built on the vocable אוה. The principal denotation of the verb is "to desire." The Pi'el stem commonly connotes simply the normal emotion of wishing or desiring. The desire can be directed toward the physical appetites (Mic. 7:1), but it can be broader (cf. Job 23:13). The Hithpa'el stem is stronger and can express lust in the sense of inordinate, excessive, or degrading desire (Deut. 5:21; Jer. 2:24). But the connotation is not necessarily negative (cf. Deut. 18:6). Unfortunately, the aetiology does not give enough of the circumstances which surround this verb to make its connotations here clear. The word אספסף is a *hapax legomenon*, but probably is intended to represent a specific group of people within the Israelites. The identity of that group is impossible to determine on the basis of this text. But the word does show that the subject of the desire is not the *whole* people of Israel. The object of the desire is not stated in any part of the aetiological saga. By virtue of its association with the quail tradition, we might assume that the object here is also quail. Can we say, then, that the verb אוה refers to the same kind of event as the verb בכה? The repeated character of בכה might argue for this. Yet אוה cannot be considered in any sense an act of "weeping" and thus an initial act which might serve as an antecedent for וישבו. If this idiom is intended to provide a connection between the two verbs and suggest that they describe the same kind of event, it

can be done only through some figurative sense of the verb
אוה.[38] And this seems most unlikely.

The same problems continue into vs. 34. Only a portion of
the people have been slain for their desire, and we may
assume that it is the same faction within the people that was
cited in vs. 4a. But there is no indication in the aetiology
itself to suggest that these people died *because of* their desire.
The only information offered in these two verses is that a
portion of the people had a desire (העם המתאוים), and that
these people were buried. The name which is derived from
this, קברות התאוה, might well suggest that the desire was the
cause of punishment which resulted in death. This would
give us some insight into the connotation of the verb אוה in
the aetiology. But even this interpretation would depend on
vs. 33. As the aetiology stands in vs. 34, there is no direct relationship to the murmuring motif, no suggestion that the
people involved represented Israel, no indication that the
desire was for the quail. How, then, is the aetiology to be related to its context?

There are two aspects of this problem. First, it seems
very unlikely that the miracle of the quail might have been associated with any particular spot; it is thus significant that
the manna and quail narrative in Exod. 16 has no local
aetiological element. It would be far more likely that it, like
the manna, was a phenomenon which was common to the
whole southern desert. Noth recognizes this extraneous character of the aetiology when he says that "es ist kaum zu
bezweifeln, dass anders als bei den Quelltraditionen hier die
Namenätiologie und damit auch die lokale Festlegung über-

---

[38] There are two other possibilities for explaining the significance of
וישבו in this text: (1) By changing the pointing, the word could be
taken as a verbal form from the root ישב; this alternative would be supported by the LXX reading καθίσαντες. But something of the same problem would persist in the use of the particle גם. (2) Gressmann, pp. 137-
38, suggests that the repeated nature of the weeping refers to a complaint
of the Israelites which preceded the gift of the manna. If this is the
case, the word in question would represent nothing more than a secondary
connection between the two motifs.

lieferungsgeschichtlich erst ein aufgesetztes Licht ist, das zur Substanz des Stoffes nicht notwendig hinzugehört." [39]

But our problem has to do with the relationship of the aetiology to the murmuring motif, and since we have suggested that the murmuring motif is a different narrative thread which has been superimposed over the motif of the quail and simply uses its principal elements as a framework to support its own emphasis, the question here is quite different. Yet in no text have we been able to determine that אוה carries even the slightest connotation that might be interpreted as *rebellion*. In the aetiology there is no evidence to connect the use of this term with the motif of the people's rejection of their deity. Indeed, the only connection available seems to come through vs. 33. Thus we may conclude that there is no primary connection between the rebellion motif and the aetiology and that the appearance of the second punishment provides a link to bind the whole together.[40] This hypothesis is supported by the fact that only vs. 33 has any connection with both the murmuring and the aetiology. The plague is the result of the demand for quail, and the resulting death prefigures the burial at קברות התאוה. To be sure, we have noted that the punishment by extension of the miracle is not in keeping with the nature of the rebellion. But neither is punishment by execution of only a *portion* of the people. It might be argued that this group was slain on behalf of the remaining people; this would be at least a more appropriate punishment for their rejection. But there is no evidence of such a vicarious death in the text. The plague was against all the people (vs. 33bα), while the people who were buried (by the rest of the Israelites?) were all the people who had the desire. Thus we must maintain that, despite the fact that the severity of Israel's rebellion seems to demand some form of

[39] Noth, *Überlieferungsgeschichte*, p. 130.

[40] Cf. Gressmann, pp. 140-41. We may also conclude that since this link, and thus the connection of the locality, קברות התאוה, with the quail narrative, depends on the interpretation of the plague as punishment, it presupposes that the quail narrative has already been reinterpreted in terms of the murmuring.

punishment, the punishment does not find its proper expression here.

Noth has a different view of the relationship between the murmuring and the aetiology:

Sie [the aetiology] führte nicht nur mit dem Element קברות auf die Voraussetzung einer göttlichen Bestrafung, sondern darüber hinaus mit התאוה auf ein "Begehren," das als Ausdruck der Unzufriedenheit und Misstimmung des Volkes die göttliche Bestrafung veranlasst hatte. . . . Hier scheint mir denn das Erzählungselement vom Murren des Volkes am festesten in einer bestimmten Einzelgeschichte verwurzelt zu sein und sich aus der überlieferungsgeschichtlichen Quelle einer bestimmten Namenätiologie ungezwungen ableiten zu lassen. Es ist daher wahrscheinlich, dass sein Ursprung hier gesucht werden muss und dass es sich von hier aus auf viele andere Einheiten des Themas "Führung in der Wüste" ausgebreitet hat.[41]

I cannot agree with this conclusion. If we were content to assume that any expression of disatisfaction with wilderness life is to be considered a part of the murmuring motif, then we would be in a better position to consider this a viable alternative. But even here, we would face difficulties since the connection between the aetiology and the main body of tradition seems to me to be built on a secondary link. This would mean that the whole argument, based on an interpretation of the name קברות התאוה as a reflection of dissatisfaction with life in the wilderness, arises from an element which lies *outside* the aetiology (vs. 33). It may well be true that קברות התאוה reflects some dissatisfaction in its own right, but this dissatisfaction is not revealed in the aetiology. On the other hand, our concern is for the rebellion motif which pits the whole people of Israel against her leaders (or her deity) over the question of the Exodus. And it seems clear that the relation of this to the aetiology is at best secondary. It would therefore be improbable that this bit of aetiological saga could account for the rise and spread of the rebellion motif.[42]

How, then, are we to explain the connection of the two?

[41] Noth, *Überlieferungsgeschichte,* p. 137.
[42] Cf. also Schnutenhaus, p. 130.

If we have only a secondary link between them, why were they brought together? The tradition of the quail has already provided a setting for the rebellion, and this has nothing to do with the aetiology; in fact, it seems to be a complete self-contained whole without the aetiology. This question must probably remain unanswered. Perhaps the itinerary which forms the secondary framework of the pentateuchal material contained a reference to this place (cf. Num. 33:16), and the story of the quail with its corresponding motif of rebellion seemed the most appropriate for the connotations of the name.

We must still consider the role which punishment plays in the motif. In vs. 33 we have the serious consequences of the plague which must be interpreted as punishment for the rebellion. But it appears in the context of a secondary link between the murmuring and aetiology. In vss. 19 ff., we have an element of punishment which, though not as serious in its consequences for the rebels, is nevertheless a response to their rebellion. But the traditio-historical background of this form of punishment reveals that it is an attempt to bring the tradition of Yahweh's aid into conformity with the rebellion motif. Thus it is clear that punishment has no consistent or essential role to play in the unit. This conclusion would be confirmed by the fact that the parallel narrative in Exod. 16 has no punishment but is nevertheless completed by a response in the form of an *Erweiswort* (cf. the spring narratives which also have no trace of punishment).

Yet the motif has a marked affinity for punishment. It seems to be the most natural response for such a serious breach of fidelity, and the two examples here do not seem to be out of place. That this is in fact the case would be emphasized by the fact that punishment is used to form a connection with the aetiology. We must conclude, then, that even though punishment does not seem to be a necessary part of the motif, it is not inconsistent with it. It merely forms a possible expression of the formal response to the murmuring.

To summarize: The manna tradition appears to be independent of the quail tradition, with no indications that manna was given in response to murmuring. The quail tradition reflects a primary stage in which it, too, was free of contact with the rebellion motif. On the other hand, the narrative development of the quail tradition is adapted to the peculiar interests of the rebellion motif. Thus the setting for the murmuring is the request for food, and an overabundance of food is interpreted to be punishment for the rebellion. This use of punishment suggests that it is not an essential part of the motif but rather a part which might be employed as one form of various responses to the rebellion. Once again, the subject of the rebellion lies in the question of the Exodus, while the unrealistic references to the food in Egypt reflect an attempt to tie this motif with its setting in the story of Yahweh's gracious aid. But in this text, this form of rebellion is seen to be an overt rejection of Yahweh. Finally, the connection with the aetiology seems to be only a secondary linking of the quail tradition already seen in terms of murmuring with a fragment from a local saga. There are insufficient grounds to maintain that this relationship reveals the origin of the murmuring motif.

What can we learn about the history of the motif from a comparison of this narrative with the P parallel in Exod. 16? The most important observation is that P reveals the same sort of leveling noted in the traditions of Meribah, as well as a tendency to broaden the influence of the murmuring wherever possible.

Numbers 21:4-9

Although this unit is not properly one of the food narratives, we shall consider it at this point because of its allusion to both food and water as problems in the wilderness period.

Vs. 4aα has been defined as a redactional link which alludes to the P narrative in 20:22-29, and vs. 4aβ as a similar link with the E narrative in 20:14-21.[43] The unit in vss. 4b-9 is apparently a later insertion into an existing order of narra-

---

[43] Gray, p. 277; Gressmann, p. 284; *et al.*

tives; its position at this particular point would be designed
to present it as a final account of Israel's life in the wilderness
before transition to the Conquest theme in vss. 21 ff.[44]

Identification of sources in vss. 4b-9 is complicated by the
variation between אלהים (vs. 5) and יהוה (vss. 6, 7, 8), and the
multiplication of names for the serpents (vs. 6: הנחשים השרפים;
vs. 7: הנחש; vs. 8: שרף; vs. 9: נחש נחשת, or simply הנחש). But
an attempt to define two parallel accounts of the serpents
on the basis of these variations alone cannot illumine the complexity of the unit. There is no evidence of a parallel narrative which would in any sense be complete, and no reason
to isolate scattered fragments. We shall concur with Noth,
then, that the unity of this section cannot be described by
reference to different sources.[45]

But which of the pentateuchal sources would be represented
here? The general tendency is to assign the whole unit to E.[46]
For some, this conclusion would depend not only on evidence
in the unit itself, but also on the connection with E in
20:14-21.[47] But the connection is at best tenuous, arising from
the redactional link in vs. 4aβ rather than the unit itself.
Moreover, the use of יהוה offers difficulties for assigning the
unit to E. Gressmann dismisses the problem by observing:
"Das ursprüngliche 'Elohim' ist nur in vs. 5 erhalten, in den
übrigen Versen ist es durch 'Jahve' verdrängt worden." [48] But
this suggestion hardly resolves the question. The several
references to יהוה with only one appearance of אלהים, the
designation of the people with the term העם, and reference to
Moses alone, i.e., without Aaron, would suggest instead that
the source is J, while the connection between the subject of
the narrative, the bronze serpent, and the Temple in Jerusalem seems to support the suggestion. Yet the one appearance
of the name אלהים is exceptional in J and raises doubt about
this choice. The J characteristics may be due to nothing more

[44] Noth, Überlieferungsgeschichte, p. 133; "Num. 21," pp. 179-80.
[45] Noth, "Num. 21," p. 178; Numeri, p. 137.
[46] Gray, p. 274; Gressmann, p. 284, n. 1; Noth, Numeri, p. 137.
[47] Baentsch, p. 575; Holzinger, p. 89.
[48] Gressmann, p. 284, n. 1; cf. also Noth, Numeri, p. 137.

than influence from the murmuring motif in other J sections
(cf. Exod. 17:3-4). Thus it appears to us that the question of
source identification here cannot be solved with certainty; we
shall conclude only that this unit appears as a late secondary
insertion into the pentateuchal complex.[49]

The type of material involved in this unit is also difficult to
determine. The focus of the unit is on the creation of the
bronze serpent (vs. 9).[50] The terms שרף and שרפים [51] are used
most often in the Old Testament in Isaiah (Isa. 6:1 ff.; 14:29;
30:6). In each of these cases it is clear that the creature is a
winged serpent, while Isa. 6:1 ff. makes the figure specifically
a six-winged creature that stands in the Temple before the
altar. That these seraphim are to be associated with the
bronze serpent in Num. 21:4b-9 seems to be clearly established
by II Kings 18:4. This short reference to the reform of
Hezekiah in 705 reports that an object destroyed by the king,
called נחש הנחשת (cf. Num. 21:9), was made by Moses. It
is unfortunate that this text does not recount more of the
details of the tradition of its origin; we must assume, nevertheless, that the reference to Moses presupposes a form of the
tradition which we have in Num. 21:4b-9. Moreover, there is

[49] Noth, Überlieferungsgeschichte, p. 133, observes: "Sie [Num. 21:
4b-9] ist schon literarisch ein Spätling, da sie wahrscheinlich einen Zusatz
innerhalb des Werkes von J bildet, der noch ganz am Schluss des Themas
'Führung in der Wüste' unmittelbar vor dem Übergang zum Thema
'Hineinführung in das Kulturland' eingeschaltet wurde."

[50] John Gray, I and II Kings, a Commentary, OTL (Philadelphia:
The Westminster Press, 1963), p. 608. There is abundant evidence for
the use of snakes in cultic rites, perhaps fertility rites, of the ancient
Near East. But the snake was also used for symbolic prophylactic purposes. It is perhaps in this context that the use of snakes and symbols
of snakes for healing purposes is to be seen. And certainly this use is
the one reflected in Num. 21:4-9.

[51] The question of the relationship of these creatures with fire has long
troubled commentators. It has been suggested that the שרפים must arise
from the burning sensation which resulted from the bite (G. Gray, p.
277). But the name is not used in regard to the result of the bite or even
the bite itself, but in description of the creature. It is possible, then,
that these were mythological creatures which were conceived as burning
in appearance. But a more probable explanation arises from Holzinger,
p. 92. He suggests that the name may be borrowed and thus have nothing
to do with the Hebrew root שרף. Cf. Noth, Numeri, p. 137.

no indication in either Num. 21:4b-9 or II Kings 18:4 that the bronze serpent was in the Temple in Jerusalem. But the connection between the שרפים in Num. 21:6 and Isa. 6:2 ff. (cf. also the winged serpents in Deut. 8:15, serpents which belong to the wilderness, and the winged seraphim in Isa. 6:1 ff.) makes it probable that the serpent was a part of the Temple cult.[52]

Rowley has proposed that not only was this creature associated with the Temple cult in Jerusalem but was in fact a part of the cult which was in Jerusalem before David conquered the city.[53] If this should be the case, then David would have faced the dilemma of having a non-Israelite cultic symbol as a part of Israel's cult. The narrative of the serpents in Num. 21 would thus be designed to give the non-Israelite cultic symbol a legitimate place in the traditions which recount the origins of Israel. But even if the non-Israelite character of the symbol is not accepted, it seems nevertheless probable that the same purpose obtains. To be sure, it would not be properly an aetiology since the narrative makes no reference to the symbol's use in the Temple or even to a subsequent use by the wilderness generation. There is no indication that the people took the symbol with them into the land and thus no transition from a wilderness setting to a setting in the Temple. Yet it seems clear that an aetiological concern undergirds the tradition.[54]

The narrative is developed by legendary motifs which recount Israel's murmuring in the wilderness. And at this point, still another purpose of the unit appears. The description of the seraphim shows that these creatures have a decidedly mythological character; they seem to be angelic in their association with the deity (vs. 6; cf. Isa. 6:6), as well as demonic in character.[55] But their association here with Moses and Israel

[52] Noth, *Numeri*, p. 137.

[53] H. H. Rowley, "Zadok and Nehushtan," *JBL* LVIII (1939), 113 ff.

[54] Noth, *Numeri*, p. 137, concludes: "Aber das spätere Vorhandensein der auf Mose zurückgeführten 'bronzenen Schlange' war gewiss der Anlass, die Geschichte von einer Schlangenplage in der Wüste zu erzählen."

[55] Th. Gaster, "Angels," *The Interpreter's Dictionary of the Bible,* ed. George Buttrick, *et al.* (Nashville: Abingdon Press, 1962), I, 132.

in the wilderness breaks their mythological character by giving them a legendary setting. This, too, may have served the practical purpose of making them somewhat more acceptable to the Israelite point of view.

Our next task is to determine the character of the murmuring motif and its place in the development of the narrative. The first problem lies in defining the significance of the verb קצר in vs. 4*b*. The only parallel of any interest which employs this vocable appears in Exod. 6:2-9, a P passage which uses a noun from this root to describe the spirit of the oppressed Israelites. This text does not provide firm control for conclusion concerning the role of the verb in the murmuring motif (cf. Appendix I). But it does suggest a similar connotation for the verb in Num. 21:4*b*. Brown, Driver, and Briggs suggest that the meaning of the verb in connection with either נפש or רוח should be "to be impatient," developing from a basic meaning of "short" (cf. Judg. 10:16; 16:16; Mic. 2:7; Zech. 11:8; Job 21:4). And in Num. 21:4*b* the subject of the verb is נפש העם.

But the cause of impatience is not clear. The reference to דרך would suggest a connection with vs. 4*a*, perhaps pointing to impatience with the leaders over the forced detour around Edom. But it is probable that vs. 4*a* is a secondary redactional link between vs. 4*b* and 20:21. Vs. 5*a* shows clearly that vs. 4*b* does not represent an overt action associated with the murmuring motif but at best a condition of the people's temperament. The series of crises in vs. 5*b* offers the most likely clue to the cause for the impatience, and the close connection between the series and the murmuring motif would increase the probability that the impatience here prefigures the murmuring.

Vs. 5, then, is the principal part of the murmuring motif in this unit. Generally, it follows the same pattern which we have noted in the previous units. Especially do we note that the issue raised by the question is once again the Exodus: "Why have you brought us up from Egypt to die in the wilderness?" But this verse shows signs of later development in the motif. First, both Moses and God (אלהים in vs. 5*a* or יהוה in vs. 7) are cited as the objects of the murmuring. But the relationship between this introduction and the accusation which follows reflects some difficulty. The verb in the accusation is, according to the MT, written defectively. The consonantal text, the Sam.Pent., the LXX, and the Syriac suggest that the verb should be singular. This reading recalls the same problem with the same verb in 20:5, but the question there was whether Aaron was to be included as a part of the subject. Here Aaron does not come into the question. We may suggest, then, that a traditional form of the murmuring in which the object was originally only Moses has been used in this unit.

Second, in contradistinction to the previous units of tradition which were formulated each around a specific crisis, here three of those crises are joined together. There is no bread (לחם); there is no water. And then in contradiction to the first, the bread (לחם) which they do have after all is worthless (הקלקל). This series represents a summary of crises from other traditions in the Wilderness theme for the purpose of supporting the legitimation of the serpent.[56]

Moreover, we have noted that the various crises usually form the *setting* in which the murmuring occurs. But this summary is so broad that it cannot serve as a precise setting for the murmuring. Indeed, its only function seems to be a condensation of the murmuring, for the principal crisis which gives the unit its substance and a precise setting is the attack of the serpents. These problems suggest that the murmuring motif, or better, the tradition about Israel's murmuring in the wilderness, is at a later stage of its development, summarized and inserted here to provide a legendary basis for the crisis of the serpent attack.

We can now raise the question of relationship between the attack of the serpents and the murmuring. Can the attack be considered a response to the murmuring? Our interest begins at vs. 6 with the dispatch of the serpents. It is not Moses but

---

[56] Noth, *Numeri*, p. 136, suggests that the series is simply a description of the circumstances of wilderness life.

Yahweh who is responsible for the attack. But this would not be surprising if we are to interpret the attack in terms of response to the murmuring since Yahweh is also the object of the rebellion. Moreover, vs. 7 suggests a causal relationship between the murmuring and the attack. The people confess that the murmuring was sinful (חטאנו) and ask Moses to intercede before Yahweh on their behalf.[57] The only conclusion possible from this construction is that the attack has been interpreted here as the result of the murmuring.

But is this the earliest form of the tradition about the fiery serpents? If we should assume that the original form of the tradition did not include the murmuring, it would have related no more than an attack by demon serpents sent by the deity (Yahweh), an appeal to Moses for aid, and his intercession before Yahweh. Such an account would still have given the needed foundation for the cultic symbol in the Temple by placing the origin of the symbol in the wilderness period, made by Moses. The reason for the insertion of the murmuring would be clear: It would be employed in order to explain the necessity for the attack (as well as to provide a legendary setting for the attack). And once again, the affinity of the motif for punishment would come into play.

What evidence do we have that an earlier form of the tradition like the one described above actually existed? Deut. 8:15, the only other text which is relevant for this question, clearly associates the נחש שרף with the wilderness.[58] There is no evidence that the murmuring tradition was involved. But neither is there evidence that an attack of the serpents was involved. The only event reflected here is Yahweh's leadership through fiery serpents and scorpions. We might suppose that his leadership was effected by means of a bronze serpent; in this case, the bronze serpent would function more in terms

[57] It is significant in light of the interpretation of this prayer as intercession that the verb is פלל instead of צעק.

[58] The syntactical relationship between במדבר הגדל והנורא and נחש is puzzling. The apparent meaning is: "through the great and terrible wilderness *where* the fiery serpents are." Cf. Brockelmann, # 146-49.

of protection than healing. But this hypothesis would be only conjecture.[59]

It seems to be clear, then, that the only source for formulating a judgment about the relationship between the murmuring and the attack of the serpents as punishment for the murmuring is Num. 21. It is not impossible to suppose that even here the tradition existed at an early stage without reference to the murmuring. This hypothesis would necessitate a view of the tradition which would have Yahweh sending the serpents against Israel for no apparent cause, thus casting a stronger shadow of the mythical over the tradition (cf. Exod 4:24-26). This might be possible. The view of the wilderness in Deut. 8:15 begins to lose contact with the concrete world by personifying the qualities of the wilderness and associating it with the threat of mythological creatures. But evidence to support such a reconstruction is tenuous, built principally on the uncertain relationship between Num. 21:4b-9 and Deut. 8:15. The development of the narrative in Num. 21 leaves little room for doubt that the attack is to be understood as Yahweh's response to rebellion against him and interpreted in terms of punishment for this act.

This form of the tradition presupposes that the petition for Yahweh's aid must be seen in terms of intercession. Moses' concern here makes his lack of concern in Num. 11:21-22 even sharper. But it does not provide evidence for suggesting that intercession is a primary part of the murmuring tradition. Quite the contrary, the intercession is tied up with the core of the serpent tradition since, as a result of the intercession, the

[59] The earliest form of the tradition may have recounted nothing more than Israel's trek through the fiery serpents with Yahweh's protection, i.e., no reference to either the murmuring or Moses. If this should be the case, then the bronze serpent created by Moses would also have no role to play, and the function of this tradition as a legitimation for the serpent in the Temple would not apply. Cf. Noth, *Numeri*, p. 137. But even if this should be the case, it seems likely that the form of the tradition which recounts Moses' construction of a bronze serpent reflects the later use of a bronze serpent in the Temple. And this would be the level of the tradition which supports the murmuring.

instructions for making the bronze serpent are given. As this unit stands, the murmuring tradition has been used in a developed form as the basis for the primary objective of the unit. But that objective, the construction of the bronze serpent, lies outside the scope of the murmuring. The intercession is thus a means for tying the late form of the murmuring tradition to the legitimation of the serpent in the Temple.[60]

We may now take a further step in defining the history of the murmuring tradition. If the serpent is at home in the Temple cult in Jerusalem, and if this unit represents an attempt to legitimize this figure for the cult, then the use of the murmuring tradition to support that end reveals that at this point in its development, it, too, was available for use, if not at home, in the Temple cult in Jerusalem.

Moreover, we know that the cultic symbol was present in the Temple until the time of Hezekiah's reform in 705. Since there is no evidence that an attempt was made to revive the symbol after the reform, we are relatively secure in saying that the narrative is either a defense of the symbol vis-à-vis Hezekiah or a previous attempt to provide an account of its origin which might make it acceptable to Israelite worshipers. This would give us a firm *terminus ad quem* for the origin of the murmuring tradition at 705.

But it is probable that the legitimation of the symbol for use in the cult was already a firm tradition before the reform.[61] And the fact that this narrative used a developed form of the murmuring suggests that the origin of the murmuring tradition lies a number of years before the time of its use in the serpent story. It seems probable, then, that the *terminus ad quem* should be several years before Hezekiah's reform, i.e., in the period of the divided monarchy.

One further question must be considered here. Does the association of the murmuring tradition with intercession show

[60] Against Schnutenhaus, pp. 140 ff.

[61] Noth, *Numeri*, p. 137, observes: "Die Diskriminierung des 'Nehusthan' als eines von den Israeliten göttlich verehrten Idols durch Hiskia ist dem hiesigen Stück [Num. 21:4b-9] offenbar noch nicht bekannt."

that the murmuring was maintained in the prophetic guilds of the Temple? It has long been known that intercession was one of the chief tasks of the prophetic office.[62] But to conclude from this observation that any reference to intercession necessarily connotes a prophetic office is a *non sequitur*.[63] Since we have discovered no evidence in any of the previous texts to suggest a connection between the murmuring tradition and the prophetic office, there is no reason to adopt this qualification.

Numbers 11:1-3

Before we move to the next division of our work, we shall consider this small unit of tradition which, though having no contact with the food narratives, is nevertheless quite similar to the tradition about the serpents.

The unit is clearly defined by ויהי and a rare participial construction which introduces the complaint of the people (vs. 1), and an aetiological formula (vs. 3). Vs. 1 comes on the heels of the narrative about the Ark, while the quail tradition follows immediately in vs. 4. There is no evidence of a primary connection between this unit and either of the two units which frame it. These three verses are self-contained, showing no trace of a doublet or even a break in the development of the narrative. As a consequence, the total section can be assigned to one source. Since the murmuring in this section is at best a condensed form, we should consider the possibility that it, like Num. 21:4b-9, is a late addition to the pentateuchal material. But Noth suggests that it is a part of the J narrative.[64] This opinion is supported by the designation of the deity as יהוה, the use of העם as a designation for the

---

[62] Gerhard von Rad, "Die falschen Propheten," *ZAW* LI (1933), 114.

[63] H. W. Hertzberg, "Sind die Propheten Fürbitter?" *Tradition und Situation, Studien zur alttestamentlichen Prophetie* (Göttingen: Vandenhoeck & Ruprecht, 1963), pp. 63-74, has shown conclusively that the task of intercession does not belong exclusively to the prophetic office.

[64] Noth, *Überlieferungsgeschichte*, p. 135; *Numeri*, p. 75.

people, and the fact that only Moses appears in the narrative. We have nothing against this choice.[65]

The type of material which appears in this narrative is analogous to that in Num. 21:4*b*-9. The basic form of the tradition is an aetiology, and here the aetiological goal of the narrative is preserved. The aetiology is built on the tradition of a fire that burns at the ends of the camp. But the fire should probably not be considered mythological; even though it functions in virtually an independent role in vs. 1*b*α (cf. Num. 21:6), it seems to be more of a tool in the hands of Yahweh than a messenger that might be dispatched (cf. Lev. 10:2; I Kings 18:38; *et al.*). The narrative, then, appears to be a legendary basis for the aetiological explanation of the place name.

But what role does the murmuring motif play in the account? The crux of the problem lies in the single word כמתאננים. The root אנן is used in only one other text in the Old Testament—Lam. 3:39—and the connotations of the word there are difficult to grasp. But the root does appear in various cognate languages. The Akkadian *enênu* has been defined as "to sigh," while the Arabic '*nn*, the Syriac '*nn*, and the Aramaic אנן are normally translated "to complain." These connotations may be used to cast light on the meaning of the word here. But the most decisive evidence in determining the meaning as well as its relationship with the murmuring tradition lies in the fact that the LXX translates the word with γογγύξων, the root which, as we have seen, is consistently used to translate לון. This shows that at least for the LXX the participle refers to the same kind of event which composes the murmuring tradition. This conclusion would be confirmed by the accusative object רע which follows the participle and the notation that Yahweh *heard* (cf. Exod. 16:12, *et al.*). But beyond these items, there is no indication of the nature of the murmuring; the narrative moves immediately to an account of the response to the murmuring. We may conclude that just

---

[65] But cf. Gressmann, p. 256, n. 4; G. Gray, p. 99; Baentsch, p. 503, for whom this is E; and Eissfeldt, p. 275*, for whom this is L.

as in the tradition of the serpents the murmuring tradition was condensed and used as a whole in the development of the narrative, so here the principal part of the tradition has been reduced to one word (cf. Deut. 9:22) .[66]

Once again, this form of the murmuring is employed to show the reason for the event which follows. The anger of Yahweh is incited against his people apparently as a result of the complaining, and the consequence is that the fire destroys a part of the people (קצה המחנה) . Since the destruction provides a foundation for the aetiology, it must be considered the principal part of the unit. The destruction is interpreted as punishment for the murmuring, and again, as in Num. 21, the punishment is followed by an intercession before Yahweh to stay the execution.[67] As in Num. 21, the affinity of the murmuring for punishment provides a connection between the murmuring and this local aetiology. We could argue that the complaining is a secondary item, leaving a narrative of a disaster by fire, a petition to Yahweh for help, and the miracle which protects the people from danger. This possibility would have the advantage of offering an aetiology for the place name which is not dependent on a later condensation of the murmuring tradition. But there would be even less basis to support such a reconstruction here than we had for the serpent tradition.

The use of the murmuring in this unit unfortunately does not offer us a firm grasp of the realm in which the tradition lived. The place which bore the name תבערה is difficult to locate; at best, we can suggest the general area of the southern desert. This conclusion would not be inconsistent with the

---

[66] Noth, *Überlieferungsgeschichte*, p. 135, n. 349. He suggests that since vs. 1 is rather rough syntactically, the text is probably not intact. In view of this possibility, we could suppose that the rebellion was once described in more detail. But there is obviously no evidence to support a reconstruction of the tradition.

[67] The close connection between the punishment for the murmuring and the central kernel of tradition in both this unit and the serpent tradition does not provide evidence for suggesting that the tradition of rebellion in the wilderness arose from these sources. Cf. Noth, *Überlieferungsgeschichte*, p. 136.

observations which were noted above concerning the use of the murmuring tradition in the Temple cult in Jerusalem. But we cannot go further at this point.

To summarize: Num. 21:4b-9 and 11:1-3 show a development in the murmuring which may be attributed to a later stage in the history of a basic rebellion tradition. The murmuring seems to have been used here because of its affinity for an element of punishment. That this element is a primary part of the two units does not indicate that the tradition of Israel's rebellion arises from the one or the other; it merely suggests that the murmuring is used as a subordinate narrative motif in order to show the reason for the danger which is expressed in the aetiology. Furthermore, the intercession appears to have no essential role to play in the murmuring tradition, coming into these units only as a result of the association of the murmuring with the aetiologies. That one of the narratives is bound to the Temple cult, or at least reflects a cultic symbol from the Temple cult, gives us an insight into the setting which at this point gave the tradition life and points to a date no later, and probably earlier, than 705 for its origin.

the remaining narratives

Exodus 13:17–14:31

These verses involve a rather complex interweaving of at least two parallel accounts of the deliverance at the Reed Sea, with fragments of a third source appearing at scattered places. The unit in 13:17-19 introduces the narrative with a description of the route followed by the Israelites after the Exodus. (Cf. vs. 17*aα*: "When Pharaoh sent the Israelites away, God did not lead them by way of the land of the Philistines.) The use of אלהים throughout this section, as well as the reference to Gen. 20:25 (E) in vs. 19, suggests the E source.[1] J appears in vss. 20-22, again a description of Yahweh's leadership after Israel's departure from Egypt.[2] A third unit appears in 14:1-4. It is only at this point that the Reed Sea narrative is properly introduced. The precise location of the event in vs. 2 (cf. Num. 33:7), along with features such as the reference to hardening Pharaoh's heart and the glorification of Yahweh in vs. 4, marks this unit as a part of P.[3] Vs. 5*a* stands out from

[1] Noth, *Exodus*, p. 105, *et al.*

[2] Noth, *Exodus*, p. 105, *et al.* Eissfeldt, p. 134*, divides the unit between J (vss. 21-22) and L (vs. 20).

[3] Noth, *Exodus*, p. 105; on the other hand, Gressmann, p. 109, n. 1, attributes vss. 1-2 and 4 to P, with vs. 3 assigned to E. Cf. also Baentsch, p. 121.

the P unit because of the reference to מלך מצרים and should probably be assigned to E (cf. Exod. 5:4).[4] Vs. 5*b* is distinguished from vs. 5*a* by the notation that the Pharaoh sent the Israelites away (vs. 5*a* suggests that the people fled), and thus is to be related to the J narrative in Exod. 12:29-34. Noth argues that vss. 6 and 7 are doublets but laments that there are no indications in either verse to facilitate assigning them to a source.[5] The repetition of the verb לקח would seem to indicate that these verses are indeed doublets. But since vs. 7 notes that in addition to the Pharaoh's own chariots and servants (cf. vs. 6) he also took all the chariots of Egypt, this conclusion may not be necessary. Vs. 6 forms the natural continuation of vs. 5*b* and is consequently a part of J. If vs. 7 can be considered a continuation of vs. 6, it, too, would be J; if not, it would be attributed to E.

Vs. 8 returns to the stylistic character of P and in fact forms a smooth continuation of vs. 4. In contrast to vss. 6-7, vs. 9aα‎א clearly duplicates vs. 8bα. We may assume that the two are from different sources, and the tendency is to assign the latter to J.[6] But a problem arises here. Should the plural verb and its dependent elements in vs. 9aαב be considered a part of the source represented in vs. 9aα‎א, i.e., J, since both 9aα‎א and 9aαב have plural verbs in common, while vs. 8, the immediate context, has only a singular verb? This is possible. But if it is the case, we would be forced to assume that P had a parallel to vs. 9aαב, for without this preparation, vs. 9aβ*b* makes no sense. And this part of the verse, because of its allusion to vs. 2, is certainly P.

Noth suggests that vs. 10bα should be separated from its context. He leaves vs. 10*a* undefined, but connects vs. 10bβ with vss. 15 ff. since the catchword צעק appears in both. This would make vs. 15 a response to vs. 10bβ.[7] But problems arise here. Vs. 10bβ has the Israelites crying directly to Yahweh,

[4]Noth, *Exodus*, p. 106. But Eissfeldt, pp. 35-36, relates this half-verse, along with vss. 1-4, to L.

[5] Noth, *Exodus*, p. 106; cf. Gressmann, p. 109, n. 1.

[6] Noth, *Exodus*, pp. 105-6.

[7] *Ibid.*, p. 105.

while vs. 15 addresses the response of Yahweh to Moses. The Syriac has felt this problem and inserted an introduction before vs. 15 to report that Moses also cried to Yahweh. But this reading can hardly be considered more than a correction of the inconsistency. The problem becomes even more complicated when we note that vs. 10bα corresponds to vs. 13. Since vss. 13-14 and vss. 15 ff. do not belong to the same source, the conclusion must be that vs. 10bα and vs. 10bβ do not belong to the same source (cf. the repetition of בני ישראל in these quarter verses).[8] The resulting division would suggest that vs. 10bβ and perhaps vs. 10a belong to P, as do vss. 15 ff., while 10bα belongs to J. Yet vs. 10bβ is a natural continuation for vs. 10bα. The people see the Egyptians, they are afraid, and they cry for help. It seems more satisfactory to suggest, then, that both α and β in vs. 10b (along with vs. 10a) belong to one source and that that source is directly related to vs. 13 (J). That vs. 15 also uses the catchword צעק would be explained by the supposition that the P narrative runs parallel to J.

Since vss. 13-14 provide a fitting response for vs. 10, it is striking that the response in vss. 13-14 does not fit the complaint of the people in vss. 11-12. Does this mean that vss. 11-12 must be considered a part of another source? There are no stylistic characteristics to place this section in either P or E. There is no evidence that vss. 11-12 constitute a doublet of a previous or a subsequent unit. Indeed, nothing more than the rough connection with the context suggests that it is not a part of the source which provides the context. If, despite this lack of literary criteria, we were to assign this section to E,[9] it would mean that contrary to the small fragments of E in vss. 5a and 19a, this, the longest piece of the narrative, would have no identifying characteristics of E. Moreover, there is nothing in the section which specifically concerns the event at the sea; if it were assigned to E as a parallel account of the J narrative of the miracle at the sea, we would have the major extant part of the E account of this miracle having no specific

    [8] *Ibid.*, p. 105.
    [9] *Ibid.*, p. 106.

reference to the theme of the narrative. It is probable, then, that these verses reflect a problem in the history of the Reed Sea tradition and are not to be separated from the J narrative in which they occur (cf. the exegesis below).

The literary problems in the verses which follow are especially difficult to resolve. Since there is no reference to the murmuring motif or any other negative element in these verses, we shall simply outline the source structure.[10] Vs. 19a is characterized by a reference to מלאך האלהים as a fragment of E. Vs. 19b, with its pillar of cloud, returns to J. Vs. 21aαא is a fragment of the P narrative related to the P section in vs. 16. Vs. 21aαבβ and vs. 21b are doublets, each reporting in its own style that the waters were divided. Since vs. 21aβ uses the word for "dry ground" which appears in the J account of the flood (cf. Gen. 8:13), it may be attributed to J. Vss. 22-23 are characteristically P (cf. יבשה with Gen. 8:14). Vs. 24 returns to a reference to the pillar of fire and cloud and must be considered a part of J. Vs. 25b is connected with vs. 27aβb by virtue of the reference to נוס. Since vs. 27aαβb is a doublet of vs. 28, and vs. 28 is a part of P, we must assign this part of vs. 27 to J. Vs. 25a has no distinctive marks, but since it comes in the context of a J section, we can attribute it to J as well. Vss. 26 and 27aαא appear to be P (cf. vss. 16, 21aα). Vss. 28-29 conclude the P narrative of the event, while vss. 30-31 offer the J conclusion. We thus have the following literary structure: P, 14:1-4, 8, 9aβb, 15-18, 21aαא, 21b, 22-23, 26-27aαא, 28-29. J, 13:20-22; 14:5b, 6, (7), 9aα, 10-14, 19b-20, 21aαבβ, 24-25, 27aαבβb, 30-31. E, 13:17-19; 14:5a, (7), 19a.

The murmuring motif appears only in vss. 11-12, that section which offers no clear evidence regarding its relationship to the various pentateuchal sources. Vs. 11a introduces the motif without reference to any of the verbs which are normally employed for this purpose. Instead, the verb is simply a 3. m. pl. *waw* consecutive imperfect of אמר. The subject is not defined in vs. 11 and obviously presupposes some previous specification. The context provided by vs. 10bβ suggests that

---

[10] *Ibid.*, pp. 113 ff. On the meaning of the corrupt vs. 20, cf. Gressmann, p. 109, n. 1.

the subject is the בני ישראל. But a noticeable change in addressee between vss. 10bβ and 11 raises difficulties for this connection. In vs. 10bβ, the people cry to Yahweh, and we expect vs. 11 to show us what their cry was. But instead, they speak to Moses. This shift could mean that vss. 11-12 represent foreign material, completely unrelated to the context. And in this sense, it is significant that there is no explicit reference to the event at the Sea in these verses. But it could also mean that these verses are nothing more than a growth in the tradition which simply changes the addressee to fit the form of the expansion. It is thus pertinent to note that the accusation in the murmuring motif is consistently addressed not to Yahweh but to Moses.

The address in vs. 11a is in a grammatical form not heretofore seen in this motif. It is introduced by the negative causative particle מבלי coupled with an interrogative hē. The following אין is redundant since מבלי already contains the notion of negation (cf. II Kings 1:3, 6, 16). The principal verb of the address is a perfect form of לקח (cf. Exod. 6:7; Deut. 4:20 for the significance of this verb in the Exodus-election traditions), which in turn is followed by an infinitive construct. The infinitive expresses the same connotation of result arising from the main verb which we have seen previously in the murmuring motif; indeed, the infinitive and its adverb of place (למות במדבר) reflect the same choice of words which has dominated the murmuring tradition in the texts previously examined. But the similarity in content does not mean that this question serves the same function as the accusation. In a sense the perfect form of the verb does question the nature of the act it describes. But the difference between this question and the normal form of the accusation lies in the fact that it does not challenge the act itself, but raises a possible *reason* for the act: "Did you take us to die in the wilderness because there are no graves in Egypt?" There are strong overtones of irony in this question; i.e., it is obvious that the Israelites would not have been denied the right of burial by law or by lack of space. And the point of the irony implies that a grave in Egypt would have been better than a grave in the wilderness. This form is thus parallel to the death wish noted above.

The accusation itself appears in vs. 11*b:* "Why have you done this to us? Why have you brought us out of Egypt?" (cf. above, Chapter II, pp. 30-32). The longer form of the interrogative introduces the question. The principal verb in this introduction is a perfect form of the verb עשה. The event described by this verb is more specifically defined by the following infinitive. And with the infinitive, the accusation is once again directed toward the Exodus (להוציאנו ממצרים). To this extent, then, the murmuring motif in this narrative corresponds exactly to the tradition about Israel's rebellion in the wilderness which has been observed in the previous texts.

But a problem arises here. The event at the Reed Sea has been held to be "the very act which was first and chiefly meant when Israel confessed Yahweh as 'the God who led us up out of Egypt,'" [11] in effect, the climax of the Exodus, the culmination of Yahweh's relationship with the Pharaoh. But the murmuring tradition, even in this context, presupposes that the Exodus event lies in the past. The sentence introduced by המבלי in vs. 11 shows that the murmuring is given a setting in the *wilderness* in contradistinction to the earlier life in Egypt. If the people should die in the wilderness, assuming that their graves would be there, their burial would be contrasted to the graves which they might have had *in Egypt;* i.e., the form of the question presupposes not only that graves in Egypt would be preferable to the ones they might have had in the wilderness, but also that there was no chance for them to obtain that preference. The accusation reflects the same problem. The challenge is directed toward the Exodus. But the Exodus does not appear as an event now in process, or an event expected in the future. Quite the contrary, it lies in the past.

What, then, is the relationship between the murmuring

[11] Noth, *Exodus,* p. 104. Cf. also Georg Fohrer, *Überlieferung und Geschichte des Exodus, BZAW* XCI (Berlin: Verlag Alfred Töpelmann, 1964), 97 ff.

tradition and the legendary material which reports the event at the Sea? There are three possible answers. We conclude either that the murmuring is completely foreign to its context,[12] or that its combination with the legend about the deliverance at the Sea has obscured the original nature of the tradition by casting the Reed Sea event as a post-Exodus event, or finally that the original nature of the Reed Sea tradition already looked back on the Exodus as a past event.

A prior question must be answered before we can consider the first alternative. What is the immediate motivation for the rebellion? This element of the motif is ordinarily expressed in immediate juxtaposition to the accusation. If this is the case here, it must come in vs. 12. Vs. 12aα refers to a statement which was allegedly made when the people were still in Egypt. It does not seem likely that the reference is to either the event recorded in Exod. 5:21 ff. or the one in 6:9 since there is no direct quotation in either text which would compare favorably to this.[13] Since there is no other text in the Old Testament which might give us an insight into the setting of the quotation, the circumstances which might have surrounded it must remain obscure. Of more importance for our concern is the fact that once again life in Egypt is considered a thing of the past. The imperative חדל and its purpose clause express even more explicitly than vs. 11a the preference of the people to remain in slavery rather than leave Egypt under the leadership of Moses. And here also, the servitude in Egypt is contrasted to death in the wilderness. In this context, then, the death which the Israelites foresee can be understood only as death from the Egyptians at the Sea.

But can this conclusion be confirmed by evidence from the text itself? Vs. 12bβ returns to the crisis of dying in the wilderness introduced initially in vs. 11aβ. But vs. 11aβ is in the context of the ironical question about graves in Egypt, and

---

[12] Gressmann, p. 109, n. 1, concludes: "Denn die Israeliten klagen nicht über die Gefahr, die ihnen vom Heere droht, sondern über die Not der Wüste." The murmuring is thus a secondary (and foreign?) element in the context. But, we must ask, what is the nature of the need posed by the wilderness in this unit?

[13] Cf. below, Appendix I.

thus set in the wilderness. Here the statement is apparently made in Egypt and formulated as an alternative to their servitude: "Let us alone that we may serve the Egyptians. For it is better to serve the Egyptians than to die in the wilderness." This statement would imply that if they did not serve the Egyptians, i.e., if they fled into the wilderness, they would die there. Since this is the only citation here, we may assume that it presents the crisis which motivates the rebellion. Moses did bring them out. They are no longer serving the Egyptians, so they now face death from the Egyptians in the wilderness. And the prospect of this death is worse than the thought of having remained in the servitude of the Egyptians. Still another connection with the broader context of the Reed Sea legend may be seen here, for it must be more than coincidence that the J narrative in vs. 5b reports that the Pharaoh's reason for pursuing the people lies in the fact that he has lost their servitude. Thus, even though the murmuring is not well unified with the narrative context, it is not foreign material. It clearly depends on the context for its formulation.

This leaves two alternatives. We must conclude either that the murmuring has obscured the tradition which gives it a setting, or that the primary form of that tradition already considered the Exodus an event which lay in the past. The evidence which we have seen on the basis of a study of the Reed Sea motif suggests that the latter is the case.[14] To be sure, it is true that the event at the Sea represents the final moment of Yahweh's victory over the Egyptians. But unless we assume that every reference to Yahweh's relationship with the Egyptians constitutes a part of the Exodus traditions, we cannot consider the event at the Sea the point of reference for the confession that Yahweh brought Israel out of Egypt.[15] The event at the Sea could not be completely disassociated from the Exodus traditions since the threat posed by the

[14] Cf. my article, "The Traditio-Historical Character of the Reed Sea Motif," *VT* XVII (1967) , 253-65.

[15] Dennis J. McCarthy, "Plagues and Sea of Reeds: Exodus 5–14,"*JBL* LXXXV (1966) , 154, observes that the Reed Sea event occurred after Israel's escape, and then raises the crucial question: "How did Israel get away in the first place?"

Egyptians derives from the escape from Egypt. But the Reed Sea tradition, as well as the murmuring tradition, looks back on the Exodus as an event of the past.

But what is the nature of the relationship between the murmuring and the Reed Sea tradition? The murmuring has not forced its context into a post-Exodus setting contrary to its original nature. But can we say that the murmuring is an integral part of the Sea tradition? Vss. 13-14 contain no element of response to the murmuring or punishment for the rebellion. Quite the contrary, these verses correspond to the familiar pattern of Yahweh's aid. The people are in the wilderness; they face a serious crisis; they cry out to Yahweh (here, as always, the murmuring is inserted, leaving the impression that the change in addressee in vss. 11-12 is the result of the same process which was noted in Exod. 17:1 ff.) ; Yahweh responds favorably by instructing Moses in the proper means for obtaining aid. With the exception of vss. 11-12, the tradition is completely positive. Moreover, the J form of the narrative concludes by affirming the positive nature of the event: "So Israel saw the great deed which Yahweh did against the Egyptians, and the people feared Yahweh. And they believed in Yahweh and in Moses his servant" (in contrast, cf. Ps. 106:7) . This conclusion is especially significant for our study of the murmuring tradition and its setting in older traditions about the wilderness wandering, for it, like Jer. 2:2, represents a conscious response of faith on the part of the Israelites. The P form of the tradition follows the same outline but is free of any element of rebellion.

To summarize: The rebellion tradition appears here as a secondary development in the tradition of Yahweh's victory at the Reed Sea. Presupposing that the Reed Sea event is a post-Exodus event, it emphasizes the same themes noted in other texts: The people accuse Moses of irresponsibility in effecting the Exodus. A parallel to the death wish is to be seen in the ironical question, showing again that the people would have preferred to stay in Egypt rather than face the crises of the wilderness. The immediate motivation for the murmuring is the crisis offered by the pursuing Egyptians.

There is no response to the murmuring; instead, the narrative moves from the accusation to Yahweh's aid.

Numbers 13–14 [16]

With a few exceptions, the source analysis of this section offers no difficulty. Vss. 1 ff. can be attributed to P, with vss. 3b-16a considered a supplementary list of spies.[17] Vs. 16b should probably be considered a gloss, explaining that הושע in vs. 8 is in fact יהושע. That the gloss comes at the end of the list indicates the unified and independent nature of the list itself.[18] Since vs. 17aα is exactly duplicated in vs. 3aα, and vs. 17aβ is an exact doublet of vs. 16aβ, with the single exception of the addition of כנען, the role of vs. 17a in the narrative is unclear. Since vs. 16aβ is in a secondary section, we might designate vs. 17aβ a part of the original material in P. But it seems unlikely that both vs. 3aα and vs. 17aα would appear together at the same level. If this were the case, vs. 17aβ would be separated from the only context to which it could belong by the insertion of the spy list. It seems more probable, then, that vs. 17a is a secondary addition to P which presupposes both vss. 1-3a and 3b-16a.

Vs. 17a is contrasted to vs. 17b where the spies, before leaving the people, receive their instructions. Vss. 17b-20 are

[16] The Sam.Pent. inserts a lengthy section before vs. 1 which corresponds with Deut. 1:20 ff. This section is contradictory to the P introduction of this unit, but many scholars feel that it may represent an original form of the JE introduction. Cf. G. Gray, pp. 129 ff.; S. R. Driver, *Deuteronomy ICC* (3rd ed., Edinburgh: T and T Clark, 1902) , pp. 22-23; Baentsch, p. 517. Since the procedure of completing the Numbers text with the parallel in Deuteronomy appears in the Sam.Pent., LXX, and Peshitta in other texts (cf. 13:33; 14:2, 23, 31, 40, 45) , but not in a consistent form, it is clear that this tendency does not reflect a single recension of the text. That some form of introduction lay behind this expansion which may have originally been a part of the JE traditions may be the case. But the character and extent of that introduction must remain obscure.

[17] von Rad, *Priesterschrift*, p. 103; G. Gray, p. 135; Noth, *Numeri*, p. 92.

[18] The age of the list need not be considered at length here. Cf. G. Gray, p. 135.

basically J. Even though various questions in this unit show
signs of redundancy (cf. Peshitta deletion in vss. 19-20), Noth
is justified in concluding that we do not have two sources
here.[19] Vs. 21 shows the characteristics of P, while vss. 22-24 are
again J. The reference to the founding of Hebron in vs. 22*b*
can be considered a parenthetical aside, a bit of information
that interrupts the natural progress of the narrative. Vss. 25-26
show a characteristic concern of P in the precise number of
days required for the mission, along with a reference to both
Moses and Aaron and the full name for the people. Vss. 27-31
conclude the J account of the spies' mission with their report
to the congregation. Vs. 29 contains another piece of parenthetical information. Vss. 32-33 represent the parallel P account of the spies' report,[20] although vs. 33*a*β may be a gloss
in the text to explain the relation of the נפלים to the ענקים.

Chapter 14:1*a* is P's account of the people's response to the
report of the spies. Vs. 1*b* is a doublet of vs. 1*a* and thus a
part of J. The reference to the people as העם in vs. 1*b* would
support this conclusion. Vs. 4 may well be considered a
doublet of vs. 3*a* since both refer to a desire to return to Egypt.
But vs. 4*a* shows that the addressee has been changed, and
vs. 4*b* introduces a new motif in the move to appoint a new
leader for the return. Since there is no stylistic evidence in
vs. 4 to support our source analysis, we must be somewhat
cautious in assigning it to one of the sources. But since vs. 1*b*
shows that J may be running parallel to the P section, we shall
follow Noth's suggestion that vs. 4 is also J.[21] The remaining
part of the section, from vs. 1 through vs. 10, can be assigned
to P.

The character of vss. 11-25 is complex and difficult to determine. It seems probable that a major break occurs between
vss. 23*a* and 23*b*, although the suffix in vs. 23*b* (יראוה) presupposes some reference to the land like the one in vs. 23*a*.
Vs. 23*b* is connected more closely with vs. 11*a* through the
participle מנאצי (cf. ינאצני in vs. 11*a*). Vss. 11*b*-23*a* do not

[19] Noth, *Überlieferungsgeschichte*, p. 34, n. 121.
[20] Noth, *Numeri*, p. 95; against G. Gray, p. 151.
[21] Noth, *Numeri*, p. 95.

encompass a unified whole. Yet there is no evidence that a second source is involved. We seem to have instead a collection of various material which has been added to the J source.[22] The precise character of this section will be considered below. On the other hand, we can agree that vs. 11a and vss. 23b-24 are clearly J. Vs. 25a can be considered still another of the parenthetical additions in the style of 13:29. Vs. 25b appears to be a concluding statement regarding the exclusion of the people from the land.

Vss. 26-38 form the final P section. Contrary to Noth's indication of secondary material in vs. 27b and vss. 30-33,[23] we can see no reason to deny the basic unity of this section. It may be that vs. 34a is to be considered a gloss, intended to explain the reason for the number forty in the punishment. Vss. 39-45 form a complete and unbroken unit that may be attributed to J. Thus we have the following literary structure: P, 13:1-3a, (3b-16a [16b]), (17a), 21, 25-26, 32, 33aα (33aβ), 33b; 14:1a, 2-3, 5-10, 26-38. J, 13:17b-20, 22a (22b), 23-24, 27-28 (29) 30-31; 14:1b, 4, 11a (11b-23a) 23b-24 (25a) 25b, 39-45.

Since the P narrative is the more complete of the two parallel accounts, we shall begin our analysis here. The first question which demands our attention concerns the nature of the murmuring motif in this narrative. Chapter 14:2 provides us with a typical introduction to the motif (וילנו על־משה ועל־אהרן), again showing Moses and Aaron to be the objects and all the people of Israel to be the subjects. The form of the murmuring is basically the same as that which has so consistently been met throughout the wilderness traditions, including a death wish which has the effect of negating the Exodus: "Would that we had died in the land of Egypt!" Also in typical fashion for P, the motif is expanded beyond this central and overriding concern of the murmuring tradition to take into consideration the current situation of the people. The question addressed to the leaders, who function in the name of Yahweh (vs. 3), does not challenge the Exodus in this case, but rather the Conquest, i.e., bringing the people

---

[22] Noth, *Numeri*, pp. 96-97, describes the unit as deuteronomistic.
[23] Noth, *Überlieferungsgeschichte*, p. 19; *Numeri*, pp. 97-98.

into contact with the inhabitants of the land. But the tradition is nevertheless the same, as we see clearly in vs. 3b: "Would it not be better for us to return to Egypt?"

The response to the murmuring (vss. 5-10) cannot be correctly evaluated without first considering whether the murmuring is a primary part of the tradition of the spies or, as in the other texts where it appears, a secondary development. The legendary material in these chapters has been categorized as a typical "spy story." [24] The outline of a "spy story" is clearly definable here: The initiative for dispatching the spies is taken in this case by Yahweh himself (vss. 1-2).[25] (1) The spies are designated (3b-16a), (2) and dispatched with careful instructions (vs. 17a, cf. the J fragment in vss. 17b-20). (3) The mission is executed (vs. 21), in this case, a reconnaissance of the whole land of Canaan. (4) The spies return and give their report (vss. 25-26).

At this point our narrative deviates from the outline, for vss. 32-33 also report the results of the reconnaissance to the people. The report is clearly unfavorable in character. But the cause for the unfavorable report is not clear. On the one hand, the spies apparently report that the land is not fertile enough to support the current inhabitants (ארץ אכלת יושביה),[26] but on the other hand, their report also concerns the threat posed by the inhabitants who are after all supported by the land. In fact, the people are of such great stature that the spies associate them with the mythological Nephilim.

It is clear that despite the reference in vs. 32bα, the predominant point of view in the tradition is that the land was fertile (cf. the phrase—ארץ זבת חלב ודבש) but so heavily fortified that the Israelites could not hope to settle in its midst, much less depose its inhabitants (thus, vs. 31; cf. also Deut. 1:28). This emphasis would not be foreign to the P account since in vs. 26b the spies show an example of the fruit

---

[24] Siegfried Wagner, "Die Kundschaftergeschichten im Alten Testament," *ZAW* LXXVI (1964), 255-69, esp. 261-62.

[25] Wagner, p. 263, notes the importance of this element but does not include it in his outline of the formal structure of the spy stories.

[26] G. Gray, p. 151.

of the land, obviously in witness to the fertility. Is it possible, then, that the expression ארץ אכלת יושביה does not refer to inferility? Ezek. 36:13 suggests that אכלת, with הרי ישראל as the subject (vs. 8) and אדם as the object, has a connotation of destruction (cf. the parallel form ומשכלת). But what is the cause of the destruction? Vss. 8-12 concern a restoration of the fertility of the land, fertility lost through the destruction of war (cf. vss. 1-7). But are we to infer from this that in vs. 13 the men who were destroyed died from the infertility of the land, i.e., from hunger? Quite the contrary, their destruction is the result of the same cause which accounts for the loss of fertility—war. The land is thus placed as the subject of the same verb אכלת in order to describe the loss of inhabitants in the plundering and battles of the period just before the Exile. In the spy narrative, the report emphasizes the fertility of the land in contrast to strong fortifications in the cities. The phrase in question, ארץ אכלת יושביה, can then be taken as a reference to political turmoil of the time, turmoil which would demand that the cities be strongly fortified against enemy attack. The report would thus not be contradictory: The land was fertile but geared for battle.

An equally pressing question concerns the relationship between vss. 25-26 and the report in vss. 32-33. It is possible to argue that the nondescript statement in vs. 26 reflects a report of the land that was completely positive in character. The only firm indication of the nature of that report is the notation that the spies showed the fruit of the land to the people, presupposing a report based on the fertility of the land. Deut. 1:25 (cf. Num. 14:6-9) also suggests that the report concerns the fertility of the land. But Deut. 1:28, along with the J parallel in vss. 27-31, shows that the tradition of a negative report is nevertheless strong and not dependent simply on the P version of the story. We shall return to the problem of this duality below.

In response to the report of the spies, the people raise their voices (14:1a). Vs. 1a is a doublet of the J fragment in vs. 1b, and in accord with the verb בכה there, the verbs here must be considered an expression of weeping. This half-verse cannot therefore be considered a part of the murmuring motif, but simply a response of fear on the part of the people toward the threat posed by the strong defenses of the land. It is true that in Num. 11:4 ff., בכה is incorporated into the murmuring motif. But it is also clear that it was not originally so used. In this case the distinction between the crying of the people in vs. 1a and their murmuring in vs. 2 is even more sharply drawn, as we see in the repeated designation of the subject. We must therefore conclude that the murmuring is a secondary element in the tradition of the spies' report as it appears in P.

The response which we might expect from the spies to a reaction of fear would be an assurance to the people that they could in fact displace the people of the land.[27] Vs. 5 is instead a typical response of Moses *and Aaron* to the murmuring of the people (cf. Num. 20:6). It is only in vs. 6 that we find a response to the fear on the part of the spies. Both Joshua and Caleb defend a positive view of the prospects for the conquest. The defense reveals two points: (1) Israel's fear is directed toward the strength of the people who now possess the land. (2) The basis for their report, especially in vss. 7-8, is not that the defenses are weak, but that the land is good (טובה הארץ מאד מאד). These points correspond to the two reports in vss. 25-26 and 32-33. Moreover, the parallel in Deut. 1 suggests that they were not two facets of the same report but two opposing reports. The tradition itself suggests that one group of spies reported the foreboding character of the defenses and the state of war, while the other emphasized the character of the land.

Vs. 9 apparently reflects both the murmuring and the response of fear in the spy narrative. The opening words represent an admonition not to rebel against Yahweh. The rebellion clearly refers to the murmuring but adds nothing further which might clarify the event which constitutes the murmuring. The admonition here is set in sharp contrast to the following jussive by the intervening pronoun ואתם (cf. Deut.

<hr />

[27] Wagner, p. 260.

1:29) . The objective of the new admonition is to dispel the fear of the people, a quite common motif in spy narratives.[28] Vs. 9*b* uses a perfect form of the verb סור for expressing certainty that the land can be captured, the fifth element in the formal structure of a spy narrative. Yahweh is not the subject of the verb, but it is nevertheless clear in the remaining part of the verse that Yahweh is the decisive power for the conquest (cf. vs. 8*a*) . This section is thus a part of the basic narrative material. The reference to the murmuring in the form of an admonition is a new element in the scope of the tradition. Since the parallel admonition not to fear is obviously a part of the basic narrative, we may conclude that the admonition not to murmur is an adaptation of this counterpart. It would thus be a part of P's tendency to broaden the perspective of the tradition at each possible point.

On the other hand, vs. 10*a* corresponds to the formal element of reaction to an inadequate response to the murmuring (cf. Exod. 17:4) . Vs. 10*b* connects more smoothly with vs. 5 than vs. 9 since the deference to Yahweh is most likely to have occurred at the tent of meeting, and there is no evidence that the report of the spies was given there. Vss. 26-35 represent an address from Yahweh to Moses and Aaron. The content of the address constitutes the response to the murmuring of the people. In this case, the response is also to be interpreted as punishment for the murmuring, and the punishment, at least toward the people involved in the murmuring, is absolute. Among the older generation, only Joshua and Caleb will escape with their lives. This exception shows that the murmuring is not independent of the spy story; their exclusion from the punishment clearly presupposes their collaboration to counteract the negative report. For P, the absolute character of the punishment presents no problem about the subsequent generations of Israel since only the generation that rebelled will die in the wilderness. Their children will wander in the

---

[28] *Ibid.*, p. 260. It has also been suggested that the setting for this kind of admonition is the holy war. Cf. N. Lohfink, "Darstellungskunst und Theologie in Dtn. 1,6–3,29," *Bib* XLI (1960) , 110 ff.

wilderness as shepherds for forty years and then inherit the
promised land (vss. 31 ff., but cf. Num. 32:6 ff.).

The relationship of vss. 36-37 to the context is not clear.
Vs. 36 repeats 13:25 and sets it within the context of the
murmuring, while vs. 37 seems to be an afterthought to the
judgment on the generation of murmurers, a conscious effort
to show that the remaining spies were punished in a special
manner for having caused the people to murmur (cf. Num.
16:35). But since this is unnecessary in the context and not
present in J, we may conclude that it represents an effort on
the part of P to harmonize the spy story with the murmuring
tradition by extending the consequences of the murmuring
as far as they will possibly go.

The J form of the spy tradition runs roughly parallel to
the P narrative, and on occasion supplements the formal
structure in P (cf. the explicit instructions for the spies in
vss. 17b-20, and the elaboration of the mission in vss. 22-24).
But the differences are nevertheless quite important in developing our understanding of the rebellion tradition. The
first question to be raised here concerns the extent of the
area covered by the reconnaissance as reported in J. P suggests that the whole land was surveyed. But does J's report
correspond in breadth? Vs. 22 takes the spies through the
Negeb and into the hill country to Hebron (on the location
of Hebron, cf. Josh. 21:11). It is possible that the Wady
Eshcol in vs. 23 was also in that vicinity, indeed, a part of the
Hebron territory. The only firm reference to the general area
in which this site might be found appears in Deut. 1:24,
where it is placed in the hill country. But this text mentions
the Wady Eshcol without reference to Hebron. Indeed, both
Deut. 1:24 and Num. 13:22-23 suggest that the Wady Eshcol
may be a distinct locality, independent of association with
Hebron.[29] The aetiological formula in vs. 24 only strengthens
this impression by suggesting that this tradition (vs. 23) is a
fragment of a local saga. Yet the cluster of grapes so large that
it had to be carried on a pole between two men (vs. 23) is

[29] G. Gray, pp. 142-43.

probably to be understood as a part of the same tradition which reports the unusual size of the Anakim, the current inhabitants of Hebron (cf. vss. 22a, 28bβ). It is probable, then, that this local tradition is to be attributed to Hebron and its surrounding area (cf. Gen. 14:13, 24).[30] The total scope of the spy tradition would support this conclusion since at least one goal of the narrative is to explain how Caleb came to be associated with Hebron (cf. Josh. 14:6 ff.). Thus only in vs. 29 do we see any indication of a mission to reconnoiter the whole land. And the participial construction of this verse emphasizes its parenthetical nature.

It may be that 14:1b should follow vs. 29, for here the people respond to the report with weeping.[31] Vs. 30 then reports Caleb's efforts to still their fears and assure the people that they could indeed overcome the inhabitants. This is, of course, the response which we would expect in the structure of a spy narrative for an expression of doubt or fear among the people. If the J narrative has a form of the murmuring tradition similar to the one in P, it would theoretically appear at this point. But the tradition in J is unfortunately too fragmentary here to permit an analysis of what its character might have been. The only possibility lies in vs. 4. The setting in this verse does not represent a face to face encounter between the leaders and the led, but only a movement within the people. But does it presuppose such an encounter (cf. vss. 2-3 [P])? The quotation is in the form of a cohortative and a following purpose clause: "Let us appoint a captain so that we may return to Egypt." This assumes that the previous captain of the people, who in J is consistently Moses, has been deposed at least insofar as the people involved in the movement are concerned.[32] If this is the case, such a maneuver would necessitate a face to face confrontation with Moses. The formal structure for expressing that maneuver is precisely the form which is present in the murmuring tradition. But evidence

[30] Noth, *Numeri*, pp. 93-94.
[31] G. Gray, p. 150.
[32] Against Noth, *Numeri*, p. 95.

for this reconstruction is tenuous. We cannot determine with certainty whether vs. 4 is a J fragment or a part of the P narrative.

We are, however, on firm ground in dealing with J's form of the murmuring in vs. 11a. This half-verse is in the form of an address from Yahweh to Moses; it is parallel to the speech of Yahweh to both Moses and Aaron in vss. 27 ff. (cf. the introductory עד אנה with עד מתי in vs. 27aα) and represents Yahweh's response to the murmuring of the people. This parallel would show without doubt that some form of murmuring was in the J material. But we can go further than this in determining what the character of the murmuring was. The people (העם) are the subject of the murmuring. The object, as shown by a first person singular suffix with the verb, is the speaker, Yahweh himself. The verb, ינאצני, is parallel to מלינים עלי in vs. 27aβ. The meaning of the verb נאץ in the Pi'el stem is listed by Brown, Driver, and Briggs as "to contemn, spurn." But in certain contexts, the meaning is stronger, connoting an overt *rejection* (cf. Isa. 1:4; 5:24). A rejection of Yahweh has been observed elsewhere in association with the murmuring tradition (cf. Num. 11:20 with the verb מאס). Moreover, it corresponds to the action described in vs. 4 since a move to reject Moses is tantamount to a rejection of Yahweh. The problem which lies at the basis of the rejection, as we have noted in the entire scope of the tradition, is the Exodus (cf. Deut. 1:27). But here, for the first time, the murmuring is followed by a move to return to Egypt. The murmuring tradition therefore involves not simply an expression of a wish that the Exodus had not occurred or a challenge of Moses' authority in executing the Exodus, but now an overt move to reverse the Exodus. Yahweh is the God "who brought Israel out of Egypt." The murmuring results in a rejection of this deity and a move to elect a new leader to take the people back to Egypt. This is in fact a rejection of the principal event and theological affirmation which constitute Israel's election: "I am Yahweh, and I will bring you out from under the burdens of the Egyptians and deliver you from their bondage and redeem you with an outstretched arm and great acts of judgment. And I will take you for my people, and I will be your God." (Exod. 6:6-7a).[33]

Yahweh's reaction to the murmuring is to reject the people. This is clearly expressed in vs. 12: אכנו בדבר ואורשנו. But the unity of this verse with the preceding is in question. The threat to make of Moses a nation to take the place of Israel is found elsewhere only in deuteronomistic material (Exod. 32:9 ff.; Deut. 9:14) and doubtlessly reflects a subsequent, perhaps deuteronomistic tendency to magnify the office of Moses (cf. Deut. 34:10). Moreover, the following intercession shows strong signs of late elements. The appeal to the reputation of Yahweh in the eyes of the nations (vss. 13 ff., esp. vs. 15) seems to presuppose the problems of the Exile more than the period of the monarchy (Exod. 32:12; Lev. 26:45; Deut. 29:23; Isa. 62:2; Jer. 22:8; et al.). At most we can say that it has strong reminiscences of the deuteronomistic theology of Yahweh's name (cf. Ps. 106:8).[34]

The reference to Yahweh's long-suffering patience in vs. 19b must be an allusion to his repeated acts of forgiveness for the repeated instances of rebellion (cf. Ps. 78:38). But in fact, the element of forgiveness has played a relatively minor role in the murmuring tradition, only appearing in those occasional texts where the tradition has been used to explain unusual threats and punishment of the people (Num. 11:1-3; 17:6-15; 21:4-9). And even there, forgiveness is veiled behind the repeal of a plague. There is no reference to forgiveness itself, no mention of reconciliation with the people until the next moment of rebellion. The only purpose seems to be a stay of some natural or supernatural disaster that unrestrained would have spelled doom for the entire people.

In contradistinction to this tendency, vs. 20 explicitly states

[33] Kurt Galling, Die Erwählungstraditionen Israels, BZAW XLVIII (Giessen: Alfred Töpelmann, 1928), 5-26.
[34] Gerhard von Rad, Studies in Deuteronomy, tr. David Stalker, SBT IX (London: SCM Press, 1953), 37 ff. The name is the means by which Yahweh is known among the nations, and with the Exodus it is peculiarly bound to Israel. If Israel is destroyed, then Yahweh's name will be ridiculed among the nations.

that Yahweh forgives the sin of the people according to the word of Moses. But even here, the forgiveness is not a repeal of the sentence of death in the wilderness or a reprieve from the loss of the inheritance of the land. The punishment which is announced *at the same moment* is absolute: אם־יראו את־הארץ אשר נשבעתי לאבתם. The reason for the judgment is contained in vs. 22: "All of the men who have seen my glory and my signs which I did in Egypt and in the wilderness, but have tested me these ten times and have not obeyed my voice. . . ." This represents a summary account of all the events of murmuring. The use of the verb נסה suggests that the summary is late, at best no earlier than Deuteronomy (cf. above on the use of נסה). There is some concession here. The rebels will not be destroyed immediately but may wander through the wilderness until the natural end of their lives. But this is the only consequence of the forgiveness announced in vs. 20, for there is no indication beyond the verb סלח that the people were reconciled either with Yahweh or with Moses. The oath in vss. 21-22 only emphasizes the punishment and continuing alienation of the rebels.

The P tradition escapes the absolute quality of this punishment by saying that all children of this generation of murmurers under twenty years of age would indeed inherit the land (vs. 31, cf. Josh. 5:2 ff.). But this exception is absent in J. It may be that something of this nature is intended by the qualifying attribute in vs. 22: "All the men who . . . tested me . . . ." This implies that those who were not involved will not be subjected to the judgment. But this statement must be considered a part of the late addition to the J text. The burden of the question concerning the judgment in the primary form of the tradition must be borne by that part of the tradition which we can clearly assign to J. Vs. 23*b* picks up the verb נאץ from vs. 11*a* and uses it in the form of a participle to define those who have forfeited the right to see the promised land. This half-verse we may designate clearly as J's announcement of punishment. To some extent, the designation of the people involved in the punishment is parallel to the qualification in vs. 22. Only the people who despised

Yahweh will be subjected to exclusion from the land. But who are the people who despised Yahweh according to J? Vs. 11 makes this clear: "How long will this people (העם הזה) despise me?" There is no exception in this statement. Neither does the fact that the rebels will be permitted to complete their lives in the wilderness represent a tempering of the judgment. The initial threat to destroy the people immediately is a part of the late addition to J and reflects a deuteronomistic emphasis on Moses. In contrast, the form of judgment in the primary J tradition is the denial of the rebels' right to see (and thus inherit) the promised land, the right which they bear as the elect people of Yahweh.[35] And this punishment is absolute.

The role of punishment in the broad scope of the murmuring tradition we can now clarify in greater detail. We have noted that even though punishment is apparently not foreign to the tradition, it has never played a decisive role. Here, however, the situation is different. The punishment is an essential part of the unit. Formally, it appears again as Yahweh's response to the rebellion. But it is not a response dictated by the nature of the tradition of Yahweh's aid or a local legend which might give it a setting. Instead, it supplies a response to Israel's rebellion which is demanded by the gravity of their action. The reference to זה עשר פעמים in vs. 22b cannot be considered a precise specification of the number of

---

[35] K. Koch, "Zur Geschichte der Erwählungsvorstellung in Israel," *ZAW* LXVII (1955), 205 ff., notes that the sophisticated expression of Israel's election vis-à-vis the other nations of the world is late and probably deuteronomistic in origin (cf. Deut. 7:6-8). If, then, the murmuring tradition negates the principal tenets of Israel's election, must we assign a correspondingly late date for its origin? The *terminus ad quem* which we established above was just after the end—or perhaps somewhat before the end—of the divided monarchy. Would this specification conflict with the late date for the election theology? It is significant that the concept of election which sees Israel chosen from among all the nations is not reflected in the murmuring tradition. Instead, the concept here is concerned only with Israel as Yahweh's people and Yahweh as Israel's God. And this doubtlessly originated much earlier, indeed, as early as the confession that Yahweh was "the God who brought us up out of the land of Egypt." Cf. John Bright, *The Authority of the Old Testament* (Nashville: Abingdon Press, 1967), pp. 131-32.

murmuring events at one time present in the wilderness traditions, but rather a round number, a general summary of the
murmuring history.[36] Although the summary is in the later
addition to the J narrative and thus reveals a generalizing
tendency common in deuteronomistic or post-deuteronomistic
forms of the murmuring tradition, we can conclude that the
summary serves as an explanation for the punishment described here. The reason for the rather minor role played by
punishment in the previous units would lie in the absolute
character of the punishment demanded; it was necessary to
express this only once. Thus the whole history of Israel's
rebellion forms the *Begründung* for this one act of judgment
(cf. Ps. 78).[37]

Vs. 24, however, makes a striking exception to the absolute
character of the punishment. Caleb will be exempted. The
exemption presupposes Caleb's role in quieting the fears of
the people concerning the spies' report. It is significant that
both in the spy report and in this part of the murmuring
tradition, Joshua plays no role, thus leading us to the conclusion that Joshua has been added, or at least emphasized,
by P in order to account for his position as the leader of the
Conquest (cf. Deut. 1:38; Josh. 1:16 ff.).

Caleb's role in the spy story arises primarily from his association with Hebron. The question which must concern us
now, however, is whether the murmuring tradition sees the
goal of the spying to be only the hill country of Caleb's
Hebron or, in conjunction with P and vs. 29, the whole land.
Vs. 24*b* notes that Caleb's exemption from punishment will
mean that he will be brought into הארץ אשר־בא שמה. The
land in this verse is identical to the land which forms the
antecedent for the suffix in vs. 23*b*. The murmurers will not
be able to see the land, but Caleb will. It would be pointless to

---

[36] Noth, *Numeri*, p. 97. Against F. V. Winnett, *The Mosaic Tradition*
(Toronto: University of Toronto Press, 1949), pp. 121 ff.

[37] This hypothesis presupposes a construction of the murmuring tradition as a sequence of connected events. However, the sequence is not
derived from the murmuring tradition but from the tradition of Yahweh's
aid in the wilderness. We shall return to the question of order below.

deny the rebels the opportunity to see (and possess?) Caleb's Hebron. This is the whole land, the land of the promise.

Thus in the place of the generation now condemned to death in the wilderness, Caleb alone will be brought into the land. And in contrast to the absence of a reference to the children of the rebels and the emphasized exception of their children in P (vs. 31), vs. 24bβ notes that Caleb's descendents will inherit (ירש) the land (cf. Deut. 1:36). The reason for Caleb's special treatment is no longer the fact that he brought a positive report from the spying mission (thus removing it even further from the association of Caleb with Hebron). Vs. 24a shows the reason to be Caleb's essential theological difference from his colleagues: "Because a different spirit is with him and he has wholly followed me. . ." (cf. Num. 32:11-12; Deut. 1:36; Josh. 14:8-9, 14). In connection with this description, we must note the designation of Caleb as עבדי in a speech by Yahweh. This term can have a technical connotation,[38] and although it is commonly used simply for the pious man before Yahweh, we must consider whether the construction of the murmuring tradition had any further motives in putting this designation into the mouth of Yahweh.

What is the significance of Caleb's unique role in the murmuring tradition? Apropos of this question is the problem of Caleb's identity. The primary form of the spy narrative was designed at least in part to explain the early association of the Calebites with Hebron. But who were the Calebites? Caleb is consistently called the son of Jephunneh and a Kenizzite (cf. Num. 32:12; Josh. 14:6, 14; 15:17). The Kenizzites are elsewhere represented as a part of the Edomite tribes (Gen. 36:11, 42).[39] It seems at least probable, then, that the Calebites were a non-Israelite people who continued to dominate the area of Hebron after the conquest was completed.

But if this is the case, they were early identified with and assimilated into the tribe of Judah (cf. Josh. 14:6; Judg. 1:10).

[38] W. Zimmerli and J. Jeremias, *The Servant of God, SBT* XX (rev. ed., London: SCM Press, 1965), 11 ff.

[39] Martin Noth, *The History of Israel;* tr. Peter Ackroyd (2nd ed., rev.; New York: Harper & Row, 1960), p. 56.

This process would perhaps be reflected in the spy narrative if not presupposed as an accomplished fact. Moreover, the list in Num. 13:6 makes Caleb a leader of the Judahites. We can therefore conclude that in the murmuring tradition, Caleb is already seen as a Judahite; indeed, since he represents Judah in the spying mission, the murmuring tradition would assume that he was the leader of that tribe. This construction suggests that the land of the promise was inherited by the leader of the tribe of Judah. Thus, in spite of the emphasis on the rebellion of the whole people, the murmuring tradition has a decidedly pro-Judean flavor.

Wagner suggests that the form of a spy account was originally connected with the Conquest theme,[40] and it seems likely that this particular narrative follows the pattern. This would suggest that just as the total scope of the murmuring tradition cannot be separated from the theme of the Exodus, so it also presupposes the traditions of the Conquest. But it is nevertheless clear that the central locus for the murmuring, even in this context, is the wilderness. This is shown by the fact that the murmuring in response to the spies' report provides the reason for the forty-year sojourn in the wilderness.

A further problem must be considered in this context. We have seen heretofore that the tradition which gives the murmuring its setting is primarily positive in nature. Is this the case here? There is some evidence that the forty-year period (the life of one generation) was not originally a form of punishment for the murmuring but a quite positive element in the tradition of Yahweh's aid to the people in the wilderness. (Cf. Deut. 2:7; 8:2, 4; 29:4; Amos 2:10; 5:25; Neh. 9:21; also Deut. 1:33. This is in sharp contrast to Ps. 95:10.) But these texts are not connected with the spy account. And when we consider the nature of this tradition, it is difficult to define any basic positive element. Quite the contrary, the report of the spies has a decidedly negative overtone even without the murmuring. The spies feel that the land before them is too strongly fortified to permit their assault. The fear which the

---

[40] Wagner, p. 263. Cf. also Noth, *Überlieferungsgeschichte*, p. 143.

people show following the negative report is, indeed, followed by the assurance that the land could be conquered. But there is nothing in this narrative or any of its counterparts to suggest that it was conquered as a result of the spies' mission.

What, then, is the nature and function of the spy tradition? Wagner suggests that the final stage in the formal structure of a spy account is a statement of action resulting from the spies' report.[41] Only vss. 39-45 could fill this role for the spy tradition here (cf. Deut. 1:41). This section is apparently dependent on the murmuring tradition: The words reported to the people in vs. 39 can only be the statement of judgment on the rebels which was first announced to Moses (vs. 11), and their response of mourning is fitting for the punishment (cf. Judg. 2:4). In vs. 40, however, the situation is not as clear. As the tradition now stands, the act of the people is irrational. Since they recognize that they have sinned and are told that Yahweh will not go with them, it is clear that if they should go into battle, they will be defeated. How, then, are we to explain the report that they do go into battle? That Yahweh is not to go with them rests on the fact that they have sinned. But does this refer to the murmuring? The word used here is חטא. This term is not commonly found in the context of murmuring, although it does appear at scattered places in the motif. (Cf. Num. 12:11; 16:22; 21:7; Ps. 78:17, 32; 106:6; Neh. 9:29, along with the Golden Calf tradition, Exod. 32:30, 31, 33; Deut. 9:16, 18. Each of these texts represents a special problem, either a late reference to the rebellion or a particular kind of infraction which lies on the periphery of the rebellion tradition.) But rather than connoting murmuring as an act of rebellion with a specific form, it is general in character: "to miss the mark."[42]

It is clear that the Israelites did not conceive the plan to go up to fight the Amalekites by themselves. Num. 14:40

[41] Wagner, p. 262.

[42] von Rad, Theology, pp. 262 ff. Rolf Knierim, Die Hauptbegriffe für Sünde im Alten Testament (Gerd Mohn: Gütersloher Verlagshaus, 1965), pp. 56 ff.

implies, and Deut. 1:41 clearly states, that their action was in accord with the command of Yahweh. But the command itself does not appear in the tradition. To be sure, the spies assure the people that the land can be captured. But the assurance is not expressed in the form of a command from Yahweh to move against the inhabitants of the land. We must assume, therefore, that the command to fight followed the spies' assurance that the battle could be won. We would thus have some explanation for the incongruous picture if we suppose that the people's action in vss. 41 ff. was in response to this command (cf. Deut. 1:41aβ) rather than a foolhardy attempt to capture the land after they had sinned and been warned that Yahweh would not go with them.

But if this is the case, what is the purpose of the reference to Israel's sin? It would seem to be a conscious construction rather than a description of historical fact. But why would the tradition have been constructed with a sin that leads to disaster? There is no indication that Israel entered the land from the south; indeed, even the tradition of Caleb's possession of Hebron is associated with the conquest which originated from the Transjordanian area (cf. Josh. 14:6; Judg. 1:10). It seems far more likely, then, that this tradition reflects an early abortive effort to enter the land from the south.[43] The negative character of the report would then anticipate the abortive invasion, while the general nature of Israel's sin would be a theological justification for the failure.

Does this sin presuppose the murmuring? In the present form of the tradition, the answer should probably be that it does. But is this the case for earlier stages? The narrative is built around the report of the spies and Israel's response in fear. In the context of a holy war, the normal procedure would be for the spokesman to assuage the fear. This is attempted (vs. 7). Vss. 42-43 suggest that the difficulty lies in an infraction of procedure in the holy war. This is especially clear in vs. 42b, for the expression אין יהוה בקרבכם is a negation of a formula which depicts the basis for Israel's pro-

⁴³ Noth, Überlieferungsgeschichte, pp. 148-49.

tection in war (cf. Deut. 7:21; Josh. 3:10; Mic. 3:11; Zeph.
3:17; also Num. 14:14). We might suppose, then, that the
violation lies in a refusal to go to battle following the assurance that Yahweh would give them victory.[44] And indeed the
confession of sin in vs. 40 cites Yahweh's command (thus,
אמר) to go up. We should conclude, then, that a reference to
Israel's sin, associated in some manner with an infraction of
holy war procedure, was present in the spy tradition before it
was incorporated into the murmuring tradition.

Moreover, the failure to win the battle would leave the
people in the wilderness (Deut. 1:46), perhaps faced with
the necessity to detour around the Dead Sea and enter the land
from the east (cf. Deut. 2). Would this mean that the forty
years of wandering were already interpreted as punishment
for this sin? This is probably not the case. The sin here would
be designed to explain the single defeat, while the rise of
the forty-year sojourn as punishment presupposes the judgment on the rebels which demands the death of the whole
generation. Thus the murmuring seems to have been incorporated here with two different traditions, the one a report from
spies which probably already included a negative element,
and the other a forty-year period of Yahweh's care and aid
in the wilderness.

In summary: This tradition presents much the same picture of the murmuring which has been seen in other texts.
We have first the spies' report, which in all probability was
already negative in character since it was associated with an
abortive attempt to enter the land. The defeat was interpreted as the result of Israel's sin, but the sin is not to be
identified with the rebellion. To this tradition the murmuring was added, interpreting the reaction of the people to the
report of the spies as rebellion against Moses and thereby
against Yahweh. Yahweh's response to the rebellion was disinheritance; the murmurers were denied the privilege of seeing
the promised land. This was done by sentencing the current
generation to wander about the wilderness until its mem-

[44] Lohfink, p. 111.

bers died, i.e., forty years. These elements, in both J and P, form the basis for a negation of the basic principles of Israel's election. P makes two exceptions to the absolute character of the punishment: (1) Caleb and Joshua, the men who reported favorably about the land, would be allowed to enter it. (2) The children of the murmurers would be made heirs to the promise in the place of their fathers. But J makes only one exception. Only Caleb will see the land, and only his descendents are mentioned as the legitimate heirs to the promise. Since Caleb appears in this tradition as the leader of Judah, this exception gives the murmuring a decidedly pro-Judean flavor.

Numbers 16–17

The literary structure of these chapters is characterized by an interweaving and expansion of two narratives, the one concerning Korah, and the other concerning Dathan and Abiram. These two story threads have classically been identified with two of the principal pentateuchal sources: Korah seems to reflect the P source, while the Dathan-Abiram story shows clear signs of J. But the surprising fact about this division is that they do not overlap; the Korah tradition shows no signs of J, and the Dathan-Abiram is free of priestly influence.[45] The accuracy of this position is confirmed by the following source analysis.

Vs. 1 apparently sets the three figures together in one genealogical introduction. But the verse is corrupt.[46] It is most probable that two distinct genealogies have been combined

[45] Num. 26:9 mentions the three together, but it is certainly a late construction dependent on the present combination of the two stories (cf. also Num. 16:1, 23, 27). On the other hand, Num. 27:3 (P) mentions only Korah, while Dathan and Abiram appear alone in Deut. 11:6. Cf. Noth, *Überlieferungsgeschichte*, p. 19, n. 59; G. Gray, p. 188.

[46] The transitive verb ויקח has no object. LXX reads καὶ ἐλάλησεν, but this does not resolve the difficulty since no quotation follows which might report what was said. Kittel suggests ויקם on the basis of the second column in the Hexapla: ὑπερηφανεύθη. This possibility offers a reasonable reconstruction, but the precise form of the original cannot be recovered. Vs. 2 apparently continues the difficulty from vs. 1. The *waw* before ואנשים in vs. 2aβ tends to separate this section of the verse from the

here at the expense of intelligibility in the text. Vs. 2aα can
be considered a part of the Dathan-Abiram introduction,
while vs. 3aα constitutes a parallel introduction for the Korah
narrative.[47] This leaves vs. 2aβb as the accusative object of the
transitive verb ויקח in vs. 1aα, a conclusion which is confirmed
by stylistic features of P (cf. esp. נשיאי עדה in the precise description of the men who are involved), and the subsequent
identification of Korah's company with 250 men (vs. 17, et
al.).[48] The subject of the verb in vs. 3 is not defined in that
verse, but we may infer from the context (vss. 1-2, 5) and the
reference to both Moses and Aaron that the subject is Korah
and his men (cf. כל־העדה as an element of P). There is no
break between vs. 3 and vss. 4-5, even though vss. 4 and 5 refer
only to Moses. The explanation for this phenomenon is most
probably to be found in the traditio-historical background
of the text.

Vss. 8-11 form a redundant account of Moses' address to
Korah and his company, heightened in vs. 8a by a new introduction to the address (cf. vs. 5aα).[49] But this section is not
properly a doublet of its counterpart, for it no longer raises
a question about the sanctity of the people but rather about
the right of the Levites to the priesthood (vs. 9), a problem
which sets the Levites in opposition to the Aaronites. And in
this context, the rebellion is interpreted to be primarily
against Aaron. It is somewhat more understandable that Aaron
is not a part of the subject here. But this does not explain why

introduction in vs. 2aα, although it could be considered simply a pleonastic
waw. Yet the dangling character in vs. 2aβb, coupled with the subsequent
identification of Korah's company as 250 men, suggests that this word may
be the object of the transitive verb in vs. 1aα. The waw would still be
a problem, but this hypothesis would at least offer the possibility for
interpreting the text as it stands. And it would leave Dathan and Abiram
disconnected from the context. They could also be considered the subjects
of the verb, but the probability is that they are in fact separate and their
combination here represents the interweaving of two originally independent genealogies. Cf. T. J. Meek, "Some Emendations in the Old
Testament," *JBL* XLVIII (1929), 167-68. On the role of the Levitical
genealogy, cf. the exegesis below.

[47] Noth, *Numeri*, p. 109.

[48] Gressmann, p. 252, n. 3.

[49] On the relationship of vs. 7b and vs. 8b, cf. the exegesis below.

he does not appear in vss. 4 ff., as well as in vs. 8. The address here should not therefore be considered another source, i.e., a separate P source, but a secondary development dependent on the primary form of the response to the Korahites in vss. 5-7.[50]

Vs. 12 returns to the story of Dathan and Abiram. But it is obvious that something is missing in the narrative between this point and the brief introduction in vss. 1b-2aα. It may be that the Dathan-Abiram narrative is badly fragmented. But it is also possible that the intervening material was dropped by the redactor who joined the two stories because it was closely parallel to the Korah material which he included. The possibility of a parallel relationship between Korah and Dathan-Abiram in the remaining part of the chapter must be carefully considered.

Vs. 15aβ is not clear. There is no indication that Dathan and Abiram had been instructed to offer a sacrifice, while in vs. 18 the company of Korah prepared an incense offering. The *mem* suffix in vs. 15aβ is undefined and could refer to either Dathan and Abiram or the company of Korah. But since a מנחה is by no means an incense offering,[51] the verse could not be attributed to the Korah narrative. This suggests that vs. 15 should be deemed a part of the Dathan-Abiram story even though no reference to a sacrifice in that tradition precedes this verse. And it also points to a parallel construction of the two narratives.

Vs. 16 returns to the Korah narrative. Since Korah and his company are once again set over against Aaron, this verse must be a continuation of the secondary expansion from vss. 8-11. Vs. 18 narrates the execution of the incense offering. But here both Moses and Aaron are considered the objects of the rebellion and involved in the trial (cf. vs. 17b). This verse is thus the continuation of the principal narrative. Vs.

---

[50] But cf. von Rad, *Priesterschrift*, p. 109.

[51] Hans-Joachim Kraus, *Gottesdienst in Israel: Grundriss einer Geschichte des alttestamentlichen Gottesdienstes* (2nd ed., rev.; München: Chr. Kaiser Verlag, 1962), pp. 137-38, notes that מנחה, even at an early period, is a meal offering.

19 is somewhat redundant over vs. 18 since vs. 18 notes the presence of Korah and his people at the door of the sanctuary, while vs. 19 says the Korah gathered (ויקהל) his people against Moses *and* Aaron.[52] Yet the combination ויקהל עליהם is not so much a renewal of the gathering at the door as an expression of the rebellion against both leaders. This verse would thus be in contrast to the rebellion against Aaron alone in vs. 11 and, along with vs. 18, correspond to the introduction of the principal Korah material in vs. 3.[53] In this regard, we note the characteristic P emphasis on the כבוד יהוה in vs. 19. This part of the tradition runs without break through vs. 22. Vs. 23 is a new address of Yahweh to Moses alone, but it need not mean that we return to the secondary expansion here (cf. vss. 4 ff.). Since vss. 22-24a are in keeping with the context, we can assign them to the principal Korah material as well.

Vs. 24*b* is obscure but probably represents an original continuation of the Korah story from vs. 24a. The difficulty lies in the fact that Dathan and Abiram are included with Korah (cf. 27a).[54] But since this half-verse stands at a break in the literary structure between the Korah story and its Dathan-Abiram counterpart (vs. 25), the reference to all three names can be explained as a combination of the two narratives. This thesis is supported by the fact that in the texts which are clearly independent of the Korah story, the tents of Dathan and Abiram are consistently designated with the word אהל, while משכן is used in this instance.[55] Vs. 25

[52] Cf. the treatment of this problem by Gunneweg, p. 173.

[53] But cf. von Rad, *Priesterschrift*, pp. 109 ff.

[54] Several LXX codices read only Korah.

[55] There is some possibility that משכן here refers to the tent of the sanctuary. This seems to me to be unlikely since previously in this narrative P has referred to the sanctuary as the אהל מועד and the combination משכן-קרח occurs twice. The word משכן in its plural form refers elsewhere to human dwellings (Num. 24:5) ; cf. G. Gray, p. 204. If the narratives are indeed as closely parallel as we have suggested, the משכן would be simply P's means for referring to the same entity which J intends by אהל. In this case we could suppose that P's change was influenced by the משכן יהוה (cf. 16:9; 17:28). But there seems to me to be no evidence to suggest that an original משכן יהוה lies behind this text.

then returns to the Dathan-Abiram story. It is significant that the congregation (העדה) [56] is directed to move away from the tent of Dathan and Abiram since the identical instruction had been given to the congregation (again העדה) in vs. 24bα. This would certainly increase the impression that the two stories are closely parallel. Vs. 27a can be interpreted in the same manner as the combined report that the people moved away from the tents. It is interesting that this combination is dominated by the Korah story (as, indeed, the entire chapter is), for the word for tent is again משכן and the verb, ויעלו, corresponds to the verb in vs. 24 rather than the one in vs. 26. Vs. 27b continues with the Dathan-Abiram story, once again referring to the two without reference to Korah. This narrative continues without break through vs. 31.

Vs. 32 is a doublet of vs. 31b. That we return here to the Korah story is shown by the reference to Korah and his family, without mention of Dathan and Abiram. This division is further confirmed by the two words for ground; as in the two creation stories in Genesis, so here J employs האדמה, while הארץ appears in the P section.[57] This also suggests that Korah suffered a fate which was identical to the punishment of Dathan and Abiram, confirming our impression that the two stories were remarkably parallel (cf. also the similarity between this verse and the condition in vs. 30). Vss. 33-34 could theoretically belong to either of the stories; since the word for ground here is ארץ, we shall include it in the Korah story, recognizing that a parallel account was probably present in the Dathan-Abiram story as well (cf. Deut. 11:6). Vs. 35 concludes the narrative of the Korah rebellion by showing how the 250 men who accompanied Korah were executed; that Korah is not mentioned in connection with his company

---

[56] העדה in this context is somewhat surprising. Cf. Gressmann, p. 251. But even in conjunction with the combination of all three names in both vss. 24 and 27, it cannot be taken as evidence for a P version of the Dathan-Abiram story.

[57] Against Noth, *Numeri*, p. 114, who sees vs. 32b as an addition to the text which anticipates the punishment in vs. 35.

here presupposes that he was punished in a different way—swallowed by the earth.[58]

Chapter 17:1 ff. is clearly dependent on the Korah story in chapter 16, but the reference to 'El'azar, the son of Aaron, instead of Aaron himself, suggests that these verses are a secondary development in the tradition. This suggestion is confirmed by vs. 5; the censers will be used as a covering for the altar as a reminder of the admonition not to be like Korah and his company.

In vss. 6 ff., we have a different level of the P narrative, for the subject shifts back to the generation of Moses and Aaron. That both Moses and Aaron are mentioned together suggests that these verses are at least dependent on the primary account of Korah and his men. But the reference in vs. 14 to the דבר־קרח as a separate event from the one which is narrated here suggests that the unit presupposes rather than continues the primary account. The possibility is open that it is to be attributed to the secondary sections in 16:8-11 and 16-17. We shall return to this problem below. This section runs without break through its natural conclusion in vs. 15.

Vss. 16 ff. clearly presuppose a later development in the controversy over the priesthood which dominates the second level of the Korah story, for here Aaron is considered, not the opponent, but the chief of the Levites (vs. 18). This section continues without break through vs. 26, where it comes to an end with a statement that Moses executed the instructions according to their prescribed form.

Vss. 27-28 are obscure and perhaps corrupt (cf. the dittography in הקרב and perhaps עבדנו). In any case, they do not seem to be connected with vss. 16-26. It is more likely that they reflect the execution of the 250 men in Korah's company

---

[58] It is not legitimate to suppose with Wellhausen, pp. 103 ff. that Korah's company was swallowed with him (vss. 28-34). This event can only be considered the destruction of Korah's immediate family and possessions. Nor is it legitimate to suppose that Korah was included in the destruction reported in vs. 35 since there is no mention of him there and reference to the 250 men does not constitute self-evident proof that Korah is to be included. It thus seems to me to be incorrect that vs. 35 should be considered a different source from vss. 32-34.

since they are afraid to come near the משכן יהוה. But how it might be related to that part of the narrative is not clear.

Chapter 18 continues in the development of the relationship between the Aaronic priesthood and the Levites. And Aaron is once again considered head of the house of Levi. But since there is no reflection of the murmuring tradition here, we can drop this chapter from our consideration. We thus have the following literary structure: J, 16:1b-2aα, 12-15, 24$b\beta$ (after למשכן־קרח) -26, 27aβb-31. All the rest is P.

But the P account is not unified. Distinctions must be drawn between a core of Korah narrative material in 16:1aα, 2aβb-7a, 18-24abα (including למשכן־קרח) 27aα, and 32-35, and a secondary expansion of that material in 16:7b, 8-11, 16-17; 17:1-5; 6-15; 16-26 (27-28). Noth observes:

> In Num. 16–18 scheint mir schon die literarische Grundlage sekundäres Gut innerhalb der P-Erzählung, also P^s, zu sein, das noch unmittelbar vor dem Schlussthema dieser Erzählung, der Mitteilung über den Tod Mirjams, Aarons und Moses, eingeschaltet wurde. Mose und Aaron erscheinen sonst bei P nicht einfach als Leviten, wie es hier der Fall ist. Die Erzählung ist inhaltlich verwandt mit dem Stück Lev. 10:1-7, das gleichfalls P^s ist. Die Anfechtung und dann Bestätigung der am Sinai gegebenen Ordnungen gehörte kaum zu den von der ursprünglichen P-Erzählung behandelten Themen.[59]

We can agree that secondary material appears in this P narrative and that it has some relationship to Lev. 10:1-7.[60] It is also clear that Moses and Aaron appear in part of this material as Levites. But it cannot be satisfactorily maintained that the principal material views Moses and Aaron as Levites, as we shall show below. The problem with priestly orders is explicit in the secondary expansion of the Korah narrative. But it is also implicit in the principal material. We therefore recognize the objections which prevent Noth from assigning any part of the Korah narrative to the original P tradition.[61] But since our

[59] Noth, *Überlieferungsgeschichte*, p. 19, n. 59.
[60] Cf. below, Appendix II.
[61] Cf. also Gunneweg, pp. 171-72.

concern here is not to define the nature of P but to analyze
the traditions in these chapters, we shall not pursue those
objections further; for convenience, we shall label the principal Korah material P without considering its relationship
to the total P source.

Since the oldest tradition in this narrative is the Dathan-
Abiram story in the J source, we shall begin our investigation
here. The first rather fragmentary insight into this tradition
comes in vss. 1b-2aα. Here Dathan and Abiram are introduced
as Reubenites, the sons of Eli'ab (cf. Deut. 11:6). They are
associated in this text with a certain 'On, also a Reubenite,
the son of Peleth. The name Peleth occurs again only in
I Chr. 2:33. But there it does not refer to a son of Reuben.
'On does not occur again in the Old Testament in this form,
but the Codex Alexandrinus reads Αὐναν here. This name does
occur elsewhere, but always as the name of a son of Judah. In
Num. 26:9, obviously a late text which already presupposes
the combination of the two narratives, Dathan and Abiram
are considered the sons of Eli'ab, along with one Nemu'el.
The name Nemu'el does not occur again. Eli'ab is the son of
Pallu', who is then the son of Reuben. Pallu' may well be
related to the Peleth in 16:1 (cf. Gen. 46:9; Exod. 6:14; I Chr.
5:3). But this addition only serves to extend the Reubenite
genealogy by one generation. The name Abiram occurs by
itself only in I Kings 16:34, but there it clearly refers to a
different individual. Otherwise, the names Dathan and Abiram
consistently appear together in the context of the tradition
which is represented in narrative form by this text. Thus the
only details we can discover about the identity of Dathan and
Abiram from the genealogy are that they were brothers from
the tribe of Reuben.

Of more importance for our interest is the fragment of
tradition in vs. 2aα. If our hypothesis is correct that the
Dathan-Abiram story runs closely parallel to the Korah story,
we may assume that this introduction is parallel to and serves
the same function as the P introduction in vs. 3aα: ויקהלו על-
משה ועל-אהרן. This combination has been shown above to be
among the stylized introductions to the murmuring motif.

We must therefore consider the possibility that the expression ויקמו לפני משה serves the same function, even though it does not occur again in this context (but cf. Deut. 19:15, 16; Ps. 27:12). This setting unfortunately does not correspond to the next part of the Dathan-Abiram story in vs. 12a, for vs. 12a presupposes that Dathan and Abiram were not in the immediate presence of Moses. Messengers were sent to summon these men (so, וישלח . . . לקרא), and they respond with a refusal (לא נעלה). To be sure, the reply is addressed directly to Moses (העליתנו), but this would not be out of order for a message in the ancient Near East. It is quite possible, then, that an important part of the tradition has been lost here, a part which would account for the shift from a face-to-face encounter to the private tents of the families.

But does the reply, לא נעלה, necessarily mean that the men will not respond to the summons? [62] It corresponds remarkably to the verb in vs. 13 (העליתנו), and this verb has reference to the Exodus.[63] The choice of words in vs. 13a is the same as we have seen previously in the murmuring tradition, especially if our corrections in the text should stand: "Is it not enough that you have brought us up from the land of Egypt to kill us in the wilderness? . . ." But this half-verse is not in the form of an accusation. The expression המעט כי recognizes simply that the circumstance described in the כי clause obtains, while putting the point of the question on the second half of the verse. And this is the part of the question which challenges what Moses is doing.

The imperfect form of the verb in vs. 13b suggests that the act which has been challenged extends into the present; i.e., it is incomplete. The verb is a second person singular con-

---

[62] The general tendency is to suggest that the verb עלה is a *terminus technicus* for appearing before a judge. Cf. G. Gray, p. 201, *et al.*

[63] The expression זבת חלב ודבש refers to Palestine in every other instance except this; here its juxtaposition with מארץ suggests that the reference is to Egypt. The Codices Vaticanus and Alexandrinus read εἰς γῆν ῥεούσαν. The Lagarde edition of LXX MSS reads ἐξ Αἰγύπτου. Although each of these is likely only an attempt to correct the text, it seems probable that the reference is to Egypt. The phrase זבת חלב ודבש may be a duplicated form of vs. 14, perhaps because of the preceeding מארץ (cf. vs. 14 אל ארץ).

struction, addressed to Moses alone. The verb, שׂרר, is a
denominative from the noun שׂר. The basic meaning of the
verb is dubious, but an Akkadian word *šarâru* suggests "to
rise in splendor" (cf. vs. 3). The noun שׂר clearly denotes
some type of chieftain or official, ranging in character from a
noble under a king (Gen. 12:15) to a military leader (Gen.
21:22), i.e., an official who has power over a group of people.
It is significant in this regard that the term does not refer to
religious authority. To be sure, all authority in Israel was
seen as religious, but this term has a secular overtone.[64] The
Hithpa'el stem of the verb suggests, then, that Moses is being
accused of elevating himself to a higher position of authority
over the people.

Vs. 14 is directly connected to the accusation in vs. 13. But
it is not an extension of that challenge. Rather, it presents
the motivation for the challenge. Moses has not kept his promise; he has not brought the people into the land (הביאתנו).
And here it is clear that the reference is to the conquest of
Palestine (ארץ זבת חלב ודבש). Vs. 14b is somewhat obscure.
Moses is accused of blinding the eyes of a certain group of
people (האנשים ההם is hardly a designation for the whole
people). The reference in Deut. 16:19 to blinding eyes by
taking a bribe suggests that a similar interpretation might be
in order for vs. 14b (cf. I Sam. 12:3). Since there is no indication that the accusation against Moses is to be taken literally,
we conclude that Moses is accused of bribing the people or in
some other manner falsely convincing them to continue under
his power (cf. Deut. 16:19).[65] At least it is clear that the
metaphor is intended to describe some kind of misuse of
power. The defense is apparently made at the sanctuary before
Yahweh, but the parallel in I Sam. 12:3 suggests that it is
also done in the presence of the people. It would be difficult
to see how the accusation itself could be made by messenger;
both the form and the setting demand the presence of the

---

[64] This would exclude the question of the priesthood from consideration in the Dathan-Abiram tradition. Cf. the Korah tradition, esp. vss.
8-11, 16-17.

[65] G. Gray, p. 201; Noth, *Numeri*, p. 111.

accusers in the assembly (thus vs. 2*a*). And in the context of this accusation, the repetition of the retort לא נעלה would seem even more pointedly directed toward a refusal to continue under Moses' leadership.

Still another problem confronts us in this section. In vs. 15*a*β, Moses petitions Yahweh not to accept the offering (מנחה) of these men. The petition implies that Yahweh should show his rejection of Dathan and Abiram by refusing their sacrifice. This could, perhaps, refer to the next time these men offer a sacrifice, but it seems more probable that the reference is to a current problem, i.e., that the men are *now* engaged in offering a sacrifice. This possibility recalls the test by means of sacrifice in the Korah story and suggests that a similar test is involved in the Dathan-Abiram tradition as a means for resolving the rebellion. And the setting for the test would certainly be the sanctuary (cf. vs. 16).

On the other hand, vs. 25, the next point at which the Dathan-Abiram story appears, clearly shows that these men are at their own tents. It is possible that some material has fallen away from the tradition between vss. 15 and 25 which would have related the shift in setting.[66] If, however, our hypothesis is correct that the material which is missing in the Dathan-Abiram story has been dropped because it is closely parallel to the Korah story, then we might refer to that narrative to reconstruct the lacuna. But there the same problem occurs. In vs. 19, the people are gathered at the אהל מועד for the test. Then in the context of an intercession, the scene suddenly shifts to the משכן־קרח (vs. 24). Moreover, the narration of the event at the tents is formulated to show that a new demonstration of Moses' authority beyond the test by sacrifice is to be given. The demonstration is made before the whole congregation. (They have followed Moses to observe the demonstration at the tents of Dathan and Abiram. They are perhaps represented by the elders [vs. 25*b*], but the address in vs. 26 is to the whole congregation. This construction pre-

---

[66] If vss. 12*b*-15 do in fact presuppose a setting at the sanctuary instead of the tents of the rebels, vs. 12*a* could be considered a secondary transition to smooth the tension caused by the shift.

supposes the incongruous picture of the whole people of
Israel gathered around the tents of Dathan and Abiram. But
the background of this picture may still be the assembly of the
people at the sanctuary. This incongruity would perhaps
point to the shift in setting as a secondary element.) Vs. 28
is again in the form of an *Erweiswort*. That which is to be
proven by the event is shown by the כי and the perfect form
of the verb which follows. And this corresponds directly to the
content of the accusation: כי־יהוה שלחני. The event which is
to serve as proof for this affirmation is reduced here to בזאת,
but it is clear that the demonstrative pronoun refers to vss.
29-30. Here the event is described in terms of alternatives,
again showing the character of the event as a test. Vs. 29 is
the negative alternative; if the circumstances described here
occur, they will prove the rebels to be correct: לא יהוה שלחני.
Vs. 30 is the positive alternative, that which will establish
Moses' authority. Vs. 31 then reports the outcome of the
demonstration.

The event which formally serves to establish Moses' authority vis-à-vis the rebels is at the same time the appropriate
punishment for the rebellion; i.e., the element of punishment
is not an independent element in the formal structure (cf. also
the trial by sacrifice in vs. 35). It may be that the formal structure of the *Erweiswort* is a late intrusion into the text and
that the event originally played only the role of punishment,
the resolution of the rebellion having been settled with the
sacrifice. But since the trial by sacrifice is also intended to
resolve the controversy by removing the opposition (vs. 35),
the two events would seem to serve a parallel function.

How, then, are we to explain this twofold nature of the
tradition? Gressmann suggests that reference to the earth
opening its mouth may be the basis of a local aetiology, an
attempt to explain a fault in the earth which is no longer
mentioned in the text. This local tradition, perhaps containing
some reference to the Reubenites, would have been secondarily combined with the tradition about the rebellion
against Moses.[67] Since the Dathan-Abiram tradition in all

[67] Gressmann, p. 255.

probability already contained a resolution of the rebellion
through the test by sacrifice, we would have an explanation
in this hypothesis for the sudden shift in setting. Indeed, the
shift to the tents seems to be for no other purpose than including the notation that all the possessions and family of the
rebels were consumed in the fault. Vss. 12a and 25 would then
be secondary connective links between the two traditions. This
is possible. But unfortunately, positive evidence for it is
lacking.

The Korah narrative begins in vs. 1 with a Levitical genealogy. But because of the peculiar character of the content in
the primary Korah material (vss. 1a, 2aβ-7), this genealogy
has been challenged as a secondary item.[68] Korah appears
here as the chief of a group of 250 leaders of the congregation.
But these leaders are not Levites. The specification of their
qualifications in vs. 2aβb is remarkable in its detail, but there
is no reference to a connection between these men and the
Levites. Indeed, one has the distinct impression that they
are laity (cf. vs. 3a).[69] We should apparently conclude, then,
that Korah, as their chief, must also be a lay leader rather
than a Levite.

Moreover, it has been argued that the laity raise an issue
against Moses and Aaron who, at this point in the narrative,
are themselves the representatives of the Levites.[70] This argument is built on two points. First, vs. 7b is, according to the
context, an address to Korah and his men (vs. 5). But according to the hypothesis, this cannot be a part of the primary
material as it now stands since both Korah and his men are
addressed as Levites (רב־לכם בני לוי). The question of Korah's
Levitical connections is still open, at least in the development
of our argument; but it seems certain that the company of
250 men must be held as lay figures in the primary Korah
narrative in vss. 3-7a. Since, however, the address of these men
to Moses and Aaron in vs. 3aβ begins with the expression
רב־לכם, it may be that vs. 7b provides the complete form of

[68] G. Gray, p. 193; Gressmann, pp. 260-61; cf. Gunneweg, p. 175.
[69] Wellhausen, p. 104, et al.
[70] G. Gray, p. 197.

that vocative introduction. This would mean that Moses and Aaron are addressed as Levites. One could cite in support of this thesis the observation that vs. 7b seems to be grossly out of place.[71] The instructions for determining the resolution of the rebellion are completed in vs. 7a, while vs. 7b appears to be an introduction to a new unit. But there is no other evidence in the entire scope of the primary material to support this. Not even the complaint which this group raises against Moses and Aaron presupposes that they are representatives of the Levites, as we shall show below. In fact, at no point in any of the Korah material is Moses seen as a Levite. The only evidence for the thesis is the identification of vs. 7b with the exclamation in vs. 3. But that this half-verse seems to be out of place does not constitute a priori evidence that it is to be equated with רב לכם in vs. 3 in contradiction to the context there. On the other hand, the secondary material in vss. 8-11 and 16-17 clearly holds both Korah and his men as Levites. This is in fact stated in the plural address in vs. 8b: שמעו־נא בני לוי. It seems more likely, then, that vs. 7b is dependent on vss. 8-11 for its identification of Korah and his men as Levites. Thus we could argue that instead of a more complete form of the introduction in vs. 3a, this statement represents an introduction to the address to Korah and his men in vs. 8. And it would be in complete accord with the context.

The second point is that the complaint of the laity is directed toward the problem of the priesthood; i.e., do Moses and Aaron, as representatives of the Levites, have the right to exclude the people from the prerogatives of the priesthood? [72] The issue here is not so much the identification of Moses and Aaron with the Levites as the nature of the complaint which Korah and company pose. The narrative of the conflict begins in vs. 3a with a typical introduction to the rebellion. Vs. 3b presents the accusation in the usual form of a question introduced by the interrogative particle מדוע. The

---

[71] S. Lehming, "Versuch zu Num. 16," ZAW LXXIV (1962), 315. Cf. also Wellhausen, p. 104; Baentsch, p. 545; G. Gray, p. 191.

[72] Gressmann, p. 261.

verb, as in vs. 13, is an imperfect Hithpaʻel in the second person, in this case, plural in number: תתנשׂאו. The reason for the difference in number is obviously the inclusion of Aaron as a part of the object of the murmuring: Moses and Aaron are accused of exalting themselves over the congregation. This accusation is surprisingly identical to the one in the Dathan-Abiram tradition; even though a different verb is employed, it is clear that the problem at hand lies in a current extension of power which Moses and Aaron exercise over the people. Further circumstances of the extension are not included, but since the form and content of the accusation are so similar to the Dathan-Abiram accusation, we may safely assume that the problem has to do with the continuation of Moses' and Aaron's leadership.[73]

The *reason* for the accusation is in vs. 3a: "Because all the congregation are holy, and Yahweh is in their midst. . . ." The complaint has a religious overtone in contrast to the civil character of the Dathan-Abiram tradition; in effect, the rights of Moses and Aaron as intermediaries between the people and Yahweh have been challenged (cf. the term הקריב). But does the religious overtone imply that the people are demanding the right of the priesthood, especially since it does not appear in the accusation?[74] This conclusion might be deduced from vs. 5. The reference to Yahweh's choice (יבחר) and his bringing the chosen one near (יקריב) would imply that if the people were chosen, they would adopt the priestly function of standing before Yahweh.[75] But it is clear even at this point that the chosen ones will be Moses and Aaron. What basis do we have, then, for speaking of a priesthood of the people? There is no indication that the people are asking Moses and Aaron to disband an organized priesthood in their favor. In-

[73] It is important to note that for the gap in the Dathan-Abiram tradition between vss. 1b-2aα and vss. 12 ff., the Korah story provides no new material. This fact would tend to support the thesis that vss. 12 ff. are not set in the locality of the private tents of Dathan and Abiram.

[74] So, Gressmann, p. 259, *et al.*

[75] Gunneweg, pp. 176-77, maintains that this verse cannot be original, at least in this form. He correctly points out that the problem here is not about the priesthood but about the holiness of the people.

deed, there is no evidence that the issue concerns the priesthood at all. Instead, the holiness of the people is nothing
more than P's peculiar means for expressing the complaint of
the people against Moses and Aaron, the foundation for the
challenge against Moses' and Aaron's extension of authority.[76]
But if there is no demand on the part of the people for the
rights of the priesthood, there would certainly be no evidence
here to suggest that Moses and Aaron are considered Levites.[77]

Vs. 4 represents the response to the murmuring. But it is a
response given only by Moses. The reason for Aaron's absence
seems most probably to lie in the use of ancient material
here, material very similar to the Dathan-Abiram tradition
where only Moses comes into play. The addition of Aaron in
vs. 3 and vss. 18 ff. would be the characteristic tendency of
P. Vs. 5 announces that Yahweh will resolve the question,
while vs. 6 sets the character of the test. Both Korah and his
company are to bring fire pans to the sanctuary (לפני יהוה),
and Yahweh will choose which one shall be holy. The description of the test presupposes an ordeal by sacrifice (cf.
I Kings 18:20 ff.).

Vs. 19 involves a repetition of the rebellion at the moment
of the test. העדה in the first half of this verse (cf. LXX) and in
vs. 21 must be considered the company of Korah rather than
the whole congregation, since Yahweh expresses an intention
to punish the group and only Korah's company was involved
in the rebellion.[78] But the intention to punish the rebels also
shows that punishment is not an independent element in the
formal structure, for the event which punishes the rebels is
formally the response to the test, i.e., the event which shows
that Moses and Aaron have been chosen. The intercession in
vs. 22 also suggests that the עדה refers to Korah's followers

[76] It seems likely that this reference to the holiness reflects the point
of view of the Holiness Code (cf. esp. Lev. 19:1 ff.). But cf. von Rad,
Priesterschrift, pp. 109-10.

[77] This would also undercut one of the arguments against viewing
Korah as a Levite; viz., as the chief protagonist for the claim of the
populace to the priesthood, he would be in opposition to the interests
of the Levites. Cf. G. Gray, p. 192.

[78] Against G. Gray, p. 203; Gressmann, p. 260.

since the intercession is on behalf of this group rather than the sin of *one* man. As a result, the company is allowed to move back and *only* Korah and his family face destruction.

Yet a trial of this sort probably presupposes the presence of the whole congregation as witnesses (cf. vs. 15). The reference to כל־העדה in vs. 19*b* is not clear, but it may well designate the entire congregation. And in the light of vs. 26, it is quite possible that the result of the intercession is the invitation of Moses to the whole people to move away from the family of Korah. This would be supported by the fact that even though the congregation is spared the destruction suffered by Korah and his family, the company of followers who are associated with Korah are destroyed at the place of the test (vs. 35). The confusion is indicative of the problem noted in the Dathan-Abiram tradition concerning the shift in setting, for the isolation of the one man and his family is associated not with the trial by sacrifice but with the ground opening its mouth. This is confirmed in vs. 24 by the address to the people: "Move away from the *tent* of Korah."

This problem has led several scholars to suggest the restoration of vs. 24*b* to read למשכן יהוה.[79] This reconstruction would have the advantage of maintaining the proper setting (cf. vs. 27*a*; 17:28). But even if the lack of textual support were overruled, the net results of the restoration would only postpone the difficulty, for vss. 32-34, certainly a part of the P narrative of Korah, presuppose the same shift in setting to the tent. The event which occurs there is identical to the punishment of Dathan-Abiram: The earth opens its mouth and swallows the family and all its possessions. Vs. 34 is something of a problem since it reports that the people had not left the vicinity of the tents. The command to move away is probably to be interpreted in terms of moving back enough to be out of immediate contact with the possessions of the condemned (so, vs. 26). Vs. 35 then returns to the motif of the test at the sanctuary. The 250 men are destroyed by fire. This is the punishment we had expected for Korah as well,

---

[79] Baentsch, p. 548; G. Gray, p. 204; Gressmann, p. 252, n. 3.

but he is noticeably missing. Thus we have the same duality that was seen in the Dathan-Abiram story and the same lack of evidence for determining its nature.

But we can go a step further in determining the character of the duality in P. The intercession in vs. 22 is a peculiarity in P which softens the abrupt shift in setting. Two observations support this interpretation: (1) The expression ויפלו על־פניהם is not ordinarily associated with intercession for the people but with deference on the part of Moses and Aaron in favor of Yahweh's response to the rebellion (cf. Num. 14:5; 16:4; 20:6; but also 17:10). (2) The intercession itself involves the designation of Yahweh as אל אלהי הרוחת לכל־בשר (cf. Num. 27:16), an epithet which reflects a late and rather advanced theological point of view. It would thus not be a part of the ancient tradition which seems to form the background of the Korah narrative. And significantly, it is not in the Dathan-Abiram material.

It seems clear that the tradition described above is the oldest form of the tradition present in P. But what is the relationship between this form of the Korah tradition and the Dathan-Abiram narrative? Do two closely parallel but independent traditions stand behind these stories? We shall approach this question by comparing the outline of the two:

1. Dathan and Abiram rebel against the authority of Moses.
2. The problem lies in an extension of Moses' civil power over the people.
3. The resolution of the rebellion has its setting in a test by sacrifice.
4. The scene shifts to the tents of these men.
5. The people are advised to move away.
6. The conditions of the test are set.
7. The earth swallows the rebels.

1. Korah and his company rebel against Moses and Aaron.
2. The problem lies in an extension of their religious authority (cf. the use of הקריב).
3. The resolution of the rebellion has its setting in a test by sacrifice.
4. The conditions of the test are set.

5. The scene shifts to the tents of Korah.
6. The people are advised to move away.
7. The earth swallows the rebel.
8. Fire destroys the company.

The outlines can hardly be independent, and the fact that the two stories do not overlap in the two sources can only add to this impression. With two exceptions, the only differences can be explained as P's peculiar interests. We may conclude, therefore, that the two narrative threads in this chapter are interdependent; i.e., a single common tradition lies behind both accounts.

But what is the significance of the two exceptions? The first is the obvious fact that the subject of the P narrative is not Dathan and Abiram but Korah. If the two narratives reflect a common tradition, how did Korah happen to replace Dathan and Abiram? At this point, we must return to the question of the Levitical genealogy of Korah. Even though it seems certain that in the primary Korah material the central figure is not a Levite, the fact remains that Korah is the eponym for an important Levitical family.[80] Moreover, the genealogy in Exod. 6:14 ff. follows the same line of generations which we see in Num. 16:1. It is clear that this text is a secondary development in the Exodus traditions.[81] But it does not follow that the genealogical configuration for Korah which makes him a Levite has been imposed on the name (cf. Num. 3:15 ff.).

Is it possible to conclude, then, that the Korah in Num. 16:1 is a completely different figure from the Korah who is the eponym of the Levitical Korahites, a lay figure who leads his 250 men against Moses and Aaron?[82] A study of the name, Korah, both in Levitical genealogies and outside them, reveals

[80] Gunneweg, pp. 180 ff., suggests that Korah is perhaps to be understood as a member of the Kahath priestly group (cf. Num. 4:4 ff.). The relationship of this group with the Levites is questionable (cf. Num. 4:2). But the fact remains that in Num. 16:1 and the remaining genealogies, as well as in the development of our unit, Korah is clearly considered a Levite.

[81] Noth, *Exodus*, p. 58.

[82] Gressmann, p. 261.

no conclusive evidence to support this hypothesis.[83] We suggest, then, that the Levitical Korah in this tradition has
replaced the name or names of the lay leaders of the rebellion
in the older tradition (Dathan and Abiram?). Gressmann
makes the same suggestion: "Man muss freilich auch mit der
Möglichkeit rechnen, dass der Held der Sage ursprünglich
anders hiess und erst später Korah getauft wurde, um die
Leviten zu ärgern." [84]
The reason which could be posited for this insertion would
lie not simply in the attempt to irritate the Levites but in
the right of the priesthood itself, an issue which appears
forcefully in the second level of the tradition. Korah and
his men, at this point obviously considered Levites, are set
over against the Aaronic priesthood. They have the right to
serve the congregation in the sanctuary (Temple singers and
door-keepers?), but they do not have the full rights of the
priesthood, the rights reserved only for Aaron. But the text
presupposes that the Levites have laid claim to these rights.[85]
And their claim is interpreted as rebellion against Aaron, a
challenge to his sole right to the priesthood. The verb לון is
used to describe this act of rebellion. The response to the
rebellion in vss. 16-17 is a duplicate form of the response in
the primary body of tradition, the only difference being that
Aaron alone is set against the crowd of Levitical rebels. P
would thus have adopted the tradition of rebellion against
Moses to interpret the position of the Korahites.[86]

[83] G. Gray, pp. 193 ff., suggests that the Levitical genealogy of Korah
replaced an earlier Judahite genealogy, reflected in the reference to a
Korah, the son of a Judahite named Hebron in Exod. 6:18 and I Chr.
2:43. But this hypothesis is weakened by the fact that the Hebron in I
Chr. 2:43 has a different lineage from the Hebron in Exod. 6:18. Gunneweg, p. 174, concludes on the basis of his study of Levitical genealogies
and the name Korah that "trotz dieser Vielfalt der Überlieferungen liegt
kein Grund vor, anzunehmen, Korach sei erst später zum Leviten gewor-
den," and that "diese Buntheit der Überlieferung darf also nicht dazu
verführen, zwischen Korach und Korach unterscheiden zu wollen."

[84] Gressmann, p. 261; cf. also Gunneweg, p. 177.

[85] Cf. Gunneweg, p. 177. He points to the use of הקריב in vs. 17, rather
than vs. 5, as the principal reference to the priesthood.

[86] For a full discussion of the conflict presupposed in this struggle over
priestly rights, cf. Gunneweg, pp. 179 ff.

The second point of difference is the company of 250 men who were also involved in the rebellion and eventually executed by fire as the result of the ordeal. There is no way to associate these men with the Levitical leaders. To be sure, Korah is consistently associated with a company of followers (cf. Num. 27:3). And in vs. 17, it is clear that this company numbers 250. But we cannot avoid the impression that the men who are numbered in vs. 2aβb are not Levites. We may therefore hypothesize that the lay leaders are part of the primary tradition, men who supported the initial rebellion against the (civil?) authority of Moses. If this were the case, we would have an explanation for the duality in the tradition, for the test with the sacrifice is especially connected with the 250 men (cf. vs. 35). This conclusion would support the thesis that the tradition about the rebellion against the authority of Moses has come together with an independent tradition concerning a catastrophic death of a family among the people (and a fault in the earth?).

But if this hypothesis is correct, it would mean that Dathan and Abiram would also be associated with a company of followers. In vs. 15aβ, we may assume that the antecedent of the *mem* suffix is Dathan and Abiram. Yet it is clear from vs. 14 that these two are not speaking just for themselves but for a group of people who, they feel, have been deceived by Moses. This group is significantly designated as האנשים ההם. The only other occurrence of האנשים in the Dathan-Abiram narrative is in vs. 2aβb (cf. Deut. 11:6; Ps. 106:16-17, esp. עדת אבירם in vs. 17 [87]). But this hypothesis must also remain tentative. Since the traditions in this chapter are fragmented, a firm

---

[87] Lauha, p. 88, argues that this psalm reflects a form of the tradition which has already undergone the combination of Korah with Dathan-Abiram. But this would not explain the presence of the plural suffix in vs. 18 or the connection between the group in question and Abiram in vs. 17. To be sure, both forms of punishment are mentioned. But we have argued that both forms were already present in the Dathan-Abiram tradition. It would seem more likely, then, that the psalm reflects precisely what it says, i.e., the Dathan-Abiram tradition without reference to Korah. And in this sense it would provide valuable support for our understanding of the Dathan-Abiram narrative in Num. 16.

resolution of the problem and thus a clear and complete understanding of the nature of the tradition are in all probability
not to be obtained.

We shall now consider the role of the murmuring motif.
From our previous analysis, it is clear that the murmuring
in this narrative is not a part of the rebellion tradition which
we have observed in other units of the Pentateuch. First, we
do not have a rebellion of all the people against their leaders,
but only a few individuals or at best a small group of men.
It is always possible that Dathan and Abiram represent a
rival faction among the people. If this were the case, the
most likely "faction" would be the tribe of Reuben itself.
Since the Reubenites disappeared as a major section of the
Israelites early in the history of the conquest, we might assume that the Dathan-Abiram tradition reflects something of
their downfall. In this sense, the basic material here may be
considered a family or a tribal saga, a report of opposition
raised by a powerful family or tribe against the authority of
Moses and the subsequent defeat of that opposition. It would
be significant in this regard that the tribe of Reuben is tra-
ditionally listed first among the tribes (Gen. 49:3; Deut. 33:6),
i.e., in the place of preeminence.[88] The date of the tradition
would of necessity be early since the Reubenites passed from
the scene, with the exception of a few minor remnants scattered among the Judahites, before the completion of the
conquest. That its downfall dated as early as the wilderness
period is unlikely since there is evidence of Reubenite settlement west of the Jordan.[89] But the process leading to its
downfall could have begun in that period. There is not
enough information for us to make a judgment about the
history of the Reubenites or the connection between Dathan
and Abiram and the disappearance of their tribe. But neither
is there evidence which would associate these men or the
people who supported them with any other group. They
certainly do not represent priestly factions. And it would

[88] Noth, *History*, p. 86.
[89] *Ibid.*, pp. 63 ff.

only needlessly complicate the tradition to posit a relationship with some other unknown group without evidence to support it. Thus the only impression which we can gain from this material is that two particular families and their followers rebelled against Moses. But, we must add, this tradition seems to have a very ancient kernel.

Second, the complaint has nothing to do with the issue of the Exodus but with a problem of Moses' authority over the people. The results of the murmuring produce a decisive demonstration of Yahweh's authority in the person of Moses which at the same time effects the punishment of the rebels. Thus all the formal elements of the murmuring motif are present. But the content is quite different from the stereotyped material we have called the rebellion tradition.

Third, there is no evidence to suggest that this example of murmuring has been secondarily imposed over a form of the tradition which was originally quite positive; in fact, there is no evidence that the murmuring is secondary in this tradition at all. It is primarily the sum and substance of the whole tradition, and any secondary elements in the tradition are dependent on and develop from it. Indeed, we can see no reason to deny the possibility that some kernel of historical event, some reflection of rebellion against the authority of Moses, lies behind the tradition. Gressmann concludes: "Als geschichtliche Tatsache lässt sich demnach mit Sicherheit nur der Untergang Dathans und Abirams betrachten." [90] But if we go this far, we must certainly presume that the *reason* for their downfall lay in their rebellion against the authority of the leaders.

Yet the rebellion tradition defined above and this unit cannot be considered unrelated. The formal structure is the same; the general choice of words is the same; even the character of the content has much in common. How, then, may we define the relationship? It seems probable to me that this body of tradition forms the traditio-historical point of departure for the development and spread of the stereo-

[90] Gressmann, p. 255.

typed murmuring tradition. It would not account for the origin of the peculiar *content* of that tradition. But it does give us a point from which the *formal* structure could arise and spread with its special content to the other narratives. Moreover, the similarity of vs. 13a with this special content suggests that it would take only the interpretative emphasis of the motivating factor or factors which supported the spread of the murmuring motif to transform what we have in this narrative into the fixed, well-developed form of the rebellion tradition.

Noth, on the other hand, doubts that this narrative could be the traditio-historical origin for the murmuring tradition. "Vielmehr haben wir es hier mit einer Verselbständigung und speziellen Anwendung jenes überlieferungsgeschichtlich schon späten Erzählungsmotivs zu tun." [91] His reasons for this are at least threefold:

1) *The complaint against Moses (and Aaron) represents reflections about the required qualifications for leadership.* The implication of this conclusion must be that the reflection is too sophisticated to have been a part of ancient tradition which might have arisen from an actual moment of rebellion. This assertion would obtain for the Korah form of the tradition. But the Dathan-Abiram level does not reflect that kind of sophistication. The rebels complain about Moses' power; indeed, the complaint is apparently directed against an extension of that power. This does not require reflection about the qualifications a leader should have. It only presupposes the moment in which the rebels feel that Moses' actions are unjust.

2) *The tradition reveals a kernel of late historical rivalries and other events which have been projected back into the classical period of Israel's history.* Late material reflecting historical rivalries does occur in this narrative, as we have

[91] Noth, *Überlieferungsgeschichte*, p. 138. Noth orients his objections primarily toward the Korah narrative. But since we see the Korah narrative as a specialized adaptation of the Dathan-Abiram tradition, we must consider the possibility of relevance in his objections for the older tradition.

seen in the conflict between the Levites and the Aaronites. But the primary level of the tradition does not reveal any evidence of such late concerns. The only possibility for identifying a historical rivalry in the primary tradition would be the downfall of the Reubenite influence. But this is demonstrably not late.

3) *This unit is a later growth in the wilderness traditions which is dependent on the murmuring tradition.*[92] It is true that the formal structure of the two is the same. But we have demonstrated above that the nature of the Dathan-Abiram tradition precludes any thesis of direct dependence on the murmuring tradition. And since, as we have suggested, the Korah narrative develops from the Dathan-Abiram tradition, it would also reflect no dependency on the murmuring tradition. Quite the contrary, it seems much more likely that the murmuring tradition depends on the Dathan-Abiram material for its formal structure and the threat of death in the wilderness.

We shall digress briefly from our study of this unit in order to raise a further question concerning the nature of the murmuring tradition. We have suggested that the murmuring takes its point of departure from the Dathan-Abiram tradition and spreads thence into other portions of the Pentateuch. Moreover, we have seen that it is commonly superimposed on the tradition of Yahweh's aid in the wilderness. But what is the nature of this contact? It is clear that the murmuring does not represent an independent tradition which has simply been inserted into this context by a subsequent redactor, for it consistently uses the motif of aid as a setting and occasion for its development. In fact, it seems to show conscious effort to reinterpret the positive traditions in terms of its own interest. But was this process accomplished after the tradition of Yahweh's aid had already been given a fixed literary form? Since the motif appears in J, we may presume that its presence in P is not due to a later literary redaction but to the form of the tradition which P employed. Thus

[92] Lehming, "Num. 16," pp. 300 ff., also develops this argument.

the question can be resolved only by a study of the phenomena in J.[93]

We have noticed two instances where the shift from the motif of aid to the murmuring is especially sharp (Exod. 14:11-12; 17:3). But we have concluded that this shift is not to be attributed to a different source. It lies instead, we have argued, in the nature of the tradition which is represented in J. But is this tension to be attributed to the stage of the tradition which lay behind J, i.e., to the source, be it oral or written, which J employed? Or is it the result of a change in the nature of the tradition which occurred after the Yahwist had already given literary form to the tradition of Yahweh's aid?[94] There is no reason to doubt that the Yahwist could have inherited this problem from his source without resolving the tension in it.[95] But there is no clear evidence that this was the case. We shall return to these questions shortly, recognizing at the same time that they probably cannot be answered with certainty.

The unit in chapter 17:6-15 is introduced with the stereotyped rebellion formula using a Niph'al *waw* consecutive imperfect form of the verb לון. The subject is כל־עדת בני־ישראל; the objects are Moses and Aaron. The accusation is introduced not with an interrogative particle but with a personal pronoun before a 2. m. pl. perfect form of the verb. And the verb clearly describes the event which is challenged: "*You* have killed the people of Yahweh" (cf. Josh. 9:19).

[93] None of the texts considered thus far can be attributed with certainty to E. It would be impossible, therefore, to suggest that the murmuring was already present in a common tradition which might have been used by both principal sources. Cf. Noth, *Überlieferungsgeschichte,* pp. 40 ff., especially his definition of the hypothetical source G.

[94] Artur Weiser, *The Old Testament: Its Formation and Development,* tr. Dorothea M. Barton (New York: Association Press, 1961), p. 108, qualifies his date for the origin of the Yahwist's work by the following observation: "Yet at the same time we must not lose sight of the fact that the Yahwist tradition . . . was subject to developments later on also, and that the history of the Yahwist strand was by no means ended when it came into being in the tenth century."

[95] We might expect that if the Yahwist himself had created the murmuring tradition, he would have resolved the tension between it and its context.

This unit, however, does not presuppose the murmuring tradition which appears so widely in the wilderness theme. It may be considered instead a continuation of P's account of the rebellion of the Korahites.[96] The response to the rebellion is typical of the P narrative: The כבוד יהוה appears and threatens to destroy the whole people (vs. 10*a*). In response Moses and Aaron fall on their faces. But it is not strictly an intercession that follows. Instead, Aaron is instructed by Moses to take a censer with fire and incense (cf. 16:17-18) into the midst of the congregation in order to stay the plague which has already begun. As a result, the sentence which had condemned the whole people is reduced, allowing a portion of Israel to live. Since vs. 14 seems to set the toll of the plague in this case in contrast to the Korah incident (דבר־קרח), we cannot consider this unit simply a part of the primary tradition. But it does seem to presuppose the conflict between the Levites and the Aaronic priesthood in 16:8-11, 16-17. Aaron is an honored figure, while the people who supported the Levitical rebellion are considered rebels.

Vss. 16-26, on the other hand, presuppose the account of the murmuring of the people as well as the problem over the priesthood. A test with green staffs is designated as the proper means for determining the one whom Yahweh has chosen for the priesthood. This test is designed to put a stop to the murmuring (vss. 20*b*, 25*b*). But contrary to the P adaptation of the tradition which sets Aaron against the Levites, here he is considered their head. Yet despite this amalgamation of the priestly groups, the murmuring motif still presupposes the rebellion over the right of the priesthood. That all the tribes were to present staffs for the test suggests that each one was to be considered a possible candidate. But this does not mean that all the tribes were debating over the right of the priesthood (cf. 16:3*a*). The issue is the choice of *one* tribe to have the right for the whole community. And this question presupposes the problem of Leviti-

---

[96] Gunneweg, pp. 182-83.

cal rights. Thus the adaptation of the rebellion tradition
in this unit reflects the late expansion of the Levitical groups
and perhaps an ascendency of the Levites in the post-exilic
community.

Vss. 1-5 represent still another secondary growth in the tradition of the Korahites.[97] That they are considered rebels
here is shown by the reference to the 250 men as sinners
who paid for their sins with their lives. 'Ele'azar, the son of
Aaron, is instructed to gather the bronze fire pans used by
the 250 men in order to convert them into a covering for the
altar. The bronze overlay was then intended to remind the
community of the rights of the Aaronic priesthood, again
presupposing the conflict with the Levites. The connection
between this section and 16:8-11, 16-17, and 17:6-15 is unclear. Since 'Ele'azar is the acting figure here instead of
Aaron and the bronze altar plays a major role, we may assume that the conflict and the pointed reference to the altar
are later than the other texts. On the other hand, the use
of the censer in 17:6-15 as a division between the dead and
the living may also reflect the connection between the censer
and the bronze altar.

In summary, the J narrative concerning Dathan and Abiram
represents the oldest form of the tradition in this chapter.
It involves the rebellion of two men on behalf of and supported by a larger group. These men may perhaps represent
the whole tribe of Reuben; otherwise, there is no indication
about who they were or whether they represented special
groups. Their rebellion concerns an extension of Moses'
power over the people, possibly for the purpose of continuing
the move toward Canaan. In order to resolve the question,
a test by sacrifice is set. But the scene shifts suddenly to the
vicinity of the tents, and the resolution of the rebellion is
effected by a fault in the earth. The shift is perhaps to be
explained by a combination of the principal tradition with
a body of local tradition about an unknown fault. The
Dathan-Abiram tradition is not dependent on the murmur-

[97] *Ibid.,* p. 182.

ing tradition. But it is not unrelated. Since the rebellion is primarily the subject of the narrative, perhaps even reflecting some kernel of historical remembrance, it may be considered the traditio-historical point of departure for the development of the murmuring tradition.

The primary form of the P material is identical to that which appears in J, reflecting only those changes which were necessary to meet the special interests of P. The chief of these is the insertion of the Levite Korah as the central figure in the rebellion. This adaptation of the old material is based on a conflict over the rights of the priesthood.

Excursus: Exodus 32:1–33:6

Exod. 32:1–33:6 demands brief attention in order to complete our exegesis of the narratives which are relevant for an examination of the murmuring tradition. It may be that behind the present form of Exod. 32:1–33:6 lies a positive account of the Golden Calf and that such a tradition should be attributed to E. If this is the case, and if it should be discernible in this narrative, then it would in all probability appear in vss. 1-6.[98] But the nature of this unit is questionable. Noth has argued that Aaron is not an original part of the unit, and that the original subject was only the people.[99] To support this position, we note that vs. 4b has a plural verb denoting the pronouncement concerning the nature of the calf, and that Aaron's act in vs. 5 presupposes that he knew nothing of the calf's creation. Moreover, vs. 8 and Deut. 9:12 hold the people responsible for the act. Since Aaron is responsible for the creation of the calf at other points in this section (cf. vss. 1-4a), we must conclude that he appears at two different levels in the tradition: (1) as "one who tolerated the *fait accompli* of the people," and (2) as one who was directly responsible for the act.[100]

This tradition may reflect an understanding of the Golden

---

[98] Walter Beyerlin, *Herkunft und Geschichte der ältesten Sinaitraditionen* (Tübingen: J. C. B. Mohr [Paul Siebeck], 1961), pp. 144 ff.

[99] Noth, *Exodus*, pp. 243 ff.

[100] *Ibid.*, pp. 244-45.

Calf (the noun in vs. 4a is singular) as a pedestal "for the
God who is imagined to be standing invisibly upon [it]." [101]
Vs. 4b nevertheless names the calf the gods (a plural noun
with a plural verb) of Israel. This is probably dependent on
the account of Jeroboam's cultic maneuver in establishing
golden calves at Dan and Bethel in order to prevent his
people from going to Jerusalem for religious activities (I
Kings 12).[102] Indeed, the identical phrase appears in both
Exod. 32:4b, 8b, and I Kings 12:28b: אשר ישראל אלהיך [אלה]
העלוך מארץ מצרים. The plural may refer to the fact that
there were two calves, one in Dan and one in Bethel. But
this possibility would not reduce the fact that in both texts
the pronouncement names the calves the *gods* of Israel. Since
Israel otherwise never confesses a plurality in the God who
brought her out of Egypt, we must assume that the form of
the tradition about the calves of Israel has been consciously
altered and now carries a polemic against the cult represented
by them. And the polemic in Exod. 32:4b is, according to
Noth's reconstruction, a part of the original form of the
tradition in this chapter.

Moreover, it is significant for the purposes of our study of
the murmuring tradition to note that the calves are not
labeled the gods who made a covenant with Israel at Sinai,
but the gods who brought Israel out of Egypt. This ties
the worship of the God of the Exodus to the calves at Dan
and Bethel. It would not mean that he was worshiped only
at these cultic centers. But the thrust of Jeroboam's action was
to say that, in contrast to Jerusalem, the God of the Exodus
could be worshiped at these sites.[103]

It has been argued that since these calves were erected
by Jeroboam, this tradition would not be old enough to be
a part of J.[104] But it is possible that Jeroboam's cultic prac-

[101] *Ibid.*, p. 247.

[102] Beyerlin, pp. 144-45, notes the various points of identity between
the two passages; this similarity leaves little doubt that the same cultic
festival, if not the same event, lies behind both texts. Cf. Noth, *Exodus*,
p. 246.

[103] Galling, p. 9.

[104] Noth, *Exodus*, p. 246.

tice does not represent an innovation but a restitution of an older cultic order.[105] We might then suppose that the polemic against the calves is older than Jeroboam; indeed, if his act is a restitution, we could assume that some form of polemic had earlier contributed to the calves' disappearance. In this case, there would be nothing against our assigning this material to J and suggesting that the association of the God of the Exodus with these cultic centers was at least older than Jeroboam.

Vss. 9-14 are generally recognized as deuteronomistic in style and secondary in this context. But what is the relationship between this material and vss. 7-8? Vss. 7-8 apparently form the natural continuation of the polemic against the calf from vss. 1-6. Deut. 1:12 is parallel to vss. 7-8 and followed by a section which is parallel to vss. 9-14. There is some evidence of a break in both texts, for the introduction to the address in both cases is repeated. But Deut. 1:12 ff. shows that at least at this point the two elements were already joined.

Vss. 15-20 continue the principal narrative, with the people held responsible for the construction of the calf. Vss. 17-18 constitute a problem here since Moses' statement in vs. 18 is in "poetical form and appear[s] to represent a stereotyped remark." [106] The original significance of the remark is obscure, and we must question whether it forms an original part of this narrative. It is possible that it does not. But since Exod. 24:13 notes that Joshua was with Moses on his way to the mountain, we may assume that some report of his return is in order. And this exchange of dialogue is the only notice which might serve that function. But if this remark is an original part of the text, we would be forced to interpret it to mean that Moses and Joshua are at this point unaware of the events in the camp. Vs. 19 may be interpreted in the same sense. Moses' anger does not rise *until he has seen the calf.* This would be surprising if, ac-

---

[105] *Ibid.,* p. 246; J. Wijngaards, "הוצא and העלה, a Twofold Approach to the Exodus," *VT* XV (1965), 100; Gunneweg, p. 92.
[106] Noth, *Exodus,* p. 249.

cording to vss. 7-8, he already knew about the apostasy. We may conclude, then, that these verses, rather than vss. 7-8, form the proper continuation of the principal tradition.

Vss. 21-24 are clearly secondary to the narrative material in this chapter. They are connected in some way to the role Aaron plays in vss. 1-6 and can be considered a part of the same development. It is impossible to define any of the principal pentateuchal sources in this unit. But we can observe contact with one of the two levels noted above since the people rather than Aaron are held responsible for the calf. Yet Deut. 9:20 knows something of Aaron's role in the tradition: It indicates that Aaron has roused the anger of Yahweh without showing what Aaron did to motivate the anger.

Vss. 25-29 also represent a secondary development in the narrative. The principal question to be answered here, however, is whether this section is a part of the same development which appears in vss. 21-24. The designation for the people is in both cases העם, while the Sam.Pent. in vs. 22 would provide a clear connection with vs. 25. Furthermore, the same attitude toward Aaron's responsibility is present in both (cf. vss. 21, 25). There seems to be little doubt, then, that at least vs. 25 provides a connective link between the two units. Vss. 26-29 incorporate into this context a form of Levitical tradition which was not originally associated with the Golden Calf story (cf. above, pp. 65 ff.). And since the incorporation depends on vs. 25, its presence in this complex can be attributed to the same Aaronic development which appears in vss. 21 ff.[107]

Vss. 30-34 are in direct contradiction to vs. 35 and probably represent a late period of the polemic against the calf. Thus Moses' intercession, which is successful in obtaining a stay of punishment, is a concession to the fact that the calves continued to exist, with the thought that the punishment must be eventually executed against the calves' devotees.[108]

[107] We note also that the Levitic insertion has already been completed in the parallel account in Deut. 9:7–10:11 (cf. 10:8-9).

[108] Noth, *Exodus*, p. 251.

Vs. 35, on the other hand, is the culmination of the punishment executed by Moses in vs. 20. Chapter 33:1-6 is to be related to the deuteronomistic section in vss. 7-14. We thus have the following literary structure: J, (1-6), 15-20, (30-34), 35. E? (1-6), Aaronic additions, 1-6, 21-29. Dtr., 32:7-14; 33:1-6.

The principal question here is whether the development of the legend of the Golden Calf can be considered a part of the murmuring tradition. If this should be the case, the contact would be found at the point of the polemic against the calf or one of the secondary expansions. Vs. 1b introduces the unit with a Niph'al waw consecutive imperfect form of the verb קהל and the preposition על. This combination can be used to describe an event of murmuring (cf. above, Chapter I, pp. 24-25). But the continuation of the introduction is obscured by the addition of the Aaronic material.

We can at best only roughly reconstruct the form of the tradition which may lie behind this addition: (1) The consequence of the people's action is the replacement of Moses. They create a calf and designate it as the gods "who brought us up from the land of Egypt." This act concerns the deity, but in all probability it is not intended to replace Yahweh but to establish a new focal point for his authority. In contrast to this formula, we note that Moses is often credited here with the act of bringing Israel out of Egypt (32:1, 8 [cf. LXX, Vul, MS], 23; 33:1; Deut. 9:12). (2) This event does not occur in the context of a personal challenge directed against Moses. Indeed, the problem at hand is that Moses has disappeared. (3) The Exodus is presupposed here; however, the problem does not involve a return to Egypt, but the designation of an authority for continuing the journey to Canaan. (4) The polemic does not involve a negation of the principles of Israel's election. But neither is it simply a blow at the use of the calves at Dan and Bethel. Rather, the focus of the unit is on the negation of the covenant established between Yahweh and Israel through Moses on Sinai.[109] If this account is secon-

---

[109] *Ibid.*, p. 249. The act of breaking the tablets means that "the covenant between God and the people [is] broken and therefore null and void."

dary to the narrative of the covenant in Exod. 34,[110] we would face the same problem which has demanded our attention in the murmuring tradition: Why should a secondary construction, i.e., a conscious, thoughtful treatise, negate such an important element as the covenant on Sinai? Here, however, we have a ready answer, for this tradition, clearly a polemic against the northern sanctuaries, also has the effect of denying their right to the privileges of the covenant relationship with Yahweh.

The next question must be whether this polemic presupposes the tradition of murmuring at all, or whether it is completely independent. This question cannot be answered with certainty because of the state of the material in the primary form of the narrative. It is possible to suppose that some relationship did exist since there are similarities in the two and the material of both appears in J. If this should be the case, the polemic against the calf would presuppose that the Sinai tradition had already come into contact with the Exodus-Wilderness-Conquest complex (cf. Deut. 9:7 ff.; Ps. 106). Just how early this combination might have occurred is difficult to determine and cannot be pursued here.

Also of relevance here is the relationship of the Aaronic priesthood to the bull cult.[111] II Chr. 13:9 suggests that Aaronic and Levitic priests alike were deposed by the institution of the bull cult in Dan and Bethel. But this text may reflect a later stage in the history of the priesthood when the two were closely identified. On the other hand, II Chr. 11:13 ff. says that only the Levites were deposed in this event. This statement is more in keeping with the traditions represented in Exod. 32, for in the polemic against the calf, Aaron is made directly responsible for the construction of the calf. Thus vs. 1b addresses a command from the people to Aaron that he make the figure. The description of the calf as an עגל מסכה suggests that the metal was melted and worked into

[110] *Ibid.,* pp. 243-44.
[111] For a more extensive discussion of the bull cult and the Aaronic priesthood, cf. Gunneweg, pp. 88 ff.

the shape of a bull. Moses' interrogation of Aaron in vss. 21-24 is not contrary to this suggestion. To be sure, Aaron claims to have simply thrown the jewelry into the fire, implying that the calf came out of the flame miraculously. Noth suggests that this is "to be understood as an attempt on the part of the narrator to provide a rather lame and hollow-sounding exculpation of Aaron." [112] But, we must ask, is this lame excuse in fact intended to controvert the explicit responsibility for the sin which Aaron carries in this unit (vs. 21)? Or is it a device designed to emphasize his guilt? The latter seems more probable since vs. 25 suggests that this explanation has not relieved him of his responsibility.

Vss. 26-29 juxtapose the Levites with Aaron and his followers. And the Levites are held in a positive light; i.e., they are not a part of the people who were involved in the festival of the bull cult. It seems to me to be irrelevant to ask whether "the 'Levites' previously looked on at the erection of the golden calf and the worship of it, and did they only realize later what was happening?" [113] If the tradition is secondary to the basic covenant tradition in Exod. 34, an artificially constructed polemic against the cult in Dan and Bethel, then the question of what really happened is not only impossible to answer but the wrong way to pose the problem. The Levitical material seems to be incorporated here for a purpose. And that purpose reflects the same conflict between the Levites and the Aaronic priesthood which was noted above (cf. Appendixes II, III).

But how did the conflict come into contact with the Golden Calf tradition? Was it simply the need for punishing the participants in the Golden Calf festival that suggested a contact with the conflict? II Chr. 11:13 ff. points to a more complex problem than this and shows that the Levites' role in the polemic against the cult at Dan and Bethel is involved with their displacement. But how are we to explain Aaron's relationship to the cult? Noth has shown that Aaron appears at

[112] Noth, *Exodus*, p. 244.
[113] *Ibid.*, p. 250.

two different levels in this tradition (see above). If it is true that Aaron appears in the primary form of the tradition as one who simply tolerated the people's construction of the calf, it is also true that Aaron took a responsible role in the *cult* of the calf by calling a feast for the following day (vs. 5). Aaron is in effect functioning as the priest for the calf cult. Could we then suppose that Jeroboam, contrary to the account in I Kings 12:31 which is obviously hostile to him, laid claim to an Aaronic genealogy for his priesthood? This hypothesis would remove the necessity of supposing that a king who seriously wanted to offer an alternative to the cult in Jerusalem would handicap his program by introducing a priesthood that had no legitimate claim to its office. Indeed, if a bull cult had existed at Dan and Bethel before Jeroboam's break with the southern kingdom, we must assume that that cult had its own priests. And if that cult claimed the legitimate worship of the God of the Exodus, it is not difficult to suppose that it would support this most central of all confessions in Israel's faith with a priesthood that had some basis in tradition. That priesthood was in all probability Aaronic (cf. Judg. 20:28).[114]

In the deuteronomistic section, two observations demand our attention. (1) We note the same principles being applied in Yahweh's first statement of judgment and Moses' intercession which were noted in Num. 14:11*b*-23*a*. Both seem clearly to reflect a later stage in the development of Israel's traditions. (2) Yahweh describes the people as עַם־קְשֵׁה־עֹרֶף (cf. above, p. 69). This expression seems to have a connotation of disobedience rather than rebellion. The issue is the presence of Yahweh among his people. But even though he denies his people the privilege of his immediate presence, the judgment is tempered by the command to continue to the land (cf. Num. 14), and by the assurance of divine leadership through an angel (33:2). It seems clear, then, that this stage of the Golden Calf tradition is not a part of the murmuring tradition.

[114] Cf. Gunneweg, pp. 90-91.

non-narrative texts

Deuteronomy 1:20-46

This unit is a part of a larger collection of material extending from chapter 1 through chapter 3. The whole complex can be described form-critically as a recitation of a portion of Israel's history, constructed in first person singular style as Moses' final address to his people. The various sub-units in this complex, including 1:20-46, are bound together by small connecting links, commonly in a first person plural form (cf. vs. 19).

Deut. 1:20-46 corresponds in general to its pentateuchal parallel,[1] suggesting that at least the tradition represented in Num. 13-14, if not some written form of that text, was known to the Deuteronomist.[2] There are, however, significant differences between the two. It has been suggested that the lengthy introduction in vss. 20-23, an introduction which makes the people rather than Yahweh responsible for the initial request for the spies, can be attributed to a source

---

[1] Deut. 1:20-46 and 9:7–10:11 probably belong to the deuteronomistic history. Cf. von Rad, *Deuteronomium*, p. 7, 54-55. We shall use the term "Deuteronomy" in a broad sense to include these deuteronomistic expansions.

[2] Lohfink, p. 107.

which is not present in Num. 13.[3] If this should be the case, the character of that source is too obscure to permit identification. In the remaining parts of the unit, however, the variations are much more subtle and may reflect deuteronomistic revisions of the tradition. If this should be the case, we would have a valuable tool for controlling the distinctive interpretation of the rebellion tradition in Deuteronomy.[4]

The negative response of the people to the spies' report is expressed in this unit by means of two verbs. The first is a Hiph'il form of the root מרה (vs. 26). The subject is Israel, the addressee of Moses' speech. The object of the rebellion is the command of Yahweh (פי יהוה) to go up into the land (vs. 26a), and probably reflects the negative form of the spies' report before it was associated with the murmuring (cf. above, p. 153 ff.).

The second verb is a Niph'al form of רגן. The subject is again Israel, but there is no specification of the object (vs. 27; cf. Ps. 106:25). There is no linguistic connection between this verb and לון; indeed the connotations of רגן are apparently clandestine, malicious talk rather than direct accusation (cf. Prov. 18:8 and 26:22). This can be seen especially in Deut. 1:27. The subject of the verb is not involved in a personal conflict with Moses. Instead, the people remain in the confines of their own tents. But the content of their conversation is clearly within the scope of the murmuring. This suggests that the new setting and even the new verb represent a deviation from the form of the murmuring which appears in Num. 14. Moreover, the complaint of the people is not set in response to a report of the spies on the fortifications of the land. Quite the contrary, the report is completely positive. There is no obvious motivation for the murmuring, and as a consequence we must label the people's response an ungrateful act of disbelief.[5]

---

[3] Cf. above, p. 137, n. 16.

[4] Lohfink, pp. 109-10.

[5] von Rad, *Deuteronomium*, p. 29; C. Steuernagel, *Das Deuteronomium*, *HKAT* I/3 (2nd ed., rev.; Göttingen: Vandenhoeck & Ruprecht, 1923), 54.

Is this change to be attributed to Deuteronomy? The influence of the Yahwistic form of the tradition in the verses that follow suggests that the change is at least a conscious deviation from the tradition in J. This influence is to be seen in the allusion to Yahweh's "reprehensible" action in bringing the people out of Egypt (vs. 27aβb) as well as the reference to the invincible character of the land (vs. 28). Vs. 28 shows that in contrast to the new form of the murmuring, the original tradition is still to be seen. Moreover, vs. 29 cites a speech of Moses in response to the recalcitrance of the people which suggests that their problem is not ungratefulness but fear. This presupposes the spies' assurance that the land could indeed be taken. But it also suggests that the people are not in their tents but gathered in the presence of Moses to hear the report of the spies. This, too, would be more in keeping with the tradition as we know it in J. But what is the source of the change in that tradition? Since the murmuring never clearly appears in E, it would be difficult to argue that an E form of the spies' report lies behind this text. The only other alternative is to suggest that the deviations represent Deuteronomy's reinterpretation of the tradition along the lines of special interest,[6] while the other, somewhat contradictory motifs have been simply taken over from the sources. The ungrateful character of the people would be taken, then, as the deuteronomistic version of the murmuring.

Gerhard von Rad feels that the aetiological concern apparent in Num. 13–14 is missing in the deuteronomistic parallel since there is no reference to Hebron. As a result, he

---

[6] Lohfink, pp. 110 ff., agrees that the section from vs. 25 through vs. 33 reflects the most pronounced revision in the style and characteristic tendencies of Dtr. In addition, he points to vs. 32 as a peculiarity in Deuteronomy, namely, the emphasis on the fact that in spite of Yahweh's many wonders (ובדבר הזה) the people still did not believe. Also worthy of note is his comment on the role of the holy war motifs. But we must also emphasize that both the motif of fear and the motif of assurance were already present in the J form of the tradition. Moreover, the relationship between vss. 29-30 and the tradition of the miracle at the Reed Sea is questionable. The parallels between the two are by and large inconsequential and do not detract from the fact that vss. 29 ff. fit naturally into the deuteronomistic version of this tradition.

concludes that vss. 36-38 are a later addition from the older
pentateuchal material.[7] But this is not necessarily the case.
References to נחל אשכל (vs. 24) and בני ענקים (vs. 28) seem
likely to be related to Hebron.[8] Thus the conscious exception
of Caleb from the punishment for the rebellion can be considered an original part of this unit.

The formal structure and content of the sentence here are
identical to the ones in Num. 14; in the form of an אם clause
(vs. 35), Yahweh swears that the rebels will not see the
promised land. It is significant, in the light of our argument
above, that Joshua is cited as an exception to the punishment,
not as Caleb's colleague, but as Moses' successor (vss. 37-38;
cf. also Deut. 3:26 ff.).[9] The exception leads to a further com-
plication in the tradition, for Joshua's task is to cause Israel to
inherit the land. This is a striking contradiction to the judgment in vs. 35 and leaves the question open as to how the men
who were denied the privilege of seeing the land will be able
to inherit it. The problem is answered in vs. 39—the children
will be the heirs (cf. P).

Vs. 39aαא is an exact duplication of Num. 14:31a and thus
raises the question of relationship between Deuteronomy and
P. The description of the children cites an earlier statement
made by the people. That statement appears in Num. 14:3 but
is completely missing in Deuteronomy. Since the expression is
meaningless without this background, we must conclude that
the original form is in P and that this reference is a secondary
addition to the unit in Deuteronomy.[10] This would be supported by the fact that vs. 39 continues with another specifica-

---

[7] von Rad, *Deuteronomium*, p. 29. Cf. also Steuernagel, pp. 54-55.

[8] Cf. above, pp. 144-45.

[9] Josh. 14:6 ff. is very close to the deuteronomistic form of this tradition. And here, the fact that Caleb approaches Joshua and asks for the
land that is rightfully his presupposes that Joshua was not one of his
colleagues (cf. vss. 7-8). Indeed, vs. 8 refers to the colleagues in a manner
which shows clearly that *all* the other spies were involved in the negative report. On the other hand, Num. 32:8 ff. is a late form of the tradition presupposing the completed redaction of the Pentateuch (cf. Lohfink,
p. 108, n. 3; Noth, *Überlieferungsgeschichte*, p. 39, n. 142). It thus reflects
only the forms of the problem which have been seen in each layer.

[10] Lohfink, p. 107, n. 1.

tion of the children, a specification which does not appear in
P. Indeed, the P designation of all who were under twenty
years of age (Num. 14:29) seems to be somewhat more liberal
than this qualification.[11] This, then, is Deuteronomy's means
for answering the problem of Israel's inheritance of the land.
The significance of this characteristic lies in the fact that
Deuteronomy has already extended the exception to the sentence beyond Caleb and his heirs (cf. P). This suggests that
although vss. 35-36 are a part of the primary tradition and
were probably present in the original text, they have not been
completely integrated into the deuteronomistic form of the
tradition.[12]

Deuteronomy 9:7–10:11

This unit constitutes an interlude in a series of sermonic
material running from Deut. 6:10 through 9:6.[13] Its form, a
first person singular recitation of events from Israel's past, has
more in common with Deut. 1–3 than with the paraenetic
series and may have originally been a part of that complex.[14]
The introduction to the unit (vs. 7) is formally an admonition addressed directly to Israel through a second person
singular imperative and establishes a link between the recitation and admonitions in the preceding series.[15]

The recitation itself begins in vs. 8 and continues without
break at least through vs. 11. That vs. 12 and vss. 13-14 are
not well unified is demonstrated by the renewed introduction
to Yahweh's speech in vs. 13a (cf. vs. 12aα).[16] In vs. 12,

---

[11] The expression "to know good and evil" is apparently one of general
knowledge and ability (cf. Gerhard von Rad, *Genesis, a Commentary*,
tr. John H. Marks, *OTL* [Philadelphia: The Westminster Press, 1961], 86).
It would thus have nothing to do with a legal age of responsibility but
probably indicates only the very young who had not experienced the
problems of the generation in the wilderness.

[12] On vss. 41 ff., cf. above, p. 153.

[13] von Rad, *Deuteronomium*, p. 54.

[14] *Ibid.*, pp. 54-55.

[15] On the didactic character of the introduction, cf. von Rad. *Deuteronomium*, p. 55.

[16] Cf. above, p. 186.

NON-NARRATIVE TEXTS **197**

Yahweh announces Israel's apostasy to Moses before Moses descends from the mountain. But in vs. 16, Moses seems to be unaware of Israel's new image (cf. Exod. 32:15 ff.). Vss. 13-14 parallel the deuteronomistic addition in Exod. 32:9-10, especially in the emphasis on Moses and his posterity as the source for a new people to replace the apostates now threatened with destruction. The recitation in first person singular style continues in vss. 15 ff., picking up from the break in the recitation at vs. 11. The intercession in vss. 18-19 is parallel to the intercession in vss. 25-29 and 10:10-11. These parallels, as well as the rough transition between vss. 12 and 13-14, are probably the result of complex growth in the Golden Calf tradition. The intercessory prayer itself appears in vss. 26-28 and corresponds in part with Exod. 32:11-13. But the parallel is not exact and probably reflects a common tradition behind both texts. Vss. 20-21 constitute an intercession for Aaron, perhaps reflecting the polemic against the Aaronic priesthood in the calf cult noted in Exod. 32, and the destruction of the calf, again with a parallel in Exod. 32:15 ff. Vss. 22-24 appear to be an insertion into the present tradition which breaks the unity of the Golden Calf event simply to list several other events of Israel's rebellion.[17] Chapter 10:1-5 may well constitute a continuation of the intercession (9:18-19) and conclude the recitation of this event.[18] Vss. 6-7 and 8-9 are considered later interpolations into the tradition,[19] although we note that vss. 8-9, the ordination of Levi, have an important parallel in Exod. 32:25-29.[20]

This presentation of the Golden Calf tradition corresponds generally with its Exodus counterpart and offers no further evidence to clarify its relationship to the murmuring tradition. The one possible exception to this observation appears in the citation posited for the Egyptians in the context of Moses' intercession (vs. 28): The place for Israel's expected death is not the mountains (cf. Exod. 32:12) but the wilderness. The

[17] von Rad, *Deuteronomium,* p. 56.
[18] *Ibid.,* p. 56.
[19] *Ibid.,* pp. 56-57.
[20] Cf. above, pp. 65 ff., 187.

change may reflect influence from the murmuring tradition and, if so, suggest that, for the deuteronomistic form of the Golden Calf, the event belongs to Israel's murmuring.

Yet this possibility is equivocal for our concern with the original contact between the Golden Calf tradition and the murmuring, for the deuteronomistic report of the rebellion history no longer maintains the limits and characteristics of the rebellion pattern established in earlier tradition. This is seen in the admonition in vs. 7: "Remember and do not forget that you angered the Lord your God in the wilderness. *From the day you came out from the land of Egypt* until you came into this place, you have been rebelling against Yahweh," and even more sharply in the (deuteronomistic?) insertion in vss. 22-24: "You have rebelled against Yahweh *from the day I knew you.*" The tendency to extend the character and consequences of the murmuring noted in P would thus already be present in germinal form in Deuteronomy. And the possible allusion to the Golden Calf in that context could be considered nothing more than a part of that tendency.

Deut. 11:2-9 [21] contains a similar appeal to history. But this recitation contains no allusion to traditions which can be assigned to the murmuring tradition (N.B. the ambiguous character of vs. 5). The one possibility is the reference to Dathan and Abiram in vs. 6. However, as we have argued, that tradition was not properly a part of the murmuring tradition as it developed and spread throughout the Pentateuch, but rather the motif from which the stereotyped pattern for the murmuring was drawn (cf. also Ezek. 20:33 ff.). We can note in support of our argument about Dathan-Abiram, however, that no reference to Korah is made,[22] and that people other than the immediate families of Dathan and Abiram suffered execution (vs. 6bα), i.e., the followers of Dathan and Abiram.

We can summarize the history of the murmuring tradition reinterpreted in Deuteronomy as follows: (1) The murmur-

---

[21] On Deut. 6:16, cf. above, p. 63. No other texts in Deuteronomy are relevant for our study.

[22] von Rad, *Deuteronomium*, p. 60, feels that the absence of Korah suggests that only the older level appears here.

ing itself has been revised from its focus on the problem of authority in the Exodus, especially Moses' authority, to an emphasis on the people's unjustified complaint. And this complaint comes in spite of the many acts of gracious aid witnessed by the people. This would be in keeping with the theological tendency noted in the Massah tradition. (2) The rebellion is extended throughout the whole period of the wilderness, and into the Exodus and Conquest generations.

Psalm 78

The form of this psalm does not correspond to any one of the principal types of psalm categories defined by Gunkel; indeed, Gunkel himself observed that "die Verbindung so verschiedener Gattungen, wie es sie enthält—es sind Sagenerzählung, Hymnus, prophetische Mahnrede und Weisheitsdichtung—zeigt eine starke Verschmelzung der Gattungen." [23] Kraus suggests that on the basis of content, the psalm can be designated a "Geschichtspsalm." [24] This definition is drawn primarily from the lengthy recitation of Israel's past, a recitation which follows the structure of the cultic credo.[25]

The principal compounding of forms appears in the introduction to the historical review. Kraus has shown satisfactorily that the introduction breaks down into the following themes: Vss. 1-2 reveal characteristics of wisdom poetry, while vss. 3-4 reflect themes from psalms of thanksgiving and hymns. Vss. 5 ff. allude to the history of Yahweh's deeds on behalf of his people and probably are to be attributed to deuteronomistic circles.[26]

It seems probable that a break can be seen between vss. 8 and 9. The fathers in vs. 8 should be identified with the rebellious wilderness generation, while the atrocity in a time of battle suggests that the Ephraimites in vs. 9 should be identi-

[23] Hermann Gunkel, *Die Psalmen*, *HKAT* II/2 (4th ed., Göttingen: Vandenhoeck & Ruprecht, 1926) , 342.

[24] Kraus, *Psalmen*, p. LIV; cf. also pp. 539-40.

[25] Gerhard von Rad, *Das formgeschichtliche Problem des Hexateuch*, *BWANT*, Folge 4, Heft 26 (Stuttgart: W. Kohlhammer Verlag, 1938) , 7 ff.

[26] Kraus, *Psalmen*, pp. 542-43.

fied with the conquest generation.[27] The relationship between
vss. 9 and 10-11 is problematic. If we assume that there is no
relationship, then the subject of the verbs and the antecedent
for the suffix in vss. 10-11 must be the wilderness fathers in
vs. 8 (even though the verbs and suffix in vss. 10-11 are plural
while vs. 8 defines the fathers by the singular noun דור with
singular verbs and suffixes). And indeed the plural suffix in
vs. 11b (הראם) suggests that the antecedent in question had
seen the events of the Exodus. But how is this to be reconciled
with the reference in vs. 12 to the witnesses of the Exodus as
אבותם? It could reflect a break between vss. 10-11 and vs. 12.
But then we would be forced to connect vss. 10-11 with vs. 8,
leaving vs. 9 either completely isolated or a detached preparation for vss. 12-13. But this fragmentation is not necessary.
Since subsequent generations are on occasion considered witnesses of events which occurred during the time of previous
generations (cf. Deut. 6:20 ff.; 26:5 ff.; Josh. 24:1 ff., esp. vs.
6), we suggest that the antecedent of the suffix in vs. 11b
was witness to the Exodus events in the same manner and
thus not the wilderness generation. This would exclude the
fathers in vs. 8 and leave only the Ephraimites in vs. 9 as the
point of reference for the suffixes and verbs in vss. 10 ff.[28]
On the other hand, vs. 13 clearly presupposes the wilderness
fathers. Since this verse cannot be separated from vs. 12, we

[27] Artur Weiser, *The Psalms, a Commentary,* tr. Herbert Hartwell, *OTL*
(Philadelphia: The Westminster Press, 1962), p. 540. Some scholars
isolate vs. 9 from its context as a disruptive fragment from some other
source (cf. Rudolf Kittel, *Die Psalmen, KAT* XIII [2nd ed.; Leipzig:
A. Deichertsche Verlagsbuchhandlung, 1914], 291; Friedrich Baethgen,
Die Psalmen, HKAT II/2 [3rd ed., rev.; Göttingen: Vandenhoeck &
Ruprecht, 1904], 244). Gunkel, p. 343, suggests that the verse is hope-
lessly corrupt and offers a radical reconstruction. Kraus, *Psalmen,* p. 538,
consigns it to a meaningless gloss on vs. 8. Otto Eissfeldt, *Das Lied Moses,
Deuteronomium 32:1-43, und das Lehrgedicht Asaphs, Psalm 78, samt
einer Analyse der Umgebung des Mose-Liedes. Berichte über die Verhandlungen der sächsischen Akademie der Wissenschaften zu Leipzig,*
Phil.-Hist. Klasse, Bd. CIV, Heft 5 (Berlin: Akademie Verlag, 1958),
33, suggests to the contrary that the verse as it now stands plays a vital
role in the psalm. We shall consider this problem in detail below.

[28] J. Schildenberger, "Psalm 78 (77) und die Pentateuchquellen," *Lex
Tua Veritas; Festschrift für Hubert Junker,* V. Heinrich Gross and F.
Mussner, eds. (Trier: Paulinus Verlag, 1961), p. 236.

must assume that the antecedent for the plural suffix in vs. 13*a*
is אבותם as it appears in vs. 12 rather than the Ephraimites
or even the fathers in vs. 8.

Vss. 12-16 constitute a credo-like recitation of Yahweh's
aid during the wilderness period, characterized by an emphasis
on Yahweh's deeds rather than the people's response, and
showing no trace of the rebellion theme introduced in vs. 8.
On the other hand, the unit in vss. 17-41 represents a fully
developed, unbroken recitation of Israel's rebellion history.
This compounding of motifs in all probability recalls the same
process of combining the rebellion tradition with the motif
of aid in the wilderness previously observed. But it also suggests a caesura between the two motifs which prevents a simple
identification of אבותם in vs. 12 with אבותם in vs. 8.

Vs. 42 returns to the motif of the Exodus which appeared
first in vss. 11 ff. Indeed, vss. 11-12 and vss. 42-43 are virtual
doublets, the only differences lying in the נגד אבותם in vs. 12
and in the whole of vs. 42*b*. We may assume, therefore, that
there is some type of connection between the two units. And
again, the view of the Exodus, Wilderness, and Conquest in
vss. 42 ff. is characterized by the kind of recitation which
concentrates on Yahweh's deeds. This unit continues without
break through vs. 55. Vss. 56-66 return once again to the motif
of rebellion but, as we shall argue below, do not form a
parallel to the recitation of the murmuring tradition in vss.
17-41. Rather, they are much more closely related to the motif
of rebellion in vss. 9-11.

The question of relationship between vs. 66 and vss. 67 ff.
is raised by the obscure identity of the adversaries in vs. 66.
It seems likely that the word צריו does not refer to the
tent of Joseph in vs. 67 but to the Philistines.[29] This conclusion is supported by the fact that vss. 65-66 constitute a
response to the report of the fall of Shiloh which expresses,
not a continued oppression of Israel (cf. vs. 59), but a rout of
Israel's enemies. The motif of the deity awakening from sleep
is a part of a response that might be expected from a lament

[29] Eissfeldt, *Das Lied Moses,* p. 35.

over the oppression or defeat of a people (cf. Pss. 44:23; 121:4).[30] In this case, the positive note in vss. 65-66 would present a sharp contrast to the repeated rejection of Israel, i.e., of the tent of Joseph in vs. 67. The unit beginning at vs. 67 continues without break through the end of the psalm. We can thus define the following structure: The introduction is composed of two parts, vss. 1-4 (wisdom) and vss. 5-8 (deuteronomistic), each having a didactic character. The recitation of Israel's history is composed of two parallel units, vss. 12-16 and vss. 42-55. These units are combined with the motif of Israel's rebellion in vss. 9-11 and vss. 56-66, but the rebellion in these verses is not set in the wilderness. Rebellion in the wilderness appears in vss. 17-41. Vss. 67-72 constitute a concluding unit.

Any conclusions which are drawn concerning the date and setting of the psalm will depend heavily on the resolution of the question concerning the relationship between the psalm and the classical sources of the Pentateuch. Gunkel sees the total psalm as a late piece of poetic creativity built on the present form of pentateuchal sources.[31] But contrary to this position, Eissfeldt suggests an unusually early date, perhaps in the time of David or Solomon,[32] and cautions that no point in the entire psalm is dependent on the pentateuchal sources.[33] His dating, however, is based on traditions in the psalm which are probably quite early, but nevertheless not representative for the complete psalm. More recent scholarship dates the psalm in the late pre-exilic period, after the fall of Samaria, but before the destruction of the Tem-

---

[30] G. Widengren, *Sakrales Königtum im Alten Testament und im Judentum* (Stuttgart: W. Kohlhammer Verlag, 1955), pp. 67 ff., develops an understanding of the awakening of the deity in connection with the "Tammuz" pattern of the deity returning to his power. This is questionable for this text. At best, we may conclude that the ascendency of the adversaries implies that the deity is asleep, while their defeat is associated with his awakening.

[31] Gunkel, p. 341. Cf. Baethgen, p. 243; B. Duhm, *Die Psalmen, KHAT* XIV (2nd ed., rev.; Tübingen: J. C. B. Mohr [Paul Siebeck], 1922), 308; Kraus, *Psalmen*, p. 541.

[32] Eissfeldt, *Das Lied Moses*, p. 41.

[33] *Ibid.*, p. 34.

ple.[34] We have agreed with Kraus that influence from deuteronomistic circles can be seen in the introduction. If this
is indeed the case, then it would be clear that the final form
of the psalm could not be earlier than the late eighth century.[35] But this conclusion does not resolve the problem, since
the psalm draws on traditions that have a much longer history
than this. It seems more adequate to suggest, then, that the
psalm will not support one sweeping conclusion concerning its
date of origin and dependency on pentateuchal sources.
The present form may be late and *reflect* the whole of the
Pentateuch. But we must allow the possibility that different
traditions of different dates and different degrees of contact
with the pentateuchal sources may compose this final form.
Whether this is in fact the case must be determined by an
examination of those traditions.

The first problem for our exegesis is again related to vs. 9.
Since, as we have argued above, the Ephraimites should be
identified with the conquest generation rather than the
generation in the wilderness, we must conclude that the event
described in vs. 9 is *not* a part of the murmuring tradition.
This would be supported by the connotation of battle given
by the words קשת and קרב. But what event does the verse refer
to? Eissfeldt has suggested that it must be related in some
manner to the fall of Shiloh described in vs. 60 (cf. I Sam.
4).[36] There are weaknesses in this position, the most notable
one being that a lengthy amount of material separates this
verse from its point of reference in vs. 60.[37] But if vss. 9-16
and vss. 42-66 are parallel, the accounts of the conquest and
the fall of Shiloh would be in their natural positions.

On the basis of vs. 9 alone, then, this thesis seems plausible.
But vss. 10-11 offer a problem. The sin reported here is a

[34] Weiser, *Psalms*, p. 540; Hans Schmidt, *Die Psalmen, HAT* XV
(Tübingen: J. C. B. Mohr [Paul Siebeck], 1934), p. 150; Schildenberger,
p. 236; H. Junker, "Die Entstehungszeit des Ps. 78 und des Deuteronomiums," *Bib* XXXIV (1953), 487 ff.; Kraus admits definitely only a
post-deuteronomistic date (p. 541).

[35] Junker, pp. 487 ff.

[36] Eissfeldt, *Das Lied Moses*, p. 33.

[37] Schildenberger, p. 236. Cf. also Junker, p. 489.

violation of God's covenant (ברית אלהים) and his law (תורתו).
Moreover, vs. 11 describes the violation in terms of forgetting
the mighty acts of God. What is the significance of these terms,
and how are they related to the military character of vs. 9? [38]
The most obvious answer would be that procedure for a holy
war has been abused. It is possible to support this thesis, for
Deut. 7:18 shows that the admonition not to fear in the context of a holy war is connected with an admonition to remember what God has done in the past. We can suggest one
further possibility: One of the most common events associated
with forgetting Yahweh's acts is idolatry (cf. Deut. 4:23;
6:12-13; 8:14; Hos. 13:6; Deut. 32:18; Judg. 3:7; 1 Sam. 12:9;
II Kings 17:38; Jer. 3:21; 23:27; Hos. 4:6; Ps. 44:21; et al.). [39]
We shall return to this question shortly.

If, then, this unit does not set the description of the people's
sin in the wilderness, how does it view that period? Vs. 12 provides our first point of contact. Junker has suggested that
אבותם in this verse refers to the same entity as אבותם in vs. 8, [40]
and indeed, we must agree that both references are to the
wilderness fathers. In fact, the use of תורתו and the reference
to the problem of forgetting Yahweh's acts in vss. 10-11 also
recall the introduction in vss. 5-8. But this similarity does not
resolve the problem of the nature of the tradition reflected in
vss. 12-16. In this section, Yahweh executes all the events, and
the people fall into the background. He effects the Exodus
(vs. 12); he leads the people through the sea (vs. 13); [41] he
provides a pillar of cloud and fire as a symbol of his leadership
(vs. 14); he strikes a rock and gives his people water to drink
(vss. 15-16). The Exodus and the Wilderness themes are combined in this recitation. But significantly the Wilderness

---

[38] Kraus, Psalmen, p. 543, suggests that these terms allude to the
Sinai traditions. But cf. von Rad, Das formgeschichtliche Problem, p. 49.

[39] But not every reference to forgetting Yahweh's acts can be identified
with idolatry. Cf. B. S. Childs, Memory and Tradition in Israel, SBT
XXXVII (London: SCM Press, 1962), 49.

[40] Junker, p. 491.

[41] The reference in vs. 13b may indeed reflect the Song of Moses; cf.
Schildenberger, p. 243. But this would say nothing about dependency
on a pentateuchal source.

theme is without reference to the rebellion of the people. Indeed, as we have noted, it follows the pattern of Yahweh's
aid to the people in the wilderness. This pattern points to a
decisive caesura between this section and vs. 8.

We have already observed the formal similarities between
vss. 10-11 and vss. 42-43. We may thus assume that the subject of the plural verb and the antecedent of the plural
suffix in vs. 42 also do not refer to the wilderness generation.
This is supported by the nature of the tradition which follows. Vs. 43 is an obvious allusion to the plagues, as is vs. 12.
At this point, in contrast to the unit in vss. 9-16, a lengthy
description of the plagues is found (vss. 44-51).[42] The events
in the wilderness are reported in vss. 52-53. Here, as in vss.
12-16, we find only the positive tradition of Yahweh's aid to
the people. Indeed, the figure of the people as a flock of
sheep graphically depicts the nature of the people's dependence on Yahweh. It is also significant here, in the light of our
argument about the nature of Exod. 14, that the miracle at the
Sea is mentioned only after the motif of Yahweh's leadership
in the wilderness has been developed (vs. 53b, but cf. also
vss. 13-14). The tradition to this point is parallel to, but not
a duplicate of, vss. 12-16.

Vss. 54-55 introduce the Conquest tradition. The land is
gained solely through the power of Yahweh, and again, the
tradition has no negative overtones.[43] It is only in vss. 56 ff.
that Israel's rebellion appears. But is the event which is described here related to the murmuring? Vs. 56a recalls the
pattern of rebellion in the wilderness on two counts: (1) The
verbs נסה and מרה are used elsewhere in this psalm to describe
the rebellion of the wilderness generation, and both have been
noted above as having a part in the murmuring tradition in
the Pentateuch. The verb נסה seems to be a particular word

---

[42] Lauha, *Die Geschichtsmotive*, pp. 50-51, has argued that this list
reflects the J version of the plagues. But cf. Schildenberger, pp. 240 ff. Since
a resolution of this problem would have no bearing on our chief interest,
we shall not pursue the issue further.
[43] It is possible that vs. 54b refers to Zion (Kraus *Psalmen*, p. 547). Cf.
also Exod. 15:17. But evidence to support the hypothesis is tenuous. Cf.
Gunkel, p. 346.

employed by the Deuteronomist for that period, while מרה
appears in the deuteronomistic introduction (vs. 8). (2) The
uses of the name עליון elsewhere in this psalm appear only
in the context of Israel's rebellion in the wilderness (vss. 17,
35). But these characteristics are inconclusive. Of more importance are vss. 56*b* ff. The reference to idols and high places
in vs. 58 shows clearly that the subject of this section is not the
wilderness generation in rebellion over the problem of the
Exodus, but the generation confronted with the problem of
Canaanite religions after they had settled in the land.[44]

We must still consider the significance of the expression
כאבותם in vs. 57*a*. Does this presuppose that the fathers in the
wilderness were also rebels? The preposition shows that the
fathers in question here are guilty of a sin comparable to the
apostasy of the people after the conquest (vss. 56-58). But
never before, even in the murmuring tradition, has the generation in the wilderness been accused of *idolatry*.[45] What, then,
is the violation? The verbs in vs. 56*a* are notoriously non-
committal. It is true that they are used in reference to the
murmuring, but they are not necessarily a part of the murmuring tradition. A parallel to vs. 56*b*, vss. 10-11, shows that
the Ephraimites were accused. Moreover, the reference to a
violation associated in some manner with a bow in vs. 57
recalls the difficulty attributed to the Ephraimites in vs. 9. But

[44] Since deuteronomistic reinterpretation of the murmuring tradition
characteristically extends the rebellion as far as possible, the apostasy of
the Conquest generation might be seen under the influence of the murmuring. But it could not be considered a part of the murmuring tradition itself.

[45] There are only two questions which could be raised here. The first
concerns Baal Pe'or, (Num. 25:1-5). But Noth, *Überlieferungsgeschichte*,
pp. 80 ff., has shown that this tradition, at least in its present form, is
to be associated with the conquest (cf. M. Noth, "Israelitische Stämme
zwischen Ammon und Moab," *ZAW* LX [1944], 11-57, esp. 28-29). Bach,
pp. 35-36, has shown satisfactorily that Hos. 9:10*b* and 13:6 do not affect
Hosea's positive view of Israel's faith in the wilderness. (We may conclude regarding Hos. 13:6 that the satiation reflects the plenty which
the people enjoyed *in the land*. Cf. Deut. 8:11 ff.; Neh. 9:25.) The second
concerns the golden calves in Exod. 32. But it seems clear that the treatment of this as idolatry is a later piece of polemic that is not connected
with the murmuring (cf. the Excursus).

at this point the similarity ceases. The one is a description of people unfaithful in battle, while the other is a description of people involved in idolatry. Yet, we must ask, from what source does the psalm draw the description of the idolaters as unfaithful bows? The allusion is clearly set, not in worship, but in battle. It seems probable to suggest, therefore, that this description has been assumed from the comparison with the fathers rather than the worship of idols. This would suggest that the "fathers" in vs. 57 is a reference to the Ephraimites, a generation which was indeed unfaithful in battle.

This conclusion raises a further problem, for the comparison כאבותם assumes according to the thesis that the Ephraimites were also idolatrous. Vss. 58 ff. show clearly that Yahweh rejects Israel, forsakes Shiloh, and allows his ark (thus, עזו ותפארתו) to be captured, all as a result of Israel's idolatry. But if these verses are to be related to the account of the fall of Shiloh in I Sam. 4, how can we explain the element of idolatry here? At no point in I Sam. 3-4 is there any indication that idolatry was the cause of the defeat. Quite the contrary, the reason is related to the transgressions of Eli's sons. This reason may be a secondary connection, an attempt to collate the downfall of the house of Eli with the fall of Shiloh. Is it not possible, then, that idolatry lies behind this explanation? Indeed, I Sam. 7:3; 12:10 suggest that the oppression of the Philistines was the result of Israel's idolatry (cf. Jer. 7:12, where the reference to the רעת applies not to the house of Eli but to the Israelites). This would, according to our thesis, account for the comparison of the idolatry of the present generation with the sin of the fathers. And it would explain the reference to a violation of God's covenant and law. But these allusions do not clearly tie the fall of Shiloh to a problem of idolatry.

A chronological problem also appears here. This section not only refers to the fall of Shiloh, but presupposes that at the same time the whole state of Israel was defeated (cf. vs. 59). The fall of Shiloh was a disastrous defeat for Israel. But opposition to the Philistines revived under Samuel's leadership. It seems likely, then, that *this text* is not primarily concerned with the problem of Israel's idolatry as an explanation for the fall of Shiloh. Rather, on the basis of Israel's subsequent apostasy (and thus in later generations), the psalm uses the fall of Shiloh as a prototype for the complete rejection of Israel, i.e., the fall of Samaria (cf. II Kings 17:7). Such a use of Shiloh is not unknown elsewhere in the Old Testament (cf. Jer. 7:12 ff.; 26:6 ff.). In this case, the response of Yahweh in vss. 65-66 is even more in keeping with the setting of this motif as a lament over the fall of a people. It makes little difference whether the adversaries in vs. 66 are the Philistines or the Assyrians; in accord with the allusion to Shiloh, we may agree with Eissfeldt that the Philistines are intended.[46] Vss. 65-66 would then express hope for restitution.[47]

It is in this tradition that Eissfeldt's exegesis of Ps. 78 is centered.[48] Since he suggests that Deut. 32:1-43 offers an important parallel, we must turn our attention briefly to this text. The critical problems here need not detain us.[49] The similarity between the introduction of the two texts, particularly in the characteristics which may be attributed to wisdom, has been sufficiently established.[50] In vss. 5-6, the

[46] Eissfeldt, *Das Lied Moses*, p. 35.

[47] Schildenberger, pp. 240 ff., suggests that this portion of the psalm reveals an "influence" from the pentateuchal sources. This is, of course, not to be confused with literary dependence. But the significance of the influence is not clear. Similarities in content and vocabulary which obviously appear here do not override the fact that in this form of the tradition, there is no rebellion in the wilderness. It seems much more probable that the sources of the Pentateuch and this portion of Ps. 78 draw from a common tradition of Yahweh's aid in the wilderness. And it may be that nothing more than this was intended by Schildenberger.

[48] Eissfeldt, *Das Lied Moses*, pp. 34 ff. Surprisingly, he pays little attention to vss. 17-41.

[49] G. Ernest Wright, "The Lawsuit of God: A Form-Critical Study of Dt. 32," *Israel's Prophetic Heritage*, Bernhard Anderson and Walter Harrelson, eds. (New York: Harper & Row, 1962), pp. 26 ff. This includes a detailed analysis of the text. The general opinion, established probably by W. F. Albright, "Some Remarks on the Song of Moses in Dt. 32," *VT* IX (1959), 339-46, is that the tradition represented here is extremely early, perhaps as early as the eleventh century. Cf. also P. W. Skehan, "The Structure of the Song of Moses in Dt.," *CBQ* XIII (1951), 153-63.

[50] Eissfeldt, *Das Lied Moses*, pp. 5 ff.

problem of Israel's sin is introduced, and we must consider once again whether this motif refers to the rebellion of the people in the wilderness. The answer is clear in the verses that follow. Vs. 7 is an admonition to remember the past, directed to the people who have been accused. The past is contrasted with the current event of faithlessness as an example of the proper relationship between Yahweh and his people. Vss. 8-9 show that the past includes not just the Exodus-wilderness period but the creation of the nations as well. In vss. 10 ff., the wilderness period appears. Since this period is to be taken as a part of the past which the rebels in vss. 5-6 are admonished to remember, it is clear that the sin in vss. 5-6 cannot be considered a part of the murmuring tradition.

How, then, is the wilderness generation viewed? Once again, the tradition recalls Yahweh's aid in the wilderness. Indeed, the figure of Israel's dependence appears here in a different, though equally graphic, manner (vss. 10b-12a). And in accord with our thesis that Israel was not accused of idolatry in this period, vs. 12b states explicitly: ואין עמו אל נכר.

There is some question about whether vss. 13-14 refer to the wilderness motif of Yahweh's aid or to the support which the people received from the land. Two points suggest the wilderness: (1) Vs. 13b refers to honey and oil from the rock. This may be a poetic allusion to the miracle of water from the rock. But the concern is not for drink but food (vs. 13aβ). (2) Vs. 14aβ refers to wheat (חטה). Since Ps. 78:24 uses a corresponding term, דגן־שמים, to refer to manna, we might connect the wheat in vs. 14aβ with the wilderness manna. Both the honey and the wheat also appear in Ps. 81:17 as an expression of Yahweh's care for his people. But there is no evidence in that psalm that the motif is to be associated with the wilderness. In our text, vs. 14aα reflects a pastoral background. But vs. 13aα suggests that the people were already in the land, while vs. 14b could hardly be considered a reference to the wilderness (but cf. Hos. 9:10). The resolution of the question is not firm, but it seems probable that both this text and Ps. 81:17 presuppose a post-Conquest setting. In vs.

15, this is certainly the case. Israel is satiated and forsakes her deity (cf. Hos. 13:4 ff.; Neh. 9:25-26).

Vss. 16 ff. show that the difficulty here, contrary to that of the wilderness period, is foreign gods. Since vss. 15 ff. are no longer a part of the history which is to be remembered but in fact the indictment of the rebels in vss. 5-6,[51] it is clear that the violation is idolatry. Moreover, this idolatry is described in vs. 18 in terms of forgetting God. Yahweh's response is to reject Israel (vs. 20). After a lengthy description of their punishment (vs. 25, cf. Ps. 78:62 ff.), the punishment is qualified. And this qualification, as in Num. 14:13 ff., is based on Yahweh's reputation before the enemy (vss. 26 ff.). Vss. 36-42 correspond with Ps. 78:65-66. The formal character of this unit is similar to that of a prophetic oracle of salvation.[52] The defeated people shall be restored, and the adversaries (vs. 41) shall be punished. Eissfeldt's argument is that this refers to the Philistines.[53] But the description of Israel's total defeat, the subsequent hope for restoration, and the concern for Yahweh's reputation suggest the fall of Samaria. Indeed, we might legitimately question whether the view of Yahweh as the only God in vs. 39 could have arisen before that period.[54] In any case, it is clear that this text follows exactly the pattern of the tradition described above, while the remaining units in Ps. 78 have no parallel here.

Eissfeldt argues that Deut. 32:1-43 derives from tribes of the northern kingdom.[55] Even if we must decide that the fall of Samaria is reflected in this unit rather than the defeat of Shiloh, this conclusion seems to be well founded. Even though Israel's idolatry is recognized, the ultimate note of hope for Israel's restitution gives the tradition a pro-Israelite point of view. Moreover, this association suggests that the traditions of the Exodus and Yahweh's aid to Israel in the wilderness are also to be associated with the northern kingdom, confirm-

[51] Wright, p. 52.
[52] von Rad, *Deuteronomium*, p. 142.
[53] Eissfeldt, *Das Lied Moses*, pp. 15 ff.
[54] von Rad, *Deuteronomium*, p. 143.
[55] Eissfeldt, *Das Lied Moses*, pp. 41-42.

ing the conclusion which we drew regarding this tradition in
Exod. 32. In Ps. 78 the same conclusion would obtain. The
people who receive Yahweh's aid in the wilderness are considered the ancestors of the northern kingdom. It thus presents
no difficulty when the term "Israel" is used to describe the
object of punishment for northern idolatry. The name in this
case refers to the northern kingdom.

In vss. 17 ff. of Ps. 78, we meet the rebellion of the wilderness generation (ביצה) for the first time. But the problems
are compounded in this section by the expression ויוסיפו
עוד. We might assume that the point of reference here is the
transgression of the Ephraimites in vs. 9.[56] But if this were
the case, we would have a puzzling anachronism, for the
transgression of the Ephraimites is associated with the conquest and thus cannot provide a chronological antecedent for
the history of rebellion in the wilderness. It seems probable,
then, that the first two words in vs. 17 must remain obscure
(but cf. vs. 8).

Vs. 18 shows that the current problem of rebellion concerns the request for food. We might have expected a reference to the rebellion at the springs in conjunction with this
request. But there is none. Indeed, the only references to the
spring tradition in the entire psalm are in vss. 15-16 and vs.
20a. Vs. 20a is a part of this unit and presupposes that the
event at the spring has already occurred. But it reveals no
evidence to determine whether that event must be considered
a part of the rebellion tradition. Insofar as the present form
of the psalm is concerned, it can only be a reference to vss.
15-16. But those verses are a part of the positive tradition
of Yahweh's aid. Does this mean that the spring traditions,
at this point in their history, had not been reinterpreted
in terms of rebellion? Or does it mean simply that the negative interpretation of the spring is missing here? The latter
seems more likely. This is not to imply that some original part
of the psalm which recounted Israel's rebellion at the spring

[56] Emilie Briggs, *The Book of Psalms, ICC* (5th printing; Edinburgh:
T and T Clark, 1952), p. 184.

has been dropped in the process of redaction. It only suggests that the formal construction of vs. 17 presupposes the tradition of rebellion at the springs and thus provides a loose connection between the present unit and the positive view of the spring in vss. 15-16. This is supported in vs. 18 by the reference to the people's rebellion with the verb וינסו, a characteristic which recalls the deuteronomistic tradition of Massah. Thus the negative motif begins where the positive motif ends.

What is the nature of the rebellion here? And specifically, what is the relationship between this view of rebellion arising out of the demand for food and the miracle of water from the rock in vss. 15-16? The subject of the verbs in this section is not explicitly defined. But from the context and the plural suffixes in vss. 12-16, we may infer that the subject is the people of Israel who lived in the wilderness (thus, בציה in vs. 17). The object is defined in this section by various names. Most of these are general terms for a deity, אלהים and אל. יהוה appears in vs. 21, but no unusual significance can be attributed to it. The only name which demands our attention is אל־עליון (vs. 35), or simply עליון (vs. 17). It has been established that עליון and אל were originally names for quite distinct deities.[57] It has also been argued that in the Old Testament עליון was combined with אל and associated with יהוה or אלהים in an attempt to identify אל עליון with the deity of Israel.[58] But under what conditions would an assimilation of that sort have been made? H. Schmid has attempted to answer this question by suggesting that עליון was the deity venerated in Jerusalem before David captured the city.[59] When the city was incorporated into David's empire,

---

[57] Marvin Pope, *El in the Ugaritic Texts, VT Sup.* ii (Leiden: E. J. Brill, 1955), 55 ff. O. Eissfeldt, "El and Yahweh," *JSS* I (1956), 25-37, has argued that עליון is the head of a pantheon of gods, of which Yahweh was one. This would explain the use of עליון in Deut. 32:8 which apparently shows this deity giving Yahweh the people of Israel as his inheritance.

[58] G. L. Della Vida, "El 'Elyon in Genesis 14:18-20," *JBL* LXIII (1944), 1-9.

[59] H. Schmid, "Jahwe und die Kulttraditionen von Jerusalem," *ZAW* LXVII (1955), 175. Cf. also Kraus, *Psalmen,* pp. 197 ff.

the existing cultic order was not destroyed but assimilated into the Israelite structure.[60] As a result, the Jerusalemite עליון became an epithet for Israel's deity. If this is indeed the case, it is significant that this psalm holds the object of Israel's rebellion in the wilderness to be עליון, for it would then give us still another point of contact between the murmuring tradition and its use in Jerusalem (cf. Num. 21:4-9).

The verbs which describe the rebellion here are varied. חטא, a general term for sin, is used elsewhere in the context of the wilderness, but those texts are either late or associated with unusual events such as the festival of the Golden Calf. We can, therefore, learn little about the rebellion from this verb. מרה connotes an open rebellion and has been used on occasion as a synonym for לון (Num. 14:9). But it does not give us a firm grasp of the nature of the rebellion which is represented here. The insight which we seek is provided only in vs. 18. The verb controlling this verse is נסה, with אל as the direct object. The connotation of this verb as a sign of distrust and thus unfaith has been noted above as a common characteristic of deuteronomistic material. This is precisely the connotation here (cf. vs. 22). The act described by the verb is the request for food. Vss. 19 ff. show that in keeping with the verb נסה, the test is posed in terms of alternatives. God had given them water. Can he or can he not deliver bread and meat?

The rebellion over the food in this unit is not the kind of rebellion which was encountered in the Pentateuch. It presupposes a connected account of the wilderness traditions since it is dependent on the previous gift of water. The requests for bread and meat are combined and treated as one event of rebellion (cf. Exod. 16 [P]). And the one request is no longer simply the setting for a rebellion over the problem of the Exodus. The accusing question is never raised.[61] In contradistinction to the original form of the positive request for and gift of the food, the total weight of the re-

---

[60] Cf. also Rowley, pp. 113 ff.

[61] The people do not ask: "Why has Yahweh not given us bread and meat?" but: "Is he able to give us bread and meat?"

bellion now rests on the distrusting request. It seems likely, therefore, that if this unit is related to the murmuring tradition, it is a late development of that tradition along the lines of specialized interests. Because of the deuteronomistic characteristics in the remaining parts of the unit, this development and these interests should also be attributed to a deuteronomistic point of view.

But is this to be related to the murmuring tradition as we have known it in the Pentateuch? Or is it a version of the people's rebellion in the wilderness which is independent of the murmuring? The answer to this question can be determined on the basis of vss. 21-31, Yahweh's response to the testing. Vs. 21 notes only that Yahweh's anger was roused over the incident. The phrase ואש נשקה ביעקב is nothing more in this statement than a parallel expression to vs. 21b; both are intended to amplify the notation in vs. 21a that Yahweh heard and was angry. Vss. 23 ff. seem to lose contact with the notion that Yahweh was angry. There is no particle to indicate a conscious contrast or transition. The sentence is connected with the previous verse only by means of a *waw* consecutive imperfect. The people fall into the background as recipients of God's gifts. There is some contact between this recitation and the Pentateuch, such as the name מן (JP), the figure of the manna falling as rain (P), the appearance of the quail by means of a wind (J), the number of the quail (JP), the location in the camp (P). But the figures of the doors of heaven, the grain of heaven, and the food of the mighty are not present in the Pentateuch. There is obviously some relationship here, a relationship which appears to be closer to P than to J. If, however, we were to speak of an influence from P here, we would be forced to recognize that much of the tradition in P is older than the P document itself. And we would also need to take the points of difference into consideration. It seems more likely, therefore, that again the similarities between the psalm and the Pentateuch reflect a common tradition behind both. And at this point, that tradition is apparently Yahweh's aid in the wilderness.

On the other hand, vs. 29 presents a somewhat different

picture. The word וחאותם, which refers to the desire of the people for meat, recalls the narrative of the quail in Num. 11. It is commonly assumed that this word expresses the epitome of Israel's sin, the reason for the punishment which follows.[62] But this is not the case. Vs. 29 uses the word only in reference to that which Yahweh gave the people, while vs. 30 notes simply that the execution began before the desire was completely satisfied. In no sense does the context demand that the word be interpreted negatively (cf. above, pp. 110-11). Indeed, the original request for the food (vss. 19-20) has no connotations of *inordinate* desire which might motivate punishment. Quite the contrary, the sin of the people lies in the fact that by means of their request they *tested* Yahweh. And the testing is clearly the cause of the punishment.

The desire in these verses alludes to the connection of the quail narrative with the locality קברות התאוה. We have shown above that even though there is no direct relationship between the locality and the murmuring, the combination of the motif of desire with the quail narrative presupposes that the murmuring is already present. Thus it is clear that the murmuring tradition does in fact lie behind this unit.

Vs. 30*b* is probably an allusion to the expression in Num. 11:33 (J). But there is a significant change. The reference is no longer to meat, בשר, but to food, אכלה. Since this verse is the conclusion not just for the quail tradition but for both the quail and the manna, the change clearly reflects the combination of the two. This would support our thesis that the sin here is not the desire for meat but the testing by asking for food (vs. 18). But it would also show that this reflection of the murmuring tradition is not directly dependent on the J form of the tradition but exhibits the influence which we have labeled deuteronomistic.

It is striking that this development in the murmuring tradition is apparently directly dependent on the positive tradition of Yahweh's aid, both in the gift of the food and in

---

[62] Weiser, *Psalms*, p. 541; Kraus, *Psalmen*, p. 545.

the miracle of the spring from the rock. This observation suggests two points about the history of the tradition: (1) Both the positive and the negative traditions continued to live side by side. The murmuring did not displace the tradition of aid. This is shown in Deut. 8–9; Ps. 105; Neh. 9; Acts 7:36 ff.; 13:18; even the *Manual of Discipline* from the Dead Sea Scrolls indicates that the negative and the positive traditions were maintained together. (2) The negative tradition was not static. Not only did it develop from its own roots, as we see in P, but new and different interests were introduced into it from the deuteronomistic circles. But of more importance for the moment is the fact that the positive tradition continued to exert an influence on it as well.

Vss. 32-41 impose the deuteronomistic pattern of history on the rebellion motif, and the result is an interesting combination of contradictions. Vs. 32 notes that even in view of the slaughter which the people suffered for their testing (vs. 31), they continued to sin. The result of their continued rebellion is shown in vs. 33: The people are to die. It is possible that this verse presupposes the tradition concerning the punishment of the people by exclusion from the land.[63] It is clear that vs. 33*b* connotes an absolute judgment. The suffixes in both vs. 33*a* and vs. 33*b* refer to the whole people, while the "completion" (ויכל) of their days and years in terror can only refer to their execution over a long period of time. In vs. 34, the verb הרג would support the notion of an absolute punishment. Yet there is no specific reference to the spy report or the denial of the right to see the land. Our conclusion here is to agree that some allusion to the spy tradition is to be seen, but we must proceed with caution.

Vs. 34 is contradictory. The perfect form of the verb הרג would assume that the slaughter of the people had been completed. Yet despite their death, they repented. Only once before have we met the motif of Israel's repentance in the context of the murmuring tradition (Num. 21:4-9). But there it was not so much a part of the murmuring tradition as a

means for connecting a summarized form of the murmuring
with the aetiology for the bronze serpent. Since it does not
otherwise play a role in the murmuring tradition, we may
assume that its presence here is due to the deuteronomistic
character of the unit.

Vss. 36-37 show that the repentance was not sincere; the
people continue in the same kind of sin (cf. vs. 37b). But
whereas this action has previously been met with a grave pen-
alty, apparently absolute in nature, here God responds with
forgiveness and refuses to destroy them. And the forgiveness is not even based on Israel's sincere repentance. The
role of forgiveness in the murmuring tradition has already
been discussed. This contradictory character would confirm the impression that it is not an original part of the
tradition. Thus we must conclude that along with repentance,
forgiveness here represents an emphasis of the deuteronomistic
form of the tradition.

Vss. 40-41 seem to be a summary statement of what the rebellion tradition has been here. But if this unit is a summary
of the rebellion, does that imply that it is the deuteronomistic conclusion to the recitation of the rebellion history?
There is neither an indication of forgiveness nor an announcement of punishment. The unit seems to be incomplete.
We must hold this question for a moment.

We have suggested above that vss. 67-72 do not form
a satisfactory continuation for vss. 65-66. What, then, is the
role of this unit? The verb מאס has been used previously in
the psalm (vs. 59b) to describe Yahweh's reaction to Israel's
idolatry. The consequence of this rejection is apparently the
fall of Samaria. But Yahweh's rejection of Israel is tempered
in vss. 65-66 with the hope that the people could eventually
be restored.

The rejection in vss. 67 ff. is, however, quite different. The
fact that אהל יוסף is set in parallel to שבט אפרים in vs. 67b
shows that the same entity is intended. This identifies the
object of the verse with the people of Israel in vs. 59, i.e., the
northern kingdom. To this extent, the two sections correspond. But vs. 67b introduces a new element with the verb

בחר. Vriezen has argued that with the exception of the use of this verb in reference to the election of the king, its use in describing the relationship of Yahweh to Israel is deuteronomistic.[64] Here it refers to the tribe of Ephraim, but in a negative sense. It is repeated in vs. 68 with two objects, שבט יהודה and הר ציון. The parallelism here suggests that the election of Judah is closely associated, if not identified, with the election of Zion. Vs. 70 then uses the same verb with reference to David. And it is clear that the election of David as king, accompanied by the election of Zion, is the dominant factor in this series of occurrences of בחר. It does not appear necessary, then, to describe this unit as deuteronomistic on the basis of this word. And the absence of deuteronomistic characteristics which have been so prevalent elsewhere in this psalm supports this conclusion.

What, then, is the character of the unit? Ephraim is rejected; she is not elected. Instead, Judah is elected. The judgment on Ephraim is never repealed. The election of Judah does not serve this function. If that were the case, why would the formulation not be composed in terms of Judah assuming the right of the election which Israel had previously enjoyed? The formulation is instead hostile to the northern kingdom. Ephraim's election is not lost or assumed by a succeeding power. It is rejected. In its place, the election of Judah and Zion is established as a new event. There would be no reason to develop or promulgate a hostile polemic against the northern kingdom after the fall of Samaria. It seems more likely that the expression reflects an attempt on the part of Judah to undercut the basis for Israel's claim for the election. And this intent would presuppose the existence of the northern kingdom.[65]

It is in this context that Eissfeldt's conclusions concerning

---

[64] Theodorus C. Vriezen, *Die Erwählung Israels nach dem Alten Testament*, *ATANT* XXIV (Zürich: Zwingli-Verlag, 1953), 47. Cf. also Koch, p. 213.

[65] Schildenberger, pp. 234-35, suggests that this unit is intended to explain why the election of Israel dropped out of the picture after the fall of Samaria.

the origin and purpose of the psalm are most relevant.[66] According to his view, the setting for the psalm, in contradistinction to Deut. 32:1-43, is Jerusalem.[67] Its purpose was to show how and why the leadership of Israel passed from Ephraim and Shiloh to Judah and Zion.[68] But he does not take the hostile attitude toward the north into consideration. Ephraim had lost the ark, and without it Shiloh never returned to its former glory. But this does not mean that the northern tribes relinquished leadership to Judah. It was only after Saul had been defeated at Gilboa and the shaky kingship of Eshbaal had collapsed that the elders of Israel approached David to offer him the kingship. But even this failed to subjugate Israel to Judah. This is shown most clearly by the rebellion of Sheba (II Sam. 20). The battle cry which appears both here and at the rebellion of Jeroboam (I Kings 12) must represent a continuing underlying dissatisfaction with the leadership of the Davidic dynasty and Jerusalem. There is no simple shift of leadership here but a hostile conflict over the right of the two kingdoms.

Moreover, the psalm cuts beyond questions of leadership to the religious foundation of the two states. The purpose of Jeroboam's calves in Dan and Bethel was to show his people that Jerusalem had no valid claim to the traditions of Yahweh's election of Israel in the Exodus, i.e., that only in Dan and Bethel could the God of the Exodus be worshiped. We may conclude in the same manner that this psalm, and especially vss. 67-72, is a polemic against Ephraim designed to show that Yahweh had rejected Israel and the form of election expressed through the Exodus.[69] The corollary to the rejection is that only in Zion could the legitimate wor-

---

[66] Eissfeldt, *Das Lied Moses,* pp. 35 ff.

[67] We agree that the setting, at least for vss. 67-72, would be Jerusalem. Weiser, *Psalms,* pp. 538 ff., places the psalm in the Temple cult, recited probably by a priest "in connection with the tradition of the Covenant Festival." We have nothing against this conclusion.

[68] Cf. also Weiser, *Psalms,* p. 540.

[69] We must agree with Eissfeldt that this polemic reflects the interests of the Jerusalem cult. A more precise definition of its *Sitz-im-Leben* cannot be offered here. Cf. Kraus, *Psalmen,* pp. 540-41.

ship of Yahweh be found and only in Judah (or David?) could the rightful heir to his election be seen.

The date for the polemic would probably be centered in the divided monarchy since David and Solomon must have been concerned not to antagonize differences more than necessary. But in view of the rebellion of Sheba, the strong response which David gave to the rebellion, the apparent oppression of the north in the time of Solomon, and the utter disregard for these differences under Rehoboam, it is not impossible to suppose with Eissfeldt that it reflects an earlier period.[70] In any case, it would appear to be pre-deuteronomistic.

But if this unit is older and not directly related to vss. 17-41, and contradictory in setting and purpose to vss. 42-66, what is its function in the psalm? Where did it come from? The pattern of tradition reflected here is identical to the one described in the pentateuchal form of the murmuring tradition. Israel, i.e., the northern kingdom, has been rejected. Rejection means reversing the election, and, especially in the north, election refers to the Exodus. The rejection is absolute, but it has a pro-Judean flavor. Yet even this favored position is dominated by one man who, interestingly enough, bears the title of Yahweh's servant (עבדו). Since this unit apparently corresponds at every point to the form of the murmuring in the Pentateuch, we conclude that it has been taken into the psalm as a part of the tradition which lies behind vss. 17-41. It would, in fact, be the concluding announcement of judgment anticipated in that unit. It is thus remarkable that these verses, contrary to vss. 17-41, have been left unaltered by the deuteronomistic tendency to emphasize the long-suffering patience of Yahweh.[71]

---

[70] Eissfeldt, *Das Lied Moses*, pp. 36-37. However, we must agree with Schildenberger, p. 232, that the argument for a date before the division of the kingdom on the basis of silence about the event is weak.

[71] It is difficult to define an order of murmuring events in the Pentateuch because of the amount of material intervening between units and lack of evidence that one is dependent on the other. If an order were suggested, however, it would appear in the following sequence: J—Event at the Sea (Exod. 14), Spring tradition (Exod. 15, 17), [Golden Calf (Exod.

Before summarizing the results of our exegesis, we must consider briefly the contribution of this psalm to our understanding of the history of the murmuring tradition. We noted above that a probable *terminus ad quem* for the tradition is the fall of the northern kingdom, or at least a pre-Deuteronomic period.[72] This date corresponds well with the pre-deuteronomistic character of the unit in vss. 67-72. A *terminus a quo* for the tradition has not yet been established. We did suggest, however, that nothing prohibits the assumption that the murmuring and the tensions created by it were already in the traditions received by the Yahwist.[73] Since the murmuring was used in Ps. 78 as a polemic against the northern state and particularly against northern election theology, it seems probable that a *terminus a quo* might be set at least in the conflict between Jeroboam and Rehoboam. If so, we would be forced to conclude that the murmuring tradition was added to the J source after its initial creation during the reign of Solomon.[74] But it is possible that at least the polemic in vss. 67-72 is earlier than the division of the Davidic kingdom, perhaps reflecting a date as early as David himself.[75] If this

---

32)], Manna and Quail (Num. 11), Spy Narrative (Num. 13–14), [Dathan-Abiram (Num. 16)]. P—Event at the Sea (Exod. 14), Manna and Quail (Exod. 16), [Nadab-Abihu, (Lev. 10)], [Miriam-Aaron (Num. 12)], Spy Narrative (Num. 13–14), [Korah (Num. 16–17)], Spring Narrative (Num. 20). In comparison, Ps. 78 offers a much stronger impression of successive events. The following order is present here: Event at the Sea (vs. 13), Spring (vss. 15-16), Manna and Quail (vss. 17 ff.), Spy Tradition (vs. 33). This corresponds with the order in J. But we do not intend to suggest that the psalm is dependent on the J source. Instead, the following two conclusions may be noted: (1) Whereas the events in J compose the span of the murmuring tradition, here at least two of the events are in positive form. This suggests that the order was already present in the tradition which the murmuring reinterpreted. Thus there could be no argument for an interrelated, independent order among the events of murmuring. (2) There is therefore no basis for suggesting that the order in the murmuring implies a forgiveness from Yahweh that functions as a transition from one event of murmuring to the next; i.e., we could not conclude that each successive event of murmuring implies that Yahweh must have forgiven the previous rebellion.

[72] Cf. above, p. 123.
[73] Cf. above, p. 181.
[74] Cf. above, p. 181, n. 94.
[75] Cf. above, p. 220.

should be the case, then the *terminus a quo* for the murmuring would be in the reign of David. And its assimilation with confessions of Yahweh's aid in the wilderness could antedate the creation of the Yahwistic strand during the reign of Solomon. The apparent conflict between the north and the south already in existence during the reign of David would support a *terminus a quo* in the Davidic period.[76]

Is it possible, then, to suggest that the *terminus a quo* for our tradition antedates the Davidic kingship? We noted above a probable date for the Dathan-Abiram narrative in the pre-monarchial period.[77] But the motif does not exhibit the same lines found in the stereotyped pattern of the murmuring tradition seen at other places in the Pentateuch. Since that stereotyped pattern so closely corresponds to the polemic in Ps. 78:67-72, we are now prepared to suggest that the murmuring tradition was originally formulated to express that polemic. The *terminus a quo* would thus be limited to the introduction of the Davidic covenant, for the polemic in Ps. 78 contrasts the northern election theology with the choice of David and Zion.

The setting for the murmuring seems to have been consistently the Jerusalem Temple cult. The close relationship between the murmuring and recitation of the *Heilsgeschichte* suggests that the worshiper may have been responsible for maintaining and spreading the tradition. The purpose of his participation in this manner would be recognition of Davidic claims to election vis-à-vis the traditional views expressed in the cultic centers at Dan and Bethel. That popular recognition was necessary for the success of the dynasty is seen in

[76] Cf. above, p. 220. George E. Mendenhall, *Law and Covenant in Israel and the Ancient Near East,* reprinted from *BA* XVII/2 (May, 1954), 26-46, and XVII/3 (Sept., 1954), 49-76, by The Biblical Colloquium (Pittsburgh, 1955), p. 46, argues that the concept of covenant guaranteeing Davidic kingship was accepted in the south but not in the north. The conflict would thus have a theological character along with its political thrust. G. von Rad, *Theology* I, 40, observes that the concept of kingship developed under David produced strained relationships with central traditions of Israel's faith "from the beginning." Cf. also Albrecht Alt, "Das Königtum in den Reichen Israel und Juda," *VT* I (1951), 2-22.

[77] Cf. above, p. 178.

the king's heavy dependence on the support of his people (cf. II Sam. 15:1 ff.; 19:40 ff.; II Kings 11:13; Prov. 14:28).

But the tradition is so closely tied to the cult in the Temple and reflects such a sophisticated degree of theological construction that the primary source of responsibility for its creation and spread should probably be attributed to cultic personnel. Since we have seen no clear evidence to point to the cultic prophets as the ones who gave their particular stamp to its form, we should probably conclude that Temple priests were responsible for its formulation.[78] The priests would have reinterpreted the tradition of Yahweh's aid to the people in the wilderness, which already had connected form, in order to show that the election expressed through the Exodus was no longer valid and that in its place, Yahweh had chosen David. But what occasion in the cultic festivals of the Temple might have given this tradition its *Sitz-im-Leben*? The most obvious answer to this question would be a covenant renewal festival. Kraus has shown that the festival for celebrating the election of Zion was associated with the Feast of Tabernacles, probably the central event for the first day of the week-long festivities.[79] The murmuring tradition should probably be considered a part of the ritual for that celebration.

In summary: This psalm is composed of a twofold introduction and at least three different units of tradition. Vss. 9-16 and 44-66 have roots in the positive tradition of Yahweh's aid to Israel in the wilderness and the negative element of Israel's idolatry in the land. The idolatry results in punishment for Israel, probably the fall of Samaria, or perhaps the earlier fall of Shiloh. But the fall is not viewed as absolute. The unit in vss. 17-41 has its roots in the murmuring tradition as it is known in the Pentateuch, but reflects a peculiar interpreta-

---

[78] Cf. von Rad, *Theology* I, 245.
[79] Kraus, *Gottesdienst in Israel*, p. 218. He also suggests (p. 82) that the fall festival reflected in Hos. 12:10 was intended to celebrate (*vergegenwärtigen*) the Exodus. This observation recalls the fact that the northern fall festival was instituted (or reinstituted) by Jeroboam in conjunction with his polemic against the southern kingdom (I Kings 12:32. Cf. the Excursus).

tion of this tradition which can be attributed to the Deuteronomist. This is characterized by the view of Israel's rebellion
as a test of God's ability to provide food rather than the desire
to return to Egypt and the introduction of the concept of
Yahweh's repeated forgiveness in spite of Israel's repeated sin.
The final unit, vss. 67-72, corresponds with the murmuring
tradition as it appears in the Pentateuch and must be considered a part of that tradition, untouched by the Deuteronomist. Indeed, it seems most likely that the polemic of this
unit reflects the stimulus which gave rise to the murmuring
tradition itself. The combination of these three units of tradition to form the present psalm points to a post-deuteronomistic date. That both the positive and negative views of the
wilderness come together here shows that at this time (after
the fall of the northern kingdom) they were maintained in
the same setting.

Psalm 106

This psalm also presents a mixture of formal types. The
principal section is again a recitation of Israel's history (vss.
7-46) and thus reflects a formal relationship with Ps. 78. The
remaining verses, which compose a framework for the recitation, contain a complex of formal elements. Vs. 1 is a call to
thanksgiving, vs. 2 is characteristic of a hymn of praise, and
vs. 3 can be described as a blessing.[80] Vss. 4-5 and vs. 47 are
from a lament, and vs. 6 can be understood as the introduction
to a confession of sins (cf. Jer. 3:25; Lam. 3:42; Neh. 9:33).[81]
Since these verses are connected immediately to the recitation
of history and the history recounts Israel's record of sin and
rebellion, we may conclude that in this psalm the recitation
is to be understood as the basis for a cultic liturgy of repentance. The generation that recites the rebellion history feels
itself equally as responsible for the sins of the fathers as the
fathers were.

[80] Kraus, *Psalmen*, p. 728.
[81] Gunkel, pp. 464-65; Kraus, *Psalmen*, p. 727. Duhm, pp. 382-83, 388,
sees these verses as a secondary addition to the psalm, a later attempt to
give the historical section a proper introduction.

A strong relationship between the recitation of history and the pentateuchal sources is generally recognized here. "Man hat mit Recht immer wieder betont, dass dieses Mittelstück von der abgeschlossenen Pentateucherzählung doch wohl auch literarisch abhängig ist. Stärker als Pss. 78, 105 und 136 lehnt sich Ps. 106 an die kanonische Fassung des Pentateuch an." [82] This conclusion would imply a late date. It seems certain enough that at least the Exile is reflected (cf. vss. 40 ff.) ,[83] but many scholars are willing to see the post-exilic diaspora in vss. 27-47.[84] But we must recognize again, as in Ps. 78, that a particular date for a psalm does not obviate an early date for traditions reflected in the psalm. We shall return to the question of date after an examination of the central section.

The difficulties in the central section begin in vs. 7. The subject of the verbs in this verse is the Exodus generation. They are accused of forgetting the mighty acts of Yahweh (so, חסדיך and נפלאותיך) while they were *in Egypt*. To be sure, the Israelites were not able to believe the announcement of their coming salvation because of their oppression and discouragement (Exod. 5:20 ff.; 6:9; cf. also 4:1, 8). But this is hardly to be considered forgetting the acts of Yahweh, much less a part of the rebellion tradition (cf. Appendix I). The problem here is that the deeds of Yahweh in Egypt ordinarily refer to the plagues (Ps. 78:11, 43). But since the plagues are associated with the preparation for the Exodus, how could the fathers forget them *in Egypt*? The problem is intensified by the juxtaposition of forgetting with the event at the Sea (vs. 7b). According to this formulation, the events which are forgotten must lie before the Exodus.

There is, however, no evidence which would enable us to determine what those events might have been (but cf. Deut. 32:7 ff.). Possibly the reference to forgetting the acts of God must be considered a stylized expression, perhaps a reference to an act of idolatry. However, there is no indication in the Pentateuch that the Israelites were involved in idolatry while

[82] Kraus, *Psalmen*, pp. 727-28.
[83] But cf. Weiser, *Psalms*, p. 680.
[84] Kraus, *Psalmen*, pp. 727-28; Gunkel, p. 464; Kittel, p. 388.

they were still in Egypt (but cf. Josh. 24:14; Ezek. 20:7-8).
It may be that these allusions reflect a tradition that simply
does not appear in the pentateuchal material which we have.
The fact that vs. 7a, like vss. 4 ff., addresses Yahweh in the
second person, while vss. 8 ff. speak of him in the third person,
would support the notion that a different tradition has been
combined with the rebellion history. But without evidence
of such a tradition, the argument is weak. There is another
possibility for resolving the problem: We have noted that
P exhibits a tendency to broaden the wilderness rebellion at
all possible points. Is it not possible that the reflection of
Israel's sin in Egypt has its roots in a similar broadening?

Vss. 8-12 recount the miracle at the Sea.[85] Vs. 8a contains
a statement which recalls the theological perspective of the
Deuteronomist in the prayers of intercession: ויושיעם למען שמו
(cf. Exod. 32:12; Num. 14:15-16, esp. the LXX form of this
verse, and Deut. 9:25 ff.). The event at the Sea is the means
for his self-revelation, the manner by which he makes himself known not just to Israel but to the nations (thus, vs. 8b).
The event itself presupposes contact with the theme of Yahweh's leadership in the wilderness. In vs. 9b, כמדבר is not intended as a comparison for בתהמות; the contrast between the
depths of the water and the arid wilderness would present a
curiously incongruous picture. But, we might protest, the
comparison refers to the dry ground which was left when the
waters were removed. In Exod. 14:22 we note that the people
were led through the sea ביבשה. But this does not carry the
connotation of waste land which would be implied by מדבר
(cf. Gen. 1:9). In the light of our agrument concerning the
relationship of the Reed Sea tradition with the tradition of
Yahweh's aid in the wilderness, it seems to be more than
accidental that the simile employs the term מדבר to describe
Yahweh's leading the people through the water. We might,
then, propose that the comparison refers to both of the preceding words: "He led them through the deep as (he led

---

[85] Weiser, *Psalms*, p. 681, suggests that "there can be no question of
a direct literary dependence by the psalm on the Pentateuch; both of
them seem to originate in a common cultic, liturgical tradition."

them) through the [the word is definite] wilderness." Moreover, with the exception of vs. 7b, the account of the miracle
at the Sea is quite positive. With Yahweh as the subject of
the verbs, the section recounts what he did. Even vs. 12, with
the people as the subject, is positive. In response to Yahweh's
act, they believed and sang praises (cf. Exod. 14:31). It seems
clear, then, that the juxtaposition of the positive tradition of
Yahweh's aid with the notation in vs. 7b that Israel rebelled
reflects the same kind of growth in the wilderness traditions
which we have seen above.

Vss. 13 ff. represent the rebellion over the problem of food.
There is no evidence of the positive motif here. Instead, vs.
13 gives the impression of a conscious transition from Israel's
positive response in vs. 12 to the problem of her sin. This
reversal clearly reflects the pattern of the Deuteronomist.[86]
The sin has no contact with the desire on the part of the
people to return to Egypt. It is introduced simply with the
motif which first appeared in vs. 7: "They quickly forgot his
works. They did not pay heed to his counsel."[87] The meaning
of the phrase, "to forget his works," is clear in this instance:
Israel demands food. But how did the phrase enter the tradition? The people have never before been accused of forgetting
God's works when they presented their demands for food. Vs.
14a presupposes the connection of the murmuring over quail
with the locality קברות התאוה, while vs. 14b reflects a rein-
pretation of Israel's request in terms of testing similar to the
one noted in Ps. 78:18 ff. But in contrast to Ps. 78, this psalm
does not emphasize the testing. The murmuring and the testing are aligned in parallel and carry the same weight.

Vss. 16-18 compose the only witness to the Dathan-Abiram
tradition in the Psalter; indeed, the only other references to
the pair outside the narrative in Num. 16 come in Num. 26:9,
a late text, and Deut. 11:6. This fact would support the

[86] Kraus, *Psalmen*, p. 729.
[87] We note in contrast to vs. 7a that the noun מעשׂיו carries a third
person suffix. But the significance of this fact cannot be more than an
indication of the complex nature of the traditions which compose the
psalm.

thesis that the psalm tends to be all-inclusive in its description of Israel's sin.

In vss. 19-23 we find one of the few references to the Sinai traditions in the context of a recitation of Israel's classical period that appear in the Old Testament.[88] Even though it is impossible to define a connection between this tradition and the rebellion in the wilderness, the unit nevertheless demands our attention. It is significant first that the name חרב is used. This name is classically attributed to the E source of the Pentateuch, but it also appears in Deut. 9:8. Moreover, the calf (singular) is considered the object of worship, a replacement for Yahweh (vs. 20a); it is thus clearly an idol (vs. 19b, cf. Deut. 4:16; 9:12). This act of idolatry is also associated with forgetting God and his works. Since the forgetting carries heavy emphasis here (vss. 21-22) and is thus not in itself the result of broadening the tradition of the calf, it could be considered the source which accounts for this motif elsewhere in the psalm (but cf. also Ezek. 20). The fact that neither this unit nor the reference to forgetting the works of God in Egypt and in the request for food appears in Ps. 78 would support this possibility. Vs. 23 refers to Moses' intercession on behalf of the people; had this not been done, the wrath of Yahweh would have completely destroyed the people. This also corresponds closely with the tradition in Deut. 9:25 ff.

Vss. 24-27 contain a reference to the spies' report. It is significant in the light of our argument about the rejection of Israel's election that here her rebellion involves rejection of the promised land.[89] Vs. 25a is directly related to the spy tradition in Deuteronomy (cf. the use of רגן in Deut. 1:27). The punishment in vs. 26 is in accord with Deut. 1:34 and Num. 14:20 ff., even to the motif of the oath. The character of the punishment is absolute—that generation will fall in the wilderness. Their descendents escape this sentence, but their

---

[88] von Rad, *Das formgeschichtliche Problem,* p. 49. Cf. also Neh. 9. This would be another point in support of the view that the psalm incorporates a broader perspective of Israel's rebellion.

[89] It is thus significant that the punishment in Num. 14 denies the rebels' right to see the land.

fate is also announced. They are to be dispersed among the nations (vs. 27). Many scholars feel that this is an allusion to the post-exilic diaspora,[90] but the same allusion in Ezek. 20:23 suggests this conclusion does not necessarily follow. The most that we can say is that the Exile is presupposed.

It is important for our interest in the history of the rebellion tradition to note that the consequences of the rebellion in the wilderness are no longer the rejection of the northern kingdom but the Exile. The reason for the change is understandable: Any conflict between the north and the south which might have given rise to the tradition would have ceased with the fall of Samaria. At this point, the concern would instead be an explanation for the theological problems posed by the Exile. That explanation is based on the belief that the current generation in exile is held responsible for the sins of the fathers (cf. vs. 6). It is therefore significant that at no point in the psalm is there a trace of the anti-Ephraimite or pro-Judean character of the murmuring or the concern to negate the election (of the northern kingdom) by returning to Egypt.

Vss. 28-31 contain a reference to a tradition which does not properly belong to the Wilderness theme, the idolatry of the people at Baal Pe'or. Once again, this section shows the extent of the psalm's inclusive character. In comparison, Ps. 78 does not make the apostasy over the idols in the conquest a part of the tradition of Israel's rebellion in the wilderness. The two are kept strictly apart. It is therefore striking that in Ps. 106 the account of Israel's rebellion at the spring comes *after* the reference to Baal Pe'or (vss. 32-33). It must be admitted that the order of events is nebulous. The spring traditions appear occasionally before and occasionally after the food traditions (cf. Ps. 78; Neh. 9). But the juxtaposition of the food and spring seems to be a constant factor. These traditions are then normally framed by the event at the Sea and the spy report. What, then, is the significance of the break in order in Ps. 106? The key to the problem lies in a comparison of this

---

[90] Cf. above, p. 225.

psalm with the order of events in P, for in the P narrative, the account of the rebellion at Meribah (no reference to Massah or Marah occurs in P) also comes after the spy account. The reason in both cases is clear: The event at the spring is used to explain Moses' failure to enter the land. The concern for an explanation of this fact is already present in Deuteronomy (1:37; 3:26), but it is never associated there with the tradition of the spring at Meribah. This suggests that our psalm, though having much in common with Deuteronomy, is nevertheless a later stage in the development of the tradition, perhaps reflecting a point between Deuteronomy and P.

Vss. 34 ff. return to the Conquest, and the rebellion involved here is idolatry. The punishment announced in vss. 26-27 is brought to fruition in vss. 40-42: Israel is delivered into the hands of the nations. Vs. 43 must be considered a part of the deuteronomistic pattern defined above; vss. 44-45 are also a part of this pattern but represent at the same time the kind of hope for restitution after the Exile which was noticed in Ps. 78:65-66.

In summary, this psalm shows deuteronomistic influence in constructing the events of Israel's rebellion in immediate relationship to Yahweh's forbearance and patience and in its similarity with various traditions in Deuteronomy. The placement of the Meribah tradition and its association with Moses' vicarious exclusion from the land show a closer affinity with P and suggest that the psalm reflects a stage in the history of the rebellion tradition which is later than Deuteronomy. The anti-Ephraimite and pro-Judean flavor is completely missing, and in its place, all the people are held responsible for the rebellion. The unique characteristic of this stage is that as a result of the rebellion *in the wilderness*, the children of that generation are sentenced to exile. Thus the complete rejection of Ephraim in Ps. 78 is exchanged for the total exile of the remaining people of Israel, i.e., Judah. The reason, then, for the lack of an anti-Ephraimite attitude is the fact that Ephraim no longer exists. Moreover, this development presupposes at least that the Exile has already occurred. In this sense, then, we see the significance of the form of this psalm as a cultic prayer of repentance. The people who are now exiled confess the sin of their fathers which has caused their troubles. Thus it is not until the Exile that the rebellion tradition was employed in this particular cultic context.

Ezekiel 20

The formal structure of this chapter can be divided into two sections, vss. 1-31 and vss. 32-44.[91] The first section is composed of an announcement of judgment (vss. 30-31), introduced by לכן and based on a lengthy recitation of Israel's history of rebellion (vss. 4-26). Vss. 27-29 represent an expansion of the unit. The introductory לכן, a commission to address the people of Israel, and a messenger formula suggest that formally the expansion is also to be considered an announcement of judgment (cf. vs. 30aα). But the content extends the history of Israel's rebellion to include the apostasy of Israel *after* the conquest (cf. esp. vs. 28b). It is thus not to be considered a part of the basic unit.[92]

The unit is introduced in vs. 1aα by a specification of date. Vs 1aβb notes the setting: The elders of Israel have come to Ezekiel to inquire of Yahweh and are sitting before him awaiting a reply.[93] Vs. 2 is a typical prophetic formula announcing the event of God's revelation to the prophet (*Wortereignisformel*), while vs. 3aα is Yahweh's commission to Ezekiel to speak to the elders of Israel as his messenger. Vs. 3b is in the form of an oath and connects with the judgment in vss. 30-31 (cf. esp. the oath in vs. 31b). The judgment in both cases is addressed directly to the elders. Vs. 4 is again Yahweh's address to Ezekiel; in the form of a question, Ezekiel is summoned to judge the people (cf. 22:2; 23:36). But he functions in the judgment as messenger (cf. vs. 5); the judgment it-

[91] Walther Zimmerli, *Ezechiel, BKAT* XIII (Neukirchen, Kreis Moers: Neukirchener Verlag, 1956-   ), 438.

[92] *Ibid.*, p. 439.

[93] *Ibid.*, p. 209. Cf. also H. Graf Reventlow, *Wächter über Israel, Ezechiel und seine Tradition, BZAW* LXXXII (Berlin: Alfred Töpelmann, 1962), 77.

self arises from Yahweh. In this text, as well as the parallel
texts in 22:2 and 23:36, the recitation of Israel's sins serves
as a basis for the judgment. In vss. 30 ff., the judgment is
repeated. After a renewed address to Ezekiel with instructions to announce the judgment to the elders (vs. 30aα), vss.
30aβb and 31aα summarize the basis for the judgment. The
basis shows that the current generation is accused of sins
which are identical to the ones of the fathers. But the judgment does not involve a catastrophic event such as the Exile;
it is concerned instead with the elders' right to inquire of
Yahweh.

The current tendency in Ezekiel studies is to consider this
unit a genuine part of the prophet's work.[94] If the date in vs.
1 is to be taken seriously, the unit would be placed in the
seventh year of the exile of King Jehoiakin, i.e., *before* the
fall of the Temple.[95]

The recitation of the rebellion history is divided into three
different sections, the generation of the fathers in Egypt (vss.
5-9), the generation of the fathers in the wilderness (vss. 10-
17), and the generation of the children who followed the
fathers in the wilderness (vss. 18-26).[96] The section concerning the generation in Egypt begins in vs. 5 with a reference
to Israel's election. The verb used to describe this event, בחר,
is common in Deuteronomy, as we have noted.[97] But it is
not an indication of deuteronomistic influence here. Indeed,
this expression of Israel's election has much more in common
with the priestly tradition in Exod. 6.[98] We note especially
the use of term —ואשא ידי ל as a form for an oath (cf. vss.
5a, 5b, 6; Exod. 6:8; Ps. 106:26), the self-revelation of the
divine name (cf. vs. 5; Exod. 6:6), and the emphasis on the

---

[94] Zimmerli, *Ezechiel,* p. 441.

[95] *Ibid.,* p. 441.

[96] W. Zimmerli, "Das Gotteswort des Ezechiel," *ZThK* XLVIII (1951),
253 ff. Georg Fohrer, *Ezechiel,* mit einem Beitrag von Kurt Galling, *HAT*
XIII (Tübingen: J. C. B. Mohr [Paul Siebeck], 1955), 112, sees a fourth
period in the history (vss. 23-31a). Although this section presupposes
the conquest generation, it is nevertheless formulated as judgment on
the second generation in the wilderness.

[97] Cf. above, p. 218, n. 64.

[98] Zimmerli, *Ezechiel,* p. 443.

verb ידע (cf. vs. 5; Exod. 6:7) . The self-revelation of Yahweh's name and the election of Israel are bound closely together and find their confirmation in the Exodus (vs. 6; cf. Exod. 6: 6-7) . They are not, however, purely a gift of grace; a demand is laid on the people in vs. 7 to reject the שקוצי עיניו and the גלולי מצרים, two parallel descriptions of the same entity. The command is followed by the formula אני יהוה אלהיכם; in this case, the formula of self-revelation is to be associated with the use of the same formula in law codes, especially the Holiness Code, as the motivation for obeying the law.⁹⁹

But Israel refuses to follow the command and rebels *in Egypt*. The question which must now be considered is whether Ezekiel is responsible for the reference to Israel's sin in Egypt or whether he is dependent on a tradition which is not heavily attested elsewhere in the Old Testament. The question involves the relationship between Ezekiel, Ps. 106:7, and Josh. 24:14. There is evidence that the ובמצרים in Josh. 24:14 is a secondary addition to the text, for the repetition of the gods whom the fathers served in vs. 15 lists those "on the other side of the river" and the gods of the Amorites but has no reference to the gods of Egypt. There is thus no basis for supposing that this verse is earlier than Ezekiel and evidence for a pre-exilic tradition of Israel's apostasy in Egypt.

The expression in Ps. 106:7 is not explicitly a reference to idols but does describe Israel's sin in Egypt in terms which can be used for idolatry. It may be that the tradition in Ps. 106 is dependent on Ezekiel, especially at this point, for the reference to the idols in Egypt is clearly a genuine part of the prophet's work (cf. also Ezek. 23, where the names אהלה and אהליבה may well reflect the period of the wilderness ¹⁰⁰) . We could then conclude that this view of Egypt reflects the current attitude of the prophet toward the relationship of the remnant in Jerusalem with the Egyptians (cf. 16:26) . But if Ps. 106 can be dated perhaps as early as the Exile and contains the substance of a *community* confession of sin which reflects the current form of the rebellion tradition, would it not seem

⁹⁹ *Ibid.*, p. 445.
¹⁰⁰ *Ibid.*, p. 541.

more likely that Ezekiel draws his material from the cultic form of the tradition? If this should be the case, Ezekiel's stamp on this tradition could be seen only in the explicit statement that the sin was idolatry. We shall return to this question below.

Vs. 8a notes that the Israelites did not obey the command-ment. The first quarter of the verse uses only general terms for this rebellion, but it is significant that one of these is מרה, a verb which is often a part of the rebellion tradition. Yet no conclusions can be drawn from the use of this verb since it appears widely in other parts of Ezekiel. The second quarter is more explicit in saying that the Egyptian idols were not abandoned. The natural reaction to such refusal would be to cancel the election. Vs. 8b falls somewhat short of this but nevertheless expresses an intention for stringent punishment. In fact, we can assume that the consequences of לכלות אפי בהם would be such a rejection.

However, the punishment is not executed (vs. 9). The reason for this leniency is bound up with the tie between the people and the revelation of Yahweh's name (cf. Ps. 106:8). There is some confusion in this statement. Vs. 9 shows by means of a Niph'al perfect form of ידע that the name was made known to the nations by means of the Exodus (להוציאם מארץ מצרים), and it is because of this revelation that Yahweh cannot destroy the people. But the Exodus is not reported in this unit until vs. 10. This would suggest that a secondary expansion of the rebellion tradition has indeed occurred, an expansion which, despite its explicit statement to the contrary, presupposes that Israel's sin was after the Exodus. The same phenomenon is also present in Ps. 106. Moreover, there is no further mention of punishment in this section, recalling the deuteronomistic tendency to emphasize Yahweh's forgiveness in spite of Israel's sin. Yet the emphasis of this unit is not on forgiveness. The repeal of judgment seems to serve only as a transition to the second stage of rebellion. And in that unit, the pattern changes.

The second period begins in vs. 10 with the movement from Egypt to the wilderness. The first motif of importance is a new revelation of laws and commandments, perhaps an allusion to the Sinai traditions.[101] This motif is closely related to the problematic emphasis on the Sabbath in vs. 12. During the Exile, the Sabbath, along with the institution of circumcision, was an important sign for designating the relationship between Yahweh and Israel. Emphasis on the Sabbath is especially strong in the priestly material (cf. e.g., Lev. 23 ff.). But its role in Ezekiel has been questioned.[102] Particularly in Ezek. 20, reference to the Sabbath appears to be only an appendix to the laws and commandments. The fact that elsewhere in Ezekiel the Sabbath plays at best a minor role has led to the suggestion that it is a part of a subsequent priestly exegesis of Ezekiel's work (cf. Neh. 9:14).[103] Thus vs. 13aβ should probably not be considered an indication of anything more than a further expansion of the disobedience in vs. 13aα.

The disobedience in vs. 13aα is once again introduced by the verb מרה. The general character of this verb is defined more explicitly by the following phrase: בחקותי לא־הלכו ואת־משפטי מאסו. If the laws and commandments allude to the Sinai traditions, we may assume that the rejection of those laws and commandments alludes to the principal event of rebellion in the Sinai traditions as well, i.e., to the Golden Calf event (cf. Ps. 106:19).

The reaction to the rebellion here is the same as the one described in vs. 8b; with one important exception, the expressions are identical. The exception comes in the infinitive לכלות.[104] In vs. 8, the object of the infinitive is Yahweh's anger, and we suggested that the completion of his anger implies the rejection of Israel. In this case, the object is expressed by means of a mem suffix which refers to Israel.

[101] Zimmerli, Ezechiel, p. 447.

[102] G. A. Cooke, The Book of Ezekiel, ICC (2nd. printing; Edinburgh: T and T Clark, 1951), pp. 213, 217. Walther Eichrodt, "Der Sabbat bei Hesekiel. Ein Beitrag zur Nachgeschichte des Prophetentextes," Lex Tua Veritas; Festschrift für Hubert Junker, V. Heinrich Gross and F. Mussner, eds. (Trier: Paulinus Verlag, 1961), pp. 65 ff.

[103] Ibid., p. 71.

[104] The addition of במדבר is explicable by virtue of the change in setting.

And the connotation of the infinitive is obviously total an-
nihilation. But in vs. 14, the judgment is again repealed.[105]
To this extent, the pattern corresponds with the first period
of Israel's rebellion.

Vs. 15 introduces a new element of judgment. Despite the
act of clemency, Yahweh denies the right of this generation
to enter the land. This presupposes the judgment which
follows the murmuring in the spy tradition, even to the point
of expressing the judgment by a divine oath. Indeed, if
the emendation of נתתי to תרתי is to be accepted (cf. vs. 6),[106]
we would be clearly within this tradition. To be sure, it would
consider Yahweh himself as the spy rather than the leaders
of the tribes. But this change would offer no great difficulty since a shift between Yahweh as the actor and a human
tool for executing the action is not uncommon in the Old
Testament (cf. Num. 11).

Vs. 16 is again problematic. A part of the reason for the
new punishment has to do with the idols of the people in
the wilderness. But, as we have noted, the wilderness generation is not ordinarily considered idolatrous. This characteristic, then, may also be considered a part of Ezekiel's emphasis
on the problem of idolatry (cf. vs. 30). The remaining elements in the reason for the judgment are the same as those
cited in vs. 13a. We must conclude, therefore, that the only
consequence of Yahweh's clemency is that the people were
not immediately destroyed (vs. 17). It thus plays a corresponding role to Moses' intercession and Yahweh's clemency in
Num. 14.

Vs. 18 moves to the generation of the children. The address
is formulated negatively as an admonition (cf. Ps. 78:8);

---

[105] The way of expressing the repeal is virtually identical to the one
in v. 9. The differences include the longer form of the verb ואעשה and
a shortened form of the אשר clause. The completion of the אשר is in both
cases לעיניהם, while the verb הוצאתים finds its counterpart in vs. 9 in
להוציאם. This correspondence would confirm our conclusion that vs. 9
presupposes the completed event of the Exodus and thus represents a
motif expansion from the second section of the chapter, obviously a
conscious effort to construct the periods of rebellion in identical terms.

[106] Zimmerli, *Ezechiel*, p. 435.

the content of the admonition is that the children should not follow the example of rebellion set by their fathers. This presupposes two points of importance: (1) The children would not be held responsible for the action of their fathers if they should accede to the admonition. This condition would correspond to Ezekiel's emphasis on the responsibility of each generation (or each person) for his sin alone. (2) They would in that case become the heirs to the promised land. This provides the exception to the stringent punishment in vs. 15 that is to be seen in the priestly narrative in Num. 14.

The formula which introduces vs. 19 is obscure; it may be considered either the motive clause for the admonition in vs. 18 or the preface to the commandment which follows in vs. 19.[107] The point of importance here is the fact that the content of the admonition in vs. 18 is transformed into a positive command in vss. 19-20 (cf. vs. 11). The children, however, did not obey the command. In vs. 21, the third period of rebellion is again described by the verb מרה and a specification that the rebellion involved a refusal to obey the commandments (cf. vs. 13a). Vs. 21b records Yahweh's reaction, again the same statement which we have seen in vss. 8b, 13b.

This period of rebellion differs from the murmuring tradition in the Pentateuch, for there is no indication in the Pentateuch that the children should be considered simply a second generation of rebels in the wilderness. Instead, they are the ones who are involved in the *Conquest*. Num. 32:14-15 suggests that this generation, especially Gad and Reuben (cf. vs. 6), may have to die in the wilderness just as their fathers if they should persist in their sin. But the sin has to do with their willingness to fight in the Conquest (Ps. 78:9?). There is no indication that they were involved in the kind of rebellion represented by the murmuring or in any sort of idolatry which might be reflected in Ezekiel. Vs. 22 is the same statement of repeal which has been seen in vss. 9 and

---

[107] *Ibid.*, p. 448.

14.[108] But as with the original wilderness generation, the clemency announced here only means that the people are not immediately destroyed (cf. Num. 32:15). They must still face punishment for their rebellion.

The punishment is introduced in a manner which is parallel to vs. 15; however, in this case it anticipates the Exile of the people into the nations. We have already noted in Ps. 106:26, again with the same form of the oath (וישא ידו להם), that the Exile appears in the context of the wilderness as the punishment for the rebellion. In Ezekiel this view is presupposed (20: 4, 30); but it nevertheless contradicts other points of Ezekiel's theology which defend the notion that each person is responsible only for his own sin (Ezek. 18). Indeed, the announcement of the Exile is not properly the judgment in the unit but only a part of the tradition which is being recited as a basis for the judgment in vss. 30-31: Israel in exile is just as rebellious as Israel in the wilderness. The judgment then holds the exile generation responsible for its own rebellion. And this is much more in keeping with Ezekiel's position expressed in chapter 18. We conclude, then, that the use of the murmuring tradition as an explanation for the tragedy of the Exile is part of popular theology, the state of the rebellion tradition in Ezekiel's day which he simply employs without resolving the tensions between it and his own theology (cf. Ps. 106).

This sentence of exile is followed in vs. 24 with the reason. As in vs. 16, the problem of idolatry is present. But the idolatry here cannot simply be equated with the event at Baal Pe'or. The idols are the idols of the fathers, i.e., the first generation in the wilderness. We have noted above that this emphasis should be considered a part of Ezekiel's own concern with the problems of idolatry.[109]

Thus, in very similar but progressively more intense sec-

---

[108] והשבתי את-ידי does not appear to be an original part of the text. Cf. Zimmerli, *Ezechiel*, p. 435. The remaining differences have been noted above.

[109] Vss. 25-26 involve a particular kind of problem which is unrelated to the murmuring tradition. Cf. Zimmerli, *Ezechiel*, p. 449.

tions, Ezekiel reflects the Exodus, the Wilderness, and the Conquest under the stamp of the murmuring tradition. The construction of this tradition in a threefold pattern with virtually identical forms, and the peculiar emphasis on idolatry seem to be the result of his own creativity. He is nevertheless heavily dependent on the current level of the rebellion tradition, including its use as an explanation for the Exile. It is significant now only to note that, as in Ps. 106, so here there is no trace of the anti-Ephraimite, pro-Judean flavor of the murmuring; it is clear that the problems which gave rise to that polemic, and probably to the whole tradition, no longer exist.

The second half of the chapter is considered an expansion of the basic text in vss. 1-31.[110] But it may nevertheless be held as genuine material. As a word of hope for restoration in contrast to the judgment in the first half of the chapter, it presupposes the fall of Jerusalem and the destruction of the Temple.[111]

Vs. 32 is in the form of a citation from the people, while vss. 33 ff. provide the response to the citation. This is the formal structure of a disputation. Moreover, the response of Yahweh to the citation is in the form of an *Erweiswort,* with a typical formula for Yahweh's self-revelation at the end.[112] Vs. 39 is apparently corrupt. If we may bracket vs. 39aβ as a fragment which does not belong here and restore לכו to read השלכו,[113] then the verse would be an admonition to abandon all idols and cease from profaning the holy name. It would then provide a fitting basis for the *Erweiswort* in vss. 40-42. Vss. 43-44 constitute a third *Erweiswort* and the conclusion of the unit.

Our interest lies only with the disputation. The citation from the people refers to a tendency toward idolatry, i.e., the worship of gods of the people among whom they live. The result of that tendency is a new judgment from Yahweh

[110] *Ibid.,* p. 452.
[111] *Ibid.,* p. 453.
[112] *Ibid.,* p. 452.
[113] *Ibid.,* p. 437.

(cf. vss. 33 ff.). We note especially the addition of a third element to the normally twofold expression ביד חזקה ובזרוע נטויה. The third element is an expression of the wrath of Yahweh: ובחמה שפוכה. But the character of that wrath is not defined. Vs. 34 refers to a return from the Exile, i.e., gathering the people from the nations. Vs. 35 then announces that the people will be taken into the wilderness for judgment.[114] This judgment will be parallel to, and thus reflects, the same tradition of judgment executed for the wilderness generation.

The problem now appears. Does this judgment presuppose the murmuring tradition? The expression in vs. 35 recalls Hos. 2:16. But the same problem of interpretation is present in Hosea as well.[115] In what sense, then, is the judgment in this section of Ezekiel to be interpreted? Vs. 37 is questionable; if מסרת can be taken as a noun from אסר, then we might suppose that the judgment results in a new covenant.[116] Vs. 38 shows that the judgment eliminates rebellious members from the people. At this point, the variation between second person and third person suffixes and verbs is decisive. The rebels are referred to in the third person; as the object of the judgment, they shall be gathered from the lands of their exile but not allowed to return to the land of Israel. To this extent, the judgment can only be considered negative. But this group of rebels is contrasted to the remaining portion of Israel, addressed in the second person. The text is unfortunately silent about the fate of the faithful, but we may well assume that the unit in vss. 39 ff. involves something of the hope for restoration which the remaining faithful could expect. To this extent, then, vss. 32-38 appear to have a positive character.

But still our question remains. What kind of background does this unit presuppose? The murmuring tradition never

---

[114] מדבר העמים is parallel to the מדבר ארץ מצרים in vs. 36 and thus serves the same function for this generation as the מדבר מצרים did for the earlier generation.

[115] Wolff, *Hosea*, pp. 49-50; Talmon, p. 50.

[116] But cf. LXX: ἐν ἀριθμῷ.

shows a concern to purge a group of rebels from the midst
of the people. This pattern suggests instead the Dathan-
Abiram tradition.[117] Since that unit of tradition is not to
be considered an immediate part of the murmuring tradition, we may conclude that Ezek. 20:36 refers to the judgment
of the fathers in the wilderness without implying that the
whole people were rebellious (cf. Deut. 11:1-7). It thus
seems clear that this unit does not reflect the murmuring
tradition but the same kind of attitude toward the wilderness
which we find in Hosea.[118]

In summary: We may conclude that the basic text of Ezekiel
reflects the stamp of the murmuring tradition and gives us
a firm grasp of the characteristics which it bore at the time
of the Exile. The characteristics are basically the same which
were noted for Ps. 106 and P, i.e., a strong tendency to extend
the murmuring as far as possible, a lack of pro-Judean flavor,
and clemency in the punishment by allowing the children
of the rebellious generation to live beyond the initial forty-
years period in the wilderness. It is also characteristic of
this stage in the development of the tradition that the rebellion in the wilderness is used to explain the necessity for
the Exile. The unit shows Ezekiel's own stamp in the threefold uniform cycle of rebellion, the idolatry of the generation
in Egypt and the wilderness, and the supposition that the
children of the wilderness generation would not be punished
for the sins of the fathers. The second section in the chapter
has no contact with the murmuring tradition. Instead, the
basically positive character shows that at the time of Ezekiel
the two elements of the wilderness tradition still existed side
by side.

Nehemiah 9

There is little difficulty in defining the limit and structure
of the unit represented by this chapter. Vs. 1 effectively marks
the beginning with a new date, while vs. 2 heightens the transi-

[117] Zimmerli, *Ezechiel*, p. 456.
[118] But cf. Cooke, p. 221.

tion from chapter 8 by noting that the mood of the assembly, in contrast to the rejoicing in the previous chapter, is now one of repentance. Vs. 3 is problematical. The event described here, the reading of the law, might point to a close connection between this unit and chapter 8. But the verse may not be an original part of the unit.[119] The subject of the verb here is apparently the Israelites of vs. 2. But they would not be the proper readers for such an event. This lapse is perhaps corrected in vss. 4-5 by the introduction of the Levites.[120] The purpose of the insertion would be an effort on the part of a post-Chronicler redactor to show that the law had a place in the ritual of repentance and that the Levites participated through this element. Yet Noth has suggested that the role of the Levites in reading and explaining the law is a principal theme of the Chronicler.[121] As a result, he sees the whole introduction as a unit from the Chronicler himself, thus assuming that the difficulty in the identification of the reader of the law is resolved by vss. 4-5. This hypothesis does not adequately resolve the question, but it seems to be the most probable alternative.

Vs. 5aβ is an admonition addressed in the second person *plural* imperative to the Israelites as a call to praise Yahweh. Vs. 5b is problematic but may be considered simply a call for the beginning of the praise. The praise itself begins in vs. 6.[122] Since the Israelites are directly admonished to praise, there is no reason to assume with the LXX that Ezra alone voices the prayer. Whether it is placed in the mouth of the people or is expressed by representative individuals cannot be determined.

Vss. 7-31 constitute the principal body of the unit, a recitation of Israel's past. These verses form basically a self-

---

[119] Wilhelm Rudolph, *Ezra und Nehemia*, *HAT* XX (Tübingen: J. C. B. Mohr [Paul Siebeck], 1949), 155-56, feels that this verse has been inserted here to provide a secondary connection with chapter 8.

[120] Kurt Galling, *Die Bücher der Chronik, Esra, Nehemia, ATD* XII (Göttingen: Vandenhoeck & Ruprecht, 1954), 239.

[121] Martin Noth, *Überlieferungsgeschichtliche Studien* (2nd ed.; Tübingen: Max Niemeyer Verlag, 1957), p. 148, n. 6.

[122] This corresponds to the hymn of praise in Ps. 106:1-3.

contained unit in the chapter, but can nevertheless be broken into various sub-units on the basis of content. Vss. 7-8 begin the recitation with a reference to the election (בחר) of Abraham.[123] Vss. 9-15 contain references to the events which form the basis for the rebellion tradition: the event at the Sea (vss. 9 ff.), the manna (vs. 15aα), the water (vs. 15aβ), and the instructions to take the land (vs. 15b). But in this case, the tradition is again positive in form, a continuation of the recitation of Yahweh's deeds. In contrast, vss. 16-31 constitute the history of Israel's rebellion. This unit may be broken down into the following subsections: Vss. 16-23 refer to Israel's rebellion in the wilderness and thus constitute the center of our concern. But these verses cannot be separated from vss. 24-31, the report of the Conquest and the apostasy of the people after they gained the wealth and fertility of the land. Vs. 32 is a petition addressed to Yahweh that the current oppression under foreign rule not be forgotten (thus, אל־ימעט). The political consequences of this request show that Ezra cannot possibly be considered the speaker of this prayer.[124] One might expect a request that this punishment be removed or lightened to follow, but it is only implicit. Vss. 33-37 represent a recognition that Israel's punishment is just, based on a renewed confession of the sins of the past. But this confession, contrary to the preceding recitation of Israel's history of rebellion, is general in nature. The prayer is concluded in vs. 37.

But the basic literary problem in the unit has not been resolved. This problem can be described briefly in terms of relationship between this chapter and its immediate context. There is general agreement among recent commentators that

[123] The Patriarchs have not previously been mentioned in the context of the rebellion tradition. On Ezek. 20:5, cf. Zimmerli, *Ezechiel*, p. 440. It is thus significant that this text does not represent an extension of the rebellion into the Patriarchal period but is a continuation of the hymnic style in vs. 6, a recitation of what Yahweh has done.

[124] Rudolph, *Esra und Nehemia*, pp. 156-57; Galling, *Die Bücher der Chronik*, p. 239.

chapters 9 and 10 belong together,[125] although some question has been raised about this position.[126] The problem lies instead in the transition from chapter 8 to chapter 9. We have noted above that the distinctions between the two chapters are sharp; the shift from rejoicing to repentance is in itself sufficient basis to suggest that chapter 9 cannot be considered the original continuation of chapter 8.[127] Since 9:2 apparently refers to a demand placed on the Israelites to separate from their Canaanite spouses, it is possible to conclude that this chapter represents the continuation of the initial introduction to the problem of mixed marriages in Ezra 10.[128] But Ezra 9 already provides a prayer of confession for that unit, a prayer attributed to Ezra. Moreover, the prayer in Ezra 9 specifically refers to the problem of mixed marriages (vss. 10 ff.), while the confession in Neh. 9 is concerned with quite different problems.[129] Ezra 10 would not therefore appear to be the most likely point of contact. Instead, it seems probable that the contact is to be defined with Noth in terms of unity between Neh. 8 and 9–10 in spite of the rough transition:

Der sachlich harte Übergang von Kap. 8 zu Kap. 9, der auf die Freude des Laubhüttenfestes nach zwei Tagen [cf. Lev. 23:27] unvermittelt die Busstimmung des Bewusstseins der Gesetzesübertretung folgen lässt, erklärt sich leicht daraus, dass Chr. von der auf den Neujahrstag (8:2) angesetzten Gesetzesverlesung durch Esra mit anschliessender Gesetzeserklärung durch die Leviten aus eigentlich auf die grosse Busse der Gemeinde hinzielte, zunächst aber die im siebenten Monat nun einmal fälligen Feiern des Neujahrstages und des Laubhüttenfestes, für die die Busstimmung nicht am Platze war, glaubte absolvieren lassen zu müssen, um dann freilich alsbald die nur zurückgehaltene Busse stattfinden zu lassen.[130]

[125] Rudolph, *Esra und Nehemia*, p. 155; Galling, *Die Bücher der Chronik*, p. 239; Noth, *Überlieferungsgeschichtliche Studien*, p. 149.

[126] Cf. Rudolph, *Esra und Nehemia*, p. 155, for a description and refutation of these questions.

[127] *Ibid.*, p. 153.

[128] *Ibid.*, pp. 156-57.

[129] Galling, *Die Bücher der Chronik*, p. 239.

[130] Noth, *Überlieferungsgeschichtliche Studien*, pp. 148-49.

The problem of authorship demands but brief attention. Noth has suggested that the whole chapter reflects the style and special interests of the Chronicler,[131] and we shall follow his lead. But regardless of the resolution of this question, it is clear that the text represents a late post-exilic period and thus gives us a firm grasp on the latest level of development in the Old Testament history of our tradition.

The recitation of the history begins in vss. 7-15 with an account of Yahweh's deeds of aid on behalf of Israel. The entire scope of tradition is represented here: Patriarchs, Exodus, Wilderness, Sinai, Conquest. Moreover, the individual traditions which form the basis of the murmuring appear here in a positive form—the event at the Sea, the gift of the manna and water, the command to take the land, even the commandment concerning the Sabbath (cf. Ezek. 20:12, *et al.*) .

In view of this full recitation of the positive tradition, the account of the murmuring is somewhat surprising, for there is no mention of the Sea or the food and water. The report of the rebellion begins in vs. 16, and vs. 16 offers our first problem. The juxtaposition of the pronoun הם and the noun ואבתינו is redundant, for the only antecedent for the pronoun is אבתינו in vs. 9. Moreover, vs. 16 is essentially duplicated in vs. 17aα by repetition of the hardening of the neck and the refusal of the people to hear. The normal procedure for explaining such repetitious style in the Pentateuch would be to suggest that two different sources are involved. But there is no further evidence to indicate two parallel accounts in this chapter. The most probable recourse is to consider this description of Israel's sin an exaggerated and overcrowded statement. This conclusion is supported by vs. 29; indeed, many of the same expressions are used in that verse.

What kind of difficulty is described by this lengthy diatribe? To harden one's neck and to refuse to hear and obey the commandments are parallel expressions. If the commandments recall the Sinai traditions, we might infer that the refusal to obey the commandments refers to the Golden Calf episode. Forgetting the wonders of Yahweh would also suggest that tradition. But we cannot be certain about this identification.

הזידו is also problematic. It is used in vs. 10 to describe Israel's treatment at the hand of the Egyptians. In vs. 16 it cannot be related to any specific event and must be considered a general description of Israel's rebellion. Indeed, the repetitious manner of describing the rebellion suggests that the emphasis in these verses is all-inclusive, a general statement that Israel was rebellious.

Vs. 17aβ, an allusion to the rejection of Moses and the desire to return to Egypt,[132] is the only explicit reference to the problem of the Exodus which appears outside the Pentateuch. It thus shows clearly that the murmuring tradition lies behind the recitation of Israel's sinful past in this particular ceremony. But it has nevertheless been greatly altered. The change is seen in the response to the desire to return to Egypt, for no reference is made to the sentence of death in the wilderness by a denial of the right to enter the land. Instead, vs. 17b emphasizes the long-suffering and forgiveness of Yahweh.

Vs. 18 notes that in spite of his gracious patience (אַף כִּי־), the people rebel again. The verse refers explicitly to the Golden Calf. That the plural form of the formula from Exod. 32 appears here in a singular form suggests that the conscious polemic against the northern calves is no longer present.[133] It is now simply assumed that the use of the Golden Calves was apostasy (cf. Ps. 106:19 ff.). Vs. 18b is again a general statement, perhaps reflecting the festival which was associated with the Calf. But even here, there is no reference to punishment. Quite the contrary, the explicit concern is to say that the rebellion did not result in punishment, especially an absolute rejection of the people in the wilderness (vs. 19a). This emphasis on Israel's sin and Yah-

[132] Cf. LXX: εἰς δουλείαν αὐτῶν ἐν Αἰγύπτῳ.
[133] LXX, Vul, and several MSS make the verb plural. But the pronoun here, contrary to Exod. 32:4, is singular: זה אלהיך.

weh's long-suffering must be related to the deuteronomistic pattern in Pss. 78 and 106.

Vss. 19b ff. return to a recitation of the events which constitute Yahweh's aid. The negative formulation of vss. 19b and 20b connects this recitation with the account of Israel's rebellion; Yahweh did not discontinue his aid when Israel sinned. But the tradition which is reflected here is the same positive report which has been encountered previously; indeed, the same events are mentioned in vss. 7-15. In vs. 22, the motif of the forty years is disassociated from the punishment for the murmuring and seems to be considered a part of the account of Yahweh's care for his people. This is in sharp contrast to the absence of reference to the forty-year period as a means of punishment in vs. 17 (cf. also vs. 19a).

Vss. 23-25 report the Conquest in a positive tone. Yahweh gave the people their inheritance, and they enjoyed the fertility of the land. Vss. 26 ff. reflect the deuteronomistic pattern of the period of the judges. It is at this point that we can most clearly see the distinction between that cycle of rebellion and forgiveness and the one associated with the rebellion of Israel in the wilderness, for in the period of the judges, Israel rebels, Yahweh gives them into the hands of their enemies, they suffer oppression and finally cry out for help, a judge is sent to save them, and they remain faithful for a short period before the process is repeated. In the murmuring tradition, even in this unit, the wilderness generation rebels (against the leaders) over the problem of the Exodus and Yahweh responds, either in punishment or, after Deuteronomy, in forgiveness. But the punishment and forgiveness are not complementary themes in the pre-deuteronomistic form of the tradition. Vs. 30 shows the final result of Israel's total history of rebellion to be the Exile. But the mercy of God is once again expressed, perhaps an allusion to the return of the exiles. Since the confession in vss. 33 ff. does not concern the wilderness period but is quite general in nature, we may drop it from our consideration.

The setting for this use of the rebellion tradition, as well as for the tradition of aid, is once again quite clearly defined.

The day of fasting and repentance points to a *Sitz-im-Leben* quite similar to the one which we met in Ps. 106. Moreover, the association between this chapter and chapter 8 suggests that the day of repentance is held in connection with the Feast of Tabernacles. Indeed, the reference to the reading of the law in 9:3 can be taken as a point of contact within this unit which binds this event of repentance to the reading of the law in Neh. 8. If this unity can be accepted, then we have further evidence to support our thesis that the rebellion tradition was associated with the Feast of Tabernacles. And in the light of that thesis, it is significant that both here and in Ps. 106, it is the people who recite the tradition.

This unit, then, represents the latest form of the rebellion tradition in the Old Testament. Its character is marked by the following points: No longer is the rebellion of the people made as broad as possible, with all details added to the basic outline of J (cf. Ps. 106). Instead, only a brief reference to the desire to return to Egypt is given, quite apart from its setting in the spy narrative. This is supplemented only by reference to the Golden Calf. In both cases, all traces of former polemic have been dropped. The only purpose is to emphasize the character of Yahweh's mercy. This brief account of the wilderness rebellion is joined with the apostasy after the conquest to show a combined reason for the Exile. But even this judgment is tempered with a recognition of and appeal to Yahweh's justice and mercy.

conclusion

This monograph has essentially two goals: (1) *to explore the nature and history* of the murmuring motif in the Wilderness traditions of the Old Testament, and (2) *to determine the significance* of that exploration for defining the relationship between positive and negative interpretations of the Wilderness traditions.

A form-critical study of the relevant texts reveals that the murmuring motif is not designed to express a disgruntled complaint. Quite the contrary, it describes an open rebellion. The act of murmuring poses a challenge to the object of the murmuring which, if unresolved, demands loss of office, due punishment, and perhaps death.

In the Wilderness theme the murmuring motif characterizes a basic tradition about the rebellion of Israel. The earliest occurrences of the tradition appear in J. But they do not seem to be a homogeneous part of the immediate context in which they stand. Since both the murmuring and the material in the context bear unmistakable signs of the style of J, the disunity cannot be attributed to a compounding of literary sources. Quite the contrary, it reflects a traditio-historical problem, a complex history of growth which shows the murmuring to be secondarily imposed on Israel's affirmations about Yahweh's aid in the wilderness.

The murmuring tradition, however, cannot be defined as an elaboration of seeds already present in the primary traditions. The primary traditions, unified by the confession of Yahweh's aid to Israel in the face of various crises posed by wilderness life, are apparently positive in their description of Israel's relationship with Yahweh. In contrast, the murmuring is completely negative, reversing the characteristic features of Yahweh's aid until they take on a negative form. The crises which motivate the gift of aid do not compose the principal content of the murmuring. They do nothing more than provide an immediate setting, a secondary connection between the murmuring tradition and its context.

There are no texts in the murmuring tradition which can be firmly attributed to E. Exod. 14:11-12 and 17:3-4 are difficult to control. The context for these verses is once again J, but contrary to the pattern mentioned above, the murmuring here shows no clear-cut stylistic markings, either of J or of E. It is thus impossible to assign them with certainty to either of the classical sources. Yet, despite this difficulty, it seems more adequate methodologically to suggest that the murmuring motif in these texts forms a part of the same source which is clearly present in the context. The disunity between these verses and their contexts can then be explained in the same manner suggested for the other J occurrences.

The J form of the murmuring is a unified and self-contained system which has the following character: (1) The whole people of Israel murmur against their leader Moses and, through him, Yahweh. (2) The murmuring consistently challenges Moses to explain his reasons for bringing the people out of Egypt. It is significant here that the murmuring never focuses its attention on the crises of hunger and thirst. (3) In a single climax the challenge becomes an overt movement to reject Moses (and Yahweh) and return to Egypt. This movement is in fact a rejection of the basic tenets of Israel's election. (4) Moreover, it is only in this climax that Yahweh's response to the murmuring plays an essential role.

The people who have murmured against Moses and Yahweh must die in the wilderness without seeing the promised land. This is a rejection of their rights as Yahweh's chosen people, the final principle of Israel's election theology. (5) The rejection is absolute. Neither this generation nor their off-spring shall have another chance to become the heirs to the election faith. The single exception lies in Caleb and his descendants. Since Caleb appears as the chief representative for the tribe of Judah, the exception gives the murmuring tradition a decidely pro-Judean flavor.

Vss. 67-72 in Ps. 78 reflect a form of the murmuring tradition which is strikingly similar to the one we have ascribed to the J source. And the climax of the murmuring here shows that the point of origin for this tradition lies in the conflict between the northern and the southern kingdoms. This conflict is clearly described in the polemic which Jeroboam issues against Jerusalem when he establishes his cult in Dan and Bethel. The weight of his argument is that only in the northern cult can the God of the Exodus be worshiped, and the implication of this position is that the northern cult enjoys the privileges of the election associated with the Exodus. The murmuring tradition, on the other hand, is the polemic directed against the northern cult. Its purpose is to argue that the northern rights to election were forfeited when the fathers in the wilderness rebelled. And in the place of that election, a new election faith is now enjoyed in Jerusalem through the Davidic heir.

The *Sitz-im-Leben* for the murmuring tradition is the cult in Jerusalem. The occasion for its repetition was the festival of election, the moment during the first day of the fall festival when the people remembered ritually the election of their king and the designation of their city as the invincible dwelling of Yahweh. The sophisticated nature of the tradition shows the stamp of priestly influence. Its origin presupposes the existence of the northern kingdom and should probably be placed as early as the beginning of the divided monarchy. But it is not impossible that it came into existence even earlier than this time.

Over against the uniform character of the murmuring described here, Num. 16 presents an example of murmuring which is quite different: (1) The murmuring is not a secondary motif in the tradition which composes the unit but the very substance of the unit. (2) It does not represent the rebellion of the whole people but only the rebellion of a few men or at most a small group of families. (3) The subject of the rebellion is not the same challenge of Moses' rights in the execution of the Exodus which was seen above, but the continuation of Moses' leadership in moving toward the promised land. It seems quite probable that this tradition goes back to an early account concerning scattered opposition to Moses' leadership, an account which has its roots in a kernel of historical event. We conclude, then, that the motif of rebellion was lifted from its setting in the Dathan-Abiram tradition, systematized and amplified along the lines indicated above, and attached to the tradition of Yahweh's gracious aid in the wilderness.

The most important theological reconstruction of the murmuring tradition can be attributed to deuteronomistic influence. The murmuring is still strikingly associated with the positive counterpart in the wilderness traditions, the tradition of aid. Its chief characteristics are as follows: (1) The specific lines of rebellion which give a concrete character to the murmuring are obscured. This change is effected primarily by an extension of the rebellion into all parts of the Wilderness theme, including traditions which were not affected by the J form of the murmuring. (2) There is no longer any sign of the polemic. The most probable explanation for this fact is that at this point in the history of Israel, the object of the polemic, the northern kingdom, had ceased to exist. (3) In the place of the specific interests and polemic in the original form of the murmuring, we find a broader theological interest. The content of the murmuring is not rebellion which threatens to reject Israel's leaders but a test or an unjustified complaint which depicts Israel's tragic lack of faith. (4) The events of rebellion and Yahweh's aid and patience are now ordered in a temporal sequence. Yahweh gives his aid *in spite of* Israel's rebellion, and Israel continues to rebel *in spite of* the aid. This gives the impression of a series of several completed instances of murmuring, each followed by an appropriate response from Yahweh. (5) The response is not always one of forgiveness and long-suffering. Yahweh reacts on occasion in anger, showing his intention to reject the people completely. This announcement of punishment is met by Moses with intercession, and as a result of the intercession, the people are spared.

The murmuring tradition in the post-exilic period follows the same tendencies of development which were already present in the deuteronomistic form of the tradition. These tendencies include a broadening to include more material under the stamp of the murmuring, the theological emphasis on the rebellion as a general violation of faith rather than an overt rejection of the leadership and reversal of the Exodus, the motif of Israel's sin *in spite of* the acts of grace seen by Israel, and the strong role of Yahweh's patience and forgiveness. But a significant new interpretation of the consequences of the murmuring appears here. The source of stimulation for this interpretation lies in the theological necessity to explain the tragedy of the Exile. Why had Yahweh allowed such an event to happen? The answer lay not only in the sins of the current generation but also in the rebellion of the fathers throughout Israel's history, especially the fathers of the wilderness period. These sins, and thus the murmuring tradition, became a part of a ritual of repentance enacted on one of the days of the fall festival.

The murmuring tradition dominates the negative interpretation of the wilderness and in fact presents the only fully developed tradition of rebellion involving *the whole people* during the period. Since the murmuring is considered secondary in the Pentateuch, and since the tradition of Yahweh's aid, which gives the murmuring its setting, is basically positive in character, we cannot conclude that the primary form of the wilderness traditions held Israel's rebellion and Yahweh's aid as mutually complementary themes; the alternation between long-suffering patience for Israel's demands and repeated acts of rebellion is the result of deuteronomistic re-interpretation of the murmuring tradition. The exact character and relationship of the tradition about Yahweh's aid in the wilderness and the judgment-purging motif from the Dathan-Abiram tradition must await further study.

appendix I: Exodus 5:21; 6:9

Exod. 5:21 and 6:9 allude to a negative relationship between Moses (and Aaron) and the Israelites while the people were still in Egypt. The first text (5:21) occurs in a chapter which, with the exception of vs. 4, can be attributed entirely to J. Vs. 4 is probably to be assigned to E because of its problematic relationship with vss. 6-7, and its use of the term מלך מצרים (cf. the use of מלך מצרים in Exod. 1:15, also E).[1]

The context for vs. 21 is as follows: As a result of Moses' attempt to persuade the Pharaoh to release the Israelites, the burden of work is increased. Eventually the burden becomes so heavy that the people cannot meet the requirements, and as a consequence the Israelite foremen are beaten. The foremen then appear before the Pharaoh to appeal for mercy, but are unsuccessful. When they leave the Pharaoh, they confront Moses, who is waiting for them outside the palace.[2] Vs. 21 constitutes their address to Moses. The form of the address is a call for judgment, the legal process which follows when the initial accusation (the form which ordinarily dominates the murmuring motif) has failed to produce results. The form, then, does not suggest that this text belongs to the murmuring tradition.

Furthermore, there is nothing in the content of the text to connect it with Israel's rebellion in the wilderness over the problem of the Exodus. The appeal for judgment is made to Yahweh and would thus have no connotation of rebellion against him. Rather,

---

[1] Noth, *Exodus*, pp. 51 ff.

[2] The problem posed by the foremen's direct appeal to the Pharaoh and the surprising fact that Moses is waiting for them when they leave will not be considered in detail. Cf. Noth, *Exodus*, p. 53.

this negative attitude seems to be a part of the tradition in which it stands. And in this context, it is clear that the complaint arises not from the desire to challenge Moses' authority in executing the Exodus but from his *failure* to do so. This is especially clear in vss. 22-23, when Moses carries the complaint to Yahweh. The form of the complaint is an accusation about the commission to go before the Pharaoh. The content is described by a Hiph'il perfect form of the verb רעע in conjunction with a Qal perfect form of שלח. But the precise character of the problem which elicits the accusation appears in vs. 23*b*: "You have not delivered your people." In this sense, this text does not reflect the rebellion tradition.

The second text (6:9) occurs in a chapter which is primarily P. The unit of P narrative which forms the context for this verse runs from vs. 2 through vs. 13.[3] The negative element is thus in immediate contact with the Exodus and Israel's election. Moses is commissioned to announce to the people that Yahweh has heard their cry and will now deliver them from their plight (vs. 5). This deliverance means that the people have been especially chosen by Yahweh to be his people (vss. 6-7) and the recipients of his promised land (vs. 8). But vs. 9 notes that when Moses announces these things to the people, they do not believe him (in contrast, cf. 4:31 [J]). Since this unbelief is directed toward the Exodus, the negative attitude here might be considered a part of the murmuring tradition (cf. Exod. 14:12). But there is no evidence that their unbelief promoted a rebellion against the idea of the Exodus or Moses' authority to execute the Exodus. Indeed, P seems to make some effort to excuse the unbelief by noting the circumstances which produced it (vs. 9*b*β). The people are impatient (thus, מקצר רוח). But they are not impatient with Moses' authority to effect the Exodus. The impatience is directed instead toward the fact that the deliverance which the people had long sought (vs. 5) had not been attained. And the impatience does not lead to rebellion but to despair. The unbelief could be interpreted to imply an accusation about the incompetency of Moses; it is possible that vss. 10-11 reflect some tendency in this direction.[4] But even if this is the case, the connection between this verse and the murmuring tradition would not be strong. There is simply no element of rebellion here.[5]

[3] *Ibid.*, pp. 58 ff. This section is probably P's version of Moses' call.
[4] *Ibid.*, p. 61.
[5] Zimmerli, *Ezechiel*, p. 446.

appendix II: Leviticus 10:1-7

As early as Gressmann, a relationship between Lev. 10:1-7 and Num. 16–17 had been noticed. That relationship is based on a similarity in setting, in the use of fire pans as censers before Yahweh, in the execution of the central figures, and even in the fact that both were steeped in a priestly spirit (cf. also LXX on Num. 17:2 with Lev. 10:1). The definition of this relationship ranges from Gressmann's rather extreme conclusion: "Die Vermutung mag daher erlaubt sein, dass die Erzählungen von Korah und Nadab-Abihu nicht nur Parallelen, sondern im letzten Grunde *identisch* sind, oder anders ausgedrückt, dass der Name Korahs den Nadabs und Abihus verdrängt hat," [1] to Noth's more conservative position: "Die Erzählung [Num. 16–17] ist inhaltlich verwandt mit dem Stück Lev. 10:1-7, das gleichfalls Pˢ ist." [2] The purpose of this appendix is to resolve two questions: (1) How can we define the relationship between these two units of tradition? (2) Does Lev. 10:1-7 have any bearing on our analysis of the murmuring tradition?

We have no quarrel with Noth's argument that the unit in Lev. 10:1-7 is an unbroken piece representing a late growth in the P narrative.[3] The identity of Nadab and Abihu is the initial problem. They are commonly listed as Aaron's sons (Exod. 6:23; 28:1; I Chr. 5:29). But their appearance in Exod. 24:1, 9 alongside Aaron without the expected designation as his sons suggests that they may have originally been connected in some way with the covenantal traditions associated with Sinai. Noth is probably cor-

[1] Gressmann, p. 263.
[2] Noth, *Überlieferungsgeschichte*, p. 19, n. 59.
[3] Martin Noth, *Das dritte Buch Mose: Leviticus, ATD* VI (Göttingen: Vandenhoeck & Ruprecht, 1962), 69-70.

rect in suggesting that they represent two priestly groups about which we now know very little.[4] But in Lev. 10:1-7 we may go a step further. Since the introduction to the unit begins with an unusual construction, thus בני־אהרן נדב ואביהוא, and thereby emphasizes an Aaronic connection, we may conclude that here they represent Aaronic groups within the priesthood. They would presumably have been involved in a controversy with other priestly groups, perhaps represented here by Misha'el and 'Elzaphan, or even by the other two sons of Aaron, 'Ele'azar (who is invited to bring the censers out of the place of execution in Num. 17:1) and 'Ithamar. But the circumstances of such a dispute cannot be determined.

Of more importance for our interest is the question concerning the nature of the violation which prompted the execution of the two. Unfortunately, the precise character of the violation is also obscure. But some general conclusions can nevertheless be drawn with relative certainty. First, we may assume that the violation did not lie in the lack of priestly right on the part of Nadab and Abihu to offer the incense; they are clearly associated with the Aaronic priesthood, and Aaron, as the chief priest, gives his tacit approval for their action. The difficulty is obviously connected with the fact that the offering contained "strange fire" (אש זרה). The definition of a "strange fire" is uncertain. Perhaps it is to be explained by reference to the fire from Yahweh in 9:24 (also a secondary passage in P). Since the fire on the altar was of heavenly origin, any fire not of the same origin would be prohibited.[5] But if this is the case, why would the priestly figures, Nadab and Abihu, not be aware of the stipulation? Vs. 1bβ gives us a somewhat different picture; the strange fire is qualified with the clause אשר לא צוה אתם. This would suggest that the difficulty lay not so much in taking the fire from the wrong source as in the very act of offering the fire and incense itself, i.e., the ritual. Yet bringing fire and incense before Yahweh in such a fire pan is not unknown elsewhere in the Old Testament (cf. e.g., Lev. 16:12). Thus we may assume that this event reflects some sort of misunderstanding or conflict over the procedure or rights involved in the ritual.

Second, as if in response to the execution by fire, Moses addresses a statement from Yahweh to Aaron (vs. 3). The use of the verb

---

[4] *Ibid.*, p. 69.
[5] *Ibid.*, p. 70.

קדש in the Niph'al in the context of a citation from Yahweh connotes Yahweh's reaction to events or objects which are opposed
to his sanctity (cf. Num. 20:13) and is clearly a reference to the
execution. The fact that this speech is addressed to Aaron and
Aaron's tacit approval of the event for which the two men were
executed suggest that Aaron may have been held partially responsible. And his silence only emphasizes his guilt.[6] The silence is more
strictly imposed on both Aaron and his remaining sons in vss.
6-7, for here they are denied the normal procedure of mourning.
The reason for this is associated not only with the death of the two
men but also with the responsibilities of the priestly office. Thus
the Aaronic priesthood, in the person of Nadab and Abihu as
well as Aaron himself, is set in a negative light.

What can we conclude, then, about the relationship between
this unit and the Korah tradition? First, it seems clear that Lev.
10:1-7 is not identical with the basic core of tradition in Num. 16
or even the application of that tradition to the problem of the
Levites and their rebellion against the Aaronites. The 250 followers
of Korah are executed for their part in a rebellion against their
leaders. There is no possibility that the cause of this execution
may be interpreted as a sacrifice of incense which was contrary
to what Yahweh had commanded. Indeed, the test by an incense
sacrifice was commanded by Moses and, through him, Yahweh.
The interpretation of the rebellion of Korah against Aaron puts
the Aaronic priesthood in a favorable light. Even the reference
to the bronze altar is designed to maintain the rights of the
Aaronic priesthood against any encroachment. The Korah tradition is thus in contrast to Lev. 10:1-7. If a conflict among priestly
groups is to be seen in Lev. 10:1-7, perhaps over the proper
execution of the sacrifice, or even the right of the priests to execute
the sacrifice, the unit is clearly anti-Aaronic in character.

But second, we can agree with Noth that the content of the two
is related. The point of the relationship seems to be closest in
Num. 17:1-5. To demonstrate the relationship, we could cite not
only the general similarities listed above but also the appointment
of certain priests (those who were held in favor?) to carry away
the remains left by the catastrophe (cf. Num. 17:2). The use of
the fire pans on the altar in the one and the presupposition that
the fire in Lev. 10 is related to the altar (ויקרבו לפני יהוה) suggest

[6] *Ibid.,* p. 71.

that the two reflect the same cultic situation.[7] Moreover, the similarity in the form of vs. 1 with Num. 16:6-7 suggests that this tradition and Num. 17:1-5 are dependent on a common regulation of priestly practice. But how are they related? It seems most likely that Lev. 10:1-7 and Num. 17:1-5 are two different developments from the same tradition, the one designed to carry a polemic against two particular groups within the Aaronic priesthood, and the other to show the origin of the bronze altar as a sign of the Aaronic right to the priesthood (cf. Num. 17:5; Lev. 10:1).

Since the violation seems to be a deviation in the procedure of sacrifice rather than a rebellion against the rights of the leaders, we may conclude that the unit in Lev. 10:1-7 does not have any bearing on the murmuring tradition.

[7] *Ibid.*, p. 70. Noth suggests that the original P narrative knew nothing of such an altar of incense.

appendix III: Numbers 12

Num. 12 also contributes to our understanding of the traditions related to the challenge of Moses' leadership and the problems in the Aaronic priesthood. A literary analysis of this chapter is difficult. Noth's suggestion that it may be taken as a secondary addition to the J source seems most adequate in the light of the indicative phenomena in the text. But the chapter nevertheless cannot be considered a unified body of secondary tradition.[1] This is shown first by the role of Aaron in relation to Miriam in vs. 1. The verb which governs the verse is a third *feminine singular* imperfect. It would not be impossible syntactically for such a form to precede a plural subject with a masculine member (cf. Gen. 33:7). But this is not the normal procedure. Moreover, the order of the two names which places Miriam first suggests that Aaron may be an addition (cf. vs. 4). In vs. 3, the problem shifts from the Cushite wife to the unique relationship between Moses and Yahweh. And here, the verb, still with Miriam and Aaron as the subjects, is a third *masculine plural* imperfect. Vs. 3 interrupts the normal progression with a parenthetical description of Moses' humility and should probably be considered a gloss. Vs. 4 provides the normal continuation of vs. 2, and here the order of the names places Miriam last. This unit continues without break through vs. 9. That vs. 9 is a part of this unit is indicated by the plural suffix, presupposing both Aaron and Miriam as the objects of Yahweh's anger.

Vs. 10 returns to the problem of Miriam's protest about the Cushite wife. It is significant confirmation of the secondary role of Aaron in this tradition that only Miriam must bear the punish-

---

[1] Noth, *Überlieferungsgeschichte*, p. 140, n. 359; cf. also p. 34, n. 120.

ment for the complaint. The intercession reflects both forms of the tradition. Vs. 11*b* is introduced with a vocative particle of entreaty (בי אדני) followed by a negative jussive (אל־נא תשת). This half-verse presupposes that *both* Aaron and Miriam have sinned and that *both* will be responsible for bearing the punishment (עלינו). Vs. 12 begins with a new negative jussive, but the petition is directed only toward the problem of Miriam's leprosy. It is possible that the two belong together at the original level of the tradition and that Aaron, though alluding to the punishment that both must bear, is nevertheless not punished by the disease because of his priesthood. It seems more likely, however, that the twofold nature of the intercession reflects the two forms of the tradition. Vss. 13-16 then relate the intercession on behalf of Miriam alone and her subsequent expulsion from the camp for seven days. The following division can therefore be observed: tradition of the Cushite wife, 1, 10, 12-16; tradition of Moses' peculiar relationship with Yahweh, 2 (3), 4-9, 11.

This unit seems to be a family saga. To be sure, Miriam cannot be considered originally to have been Moses' sister.[2] But Miriam's complaint about Moses' Cushite wife is uniquely personal.[3]

The expression דבר ב־ has been noted as an equivalent to the introductions in the rebellion tradition. But the two other occurrences are in later forms of the tradition and clearly depend on the context in which they appear for the connotation of rebellion. If Miriam's complaint is to be considered in this classification, the character of her rebellion is not clear. The *reason* for the complaint is Moses' marriage to a Cushite woman. But no direct quotation concerning this problem accompanies the narrative.

Yet even without the quotation, we may conclude that this unit does not reflect the same kind of resistance to Moses' authority which we see in the Dathan-Abiram story. It would be most difficult to see that kind of problem in a complaint about Moses' wife. Moreover, there is no indication of a response to the complaint from Moses or Yahweh. Instead, the narrative jumps from the complaint to the punishment. Vs. 10 presupposes that in the intervening jump, Miriam has been called to the tent of meeting. Aaron has accompanied her, but the relationship between the two at this point is unclear. The only insight into Aaron's role is that in response to the discovery of Miriam's leprosy, he appeals to

[2] Noth, *Exodus*, pp. 122-23.
[3] On the identity of this wife, cf. G. Gray, p. 121.

Moses for leniency. Moses intercedes before Yahweh, and the punishment is reduced to a mere seven days' exclusion from the community.

Whether this unit is indeed a family saga which reflects some actual problem regarding Moses' wife cannot be definitely determined. The whole tradition may well be a late development in the J material. But if this is our only conclusion, we have left unanswered the question of how a tradition about Miriam's complaint concerning Moses' wife might have arisen. The most obvious answer is that it is not related to any major traditional body concerning late rivalries, but *sui generis*. This conclusion could be pursued at some length. But for our purposes, it will suffice. It seems clear that this unit does not reflect the murmuring tradition.

The tradition in vss. 2, 4-9, 11 is dependent on the foregoing,[4] but the problem which it presents is somewhat different. In vs. 2, Miriam *and* Aaron complain together about Moses' exclusive rights for the mediation of Yahweh's word.[5] But the quotation in this verse does not represent a face-to-face challenge of Moses' rights. It is overheard by Yahweh, who then summons the three to the tent of meeting for judgment. The poem in vss. 6-8, Yahweh's response to the complaint, is a late exalted account of the unique relationship between Moses and Yahweh (cf. Exod. 33:11; Num. 11: 24 ff.; Deut. 34:9 ff.).[6] But contrary to other descriptions of this relationship (cf. Deut. 34:10), it does not describe Moses' position as prophetic. Instead, he is contrasted with the prophet who must receive his message in visions and dreams. The contrast is directed toward the two antagonists, as we see in the address in vs. 8b. In the case of Miriam the contrast is poignant, for Miriam is known elsewhere as a prophetess (Exod. 15:20). But Aaron is commonly held to be the prototype of at least a branch of the priesthood. Since this level of the tradition is distinguished from the primary level by shifting the focus of attention from Miriam alone to Miriam and Aaron, the emphasis of the change seems to lie on the inclusion of Aaron in the indictment.

If this is the case, does this text represent another example of the conflict in the priesthood? Is it possible that the supra-prophetic,

---

[4] Noth, *Überlieferungsgeschichte*, p. 140; cf. also vs. 8b.

[5] The *beth* in במשה and בנו must be interpreted as a *beth* of instrument: "Has Yahweh spoken only through Moses? Has he not also spoken through us?"

[6] Noth, *Überlieferungsgeschichte*, pp. 140 ff.

supra-Aaronic Moses is seen here as the representative for the Levitical position in that conflict? Judg. 18:30 reflects a priesthood which traced its lineage to Moses, while the context of this tradition shows that this lineage has a connection with the Levites (cf. the excursus on Exod. 32:25 ff.). If this is indeed the case, then the change which brings Aaron into the center of the tradition would reflect the same late period as the material about the conflict between the Levites and the Aaronic priesthood in Num. 16–17. In this case, however, the problem would be seen from the side of the Levites. And this dating certainly corresponds to the late character of the reflective description of Moses' office. Moreover, this level of the narrative would presuppose the tradition of the challenge of Moses' authority. Vs. 8*b* is doubtlessly to be seen in this light. That ‏דבר ב-‎ is found with this connotation only in late texts would support this thesis. But since nothing new is added to our understanding of the murmuring or even the challenge of Moses' rights in this text, we shall leave this suggestion as a tentative solution to the problem.

bibliography

A. Primary Sources

Colunga, R. P. A., and Turrado, L., eds. *Biblia Sacra juxta Vulgatam Clementinam*. 3rd ed.; *Biblioteca de Autores Cristianos;* Madrid: La Editorial Catolica, S. A., 1959.

von Gall, A. F., ed. *Der hebräische Pentateuch der Samaritaner*. Giessen: A. Töpelmann, 1918.

Kittel, R., ed. *Biblia Hebraica*. 7th ed.; Stuttgart: Privilegierte Württembergische Bibelanstalt, 1951.

Rahlfs, A., ed. *Septuaginta*. 2 vols.; 6th ed.; Stuttgart: Privilegierte Württembergische Bibelanstalt, n.d.

B. Books and Monographs

Auerbach, E. *Moses*. Amsterdam: G. J. A. Ruys, 1953.

Bauer, H., and Leander, P. *Historische Grammatik der hebräischen Sprache des Alten Testaments*. Halle: M. Niemeyer, 1922.

Begrich, J. *Studien zu Deuterojesaja. BWANT*, 4. Folge, Heft 25 (77); Stuttgart: W. Kohlhammer Verlag, 1938.

Beyerlin, W. *Herkunft und Geschichte der ältesten Sinaitraditionen*. Tübingen: J. C. B. Mohr (Paul Siebeck), 1961.

Boecker, Hans J. *Redeformen des Rechtslebens im Alten Testament. WMANT* XIV; Neukirchen-Vluyn: Neukirchener Verlag, 1964.

Bright, John. *The Authority of the Old Testament*. Nashville: Abingdon Press, 1967.

Brockelmann, C. *Grundriss der vergleichenden Grammatik der semitischen Sprachen*. Berlin: Reuther und Reichard, 1908.

Brown, F., Driver, S. R., and Briggs, C. A., eds. *A Hebrew and English Lexicon of the Old Testament*. 3rd ed., Oxford: The Clarendon Press, 1957.

265

Buber, M. *Moses.* Oxford: East and West Library, 1946.

Budde, K. *Das Lied Moses, Deut. 32.* Tübingen: J. C. B. Mohr (Paul Siebeck), 1920.

Childs, B. S. *Memory and Tradition in Israel.* SBT XXXVII; London: SCM Press, 1962.

Daube, D. *The Exodus Pattern in the Bible. All Souls Studies* II; London: Faber and Faber, 1963.

Driver, S. R. *An Introduction to the Literature of the Old Testament.* Meridian Library Edition; New York: Meridian Books, The World Publishing Co., 1960.

Eerdmans, B. D. *The Composition of Numbers. Oudtestamentische Studiën,* Vol. VI; Leiden: E. J. Brill, 1949.

Eissfeldt, O. *Hexateuch-Synopse.* Leipzig: J. C. Hinrichs Verlag, 1922.

————. *Das Lied Moses, Deuteronomium 32:1-43, und das Lehrgedicht Asaphs, Psalm 78, samt einer Analyse der Umgebung des Mose-Liedes. Berichte über die Verhandlungen der sächsischen Akademie der Wissenschaften zu Leipzig,* Phil.-Hist. Klasse, Bd. CIV, Heft 5; Berlin: Akademie Verlag, 1958.

————. *The Old Testament, an Introduction.* tr. Peter Ackroyd. New York: Harper & Row, 1965.

Fohrer, G. *Überlieferung und Geschichte des Exodus.* BZAW XCI; Berlin: Verlag Afred Töpelmann, 1964.

Galling, K. *Die Erwählungstraditionen Israels.* BZAW XLVIII; Giessen: Verlag Alfred Töpelmann, 1928.

Gesenius, W. *Hebräisches und aramäisches Handwörterbuch,* ed. Frants Buhl, *et al.* 14th ed., rev.; Leipzig: F. C. W. Vogel, 1921.

Gesenius' Hebrew Grammar. ed. E. Kautzsch. 2nd English ed., rev. by A. E. Cowley; Oxford: The Clarendon Press, 1910.

Gressmann, H. *Die Anfänge Israels.* 2nd ed., rev. *SAT* I/2; Göttingen: Vandenhoeck & Ruprecht, 1922.

————. *Mose und seine Zeit, ein Kommentar zu den Mose-Sagen. FRLANT* XVIII; Göttingen: Vandenhoeck & Ruprecht, 1913.

Gunneweg, A. H. J. *Leviten und Priester, Hauptlinien der Traditionsbildung und Geschichte des israelitisch-jüdischen Kultpersonals. FRLANT* LXXXIX; Göttingen: Vandenhoeck & Ruprecht, 1965.

Haldar, A. *The Notion of the Desert in Sumero-Accadian and West-Semitic Religions. Uppsala Universitets Arsskrift* III; Uppsala: A.-B. Lundequistska Bokhandeln, 1950.

Jean, C. F. and Hoftijzer, J. *Dictionnaire des inscriptions sémitiques de l'ouest.* Leiden: E. J. Brill, 1965.

Jolles, A. *Einfache Formen.* Tübingen: Max Niemeyer Verlag, 1958.

Knierim, R. *Die Hauptbegriffe für Sünde im Alten Testament.* Gerd Mohn: Gütersloher Verlagshaus, 1965.

Koch, K. *Die Priesterschrift von Exodus 25 bis Leviticus 16, eine überlieferungsgeschichtliche und literarkritische Untersuchung.* FRLANT LXXI; Göttingen: Vandenhoeck & Ruprecht, 1959.

Köhler, L. *Deuterojesaja stilkritisch untersucht.* BZAW XXXVII; Giessen: Verlag A. Töpelmann, 1923.

──────. *Hebrew Man.* Tr. Peter Ackroyd. London: SCM Press, 1956.

Köhler, L. and Baumgartner, W. *Lexicon in Veteris Testamenti Libros.* Leiden: E. J. Brill, 1953.

Kraus, H.-J. *Gottesdienst in Israel: Grundriss einer Geschichte des alttestamentlichen Gottesdienstes.* 2nd ed., rev.; München: Chr. Kaiser Verlag, 1962.

──────. *Die Königsherrschaft Gottes im Alten Testament. Beiträge zur historischen Theologie* XIII; Tübingen: J. C. B. Mohr (Paul Siebeck), 1951.

Lauha, A. *Die Geschichtsmotive in den alttestamentlichen Psalmen.* Helsinki: Druckerei der finnischen Literaturgesellschaft, 1945.

Mauser, U. W. *Christ in the Wilderness. SBT* XXXIX; London: SCM Press, 1963.

Mendenhall, G. E. *Law and Covenant in Israel and the Ancient Near East,* reprinted from *BA* XVII/2 (May, 1954), 26-46, and XVII/3 (Sept., 1954), 49-76, by the Biblical Colloquium. Pittsburgh, 1955.

Mowinckel, S. *Psalmenstudien.* 6 vols.; Kristiania (Oslo): Jacob Dybwad, 1921.

──────. *The Psalms in Israel's Worship.* Tr. D. R. Ap-Thomas. 2 vols.; Nashville: Abingdon Press, 1962.

Newman, M. L. *The People of the Covenant, a Study of Israel from Moses to the Monarchy.* Nashville: Abingdon Press, 1962.

Nöldeke, T. *Beiträge zur semitischen Sprachwissenschaft.* Strassburg: Karl J. Trübner, 1904.

Noth, M. *The History of Israel.* Tr. Peter Ackroyd. 2nd ed., rev.; New York: Harper & Row, 1960.

──────. *Die israelitischen Personennamen im Rahmen der gemein-semitischen Namengebung. BWANT,* 3 Folge, Heft 10 (46); Stuttgart: W. Kohlhammer Verlag, 1928.

──────. *Das System der zwölf Stämme Israels. BWANT,* 4 Folge, Heft 1 (51); Stuttgart: W. Kohlhammer Verlag, 1930.

──────. *Überlieferungsgeschichte des Pentateuch.* Stuttgart: W. Kohlhammer Verlag, 1948.

──────. *Überlieferungsgeschichtliche Studien.* 2nd ed.; Tübingen: Max Niemeyer Verlag, 1957.

Osswald, E. *Das Bild des Mose in der kritischen alttestamentlichen Wissenschaft seit Julius Wellhausen. Theologische Arbeiten* XVIII; Berlin: Evangelische Verlagsanstalt, 1962.

Pedersen, J. *Israel, Its Life and Culture.* 4 vols.; 2nd ed.; London: Oxford University Press, 1959.

Pope, M. *El in the Ugaritic Texts. VT Sup.* ii; Leiden: E. J. Brill, 1955.

von Rad, G. *Das formgeschichtliche Problem des Hexateuch. BWANT,* Folge 4, Heft 26; Stuttgart: W. Kohlhammer Verlag, 1938.

————. *Das Gottesvolk im Deuteronomium. BWANT,* Folge 3, Heft 11 (47); Stuttgart: W. Kohlhammer Verlag, 1929.

————. *Der heilige Krieg im alten Israel. ATANT* XX; Zürich: Zwingli-Verlag, 1951.

————. *Moses. World Christian Books* XXXII; London: Lutterworth Press, 1960.

————. *Old Testament Theology.* Tr. D. M. G. Stalker. 2 vols; New York: Harper & Row, 1962.

————. *Die Priesterschrift im Hexateuch. BWANT,* Folge 4, Heft 13 (63); Stuttgart: W. Kohlhammer Verlag, 1934.

————. *Studies in Deuteronomy.* Tr. David Stalker. *SBT* IX; London: SCM Press, 1953.

Reventlow, H. *Wächter über Israel, Ezechiel und seine Tradition. BZAW* LXXXII; Berlin: Alfred Töpelmann, 1962.

Rowley, H. H. *The Biblical Doctrine of Election.* London: Lutterworth Press, 1950.

Rudolph, W. *Der "Elohist" von Exodus bis Josua. BZAW* LXVIII; Berlin: Alfred Töpelmann, 1938.

Smend, R. *Das Mosebild von Heinrich Ewald bis Martin Noth. Beiträge zur Geschichte der biblischen Exegese* III; Tübingen: J. C. B. Mohr (Paul Siebeck), 1959.

Torrey, C. C. *The Composition and Historical Value of Ezra-Nehemiah. BZAW* II; Giessen: J. Ricker, 1896.

Volz, P. *Mose und sein Werk.* 2nd ed., rev.; Tübingen: J. C. B. Mohr (Paul Siebeck), 1932.

Vriezen, T. *Die Erwählung Israels nach dem Alten Testament. ATANT* XXIV; Zürich: Zwingli-Verlag, 1953.

von Waldow, E. *Der traditionsgeschichtliche Hintergrund der prophetischen Gerichtsreden. BZAW* LXXXV; Berlin: Alfred Töpelmann, 1963.

Weiser, A. *The Old Testament: Its Formation and Development.* Tr. Dorothea M. Barton. New York: Association Press, 1961.

Wellhausen, J. *Die Composition des Hexateuchs und der historischen Bücher des Alten Testaments.* 4th ed.; Berlin: Walter de Gruyter & Co., 1963.

Widengren, G. *Sakrales Königtum im Alten Testament und im Judentum.* Stuttgart: W. Kohlhammer Verlag, 1955.

Wildberger, H. *Jahwes Eigentumsvolk: eine Studie zur Traditionsgeschichte und Theologie des Erwählungsgedankens. ATANT* XXXVII; Zürich: Zwingli-Verlag, 1960.

Winnet, F. V. *The Mosaic Tradition.* Toronto: University of Toronto Press, 1949.

Würthwein, E. *The Text of the Old Testament.* Tr. Peter Ackroyd. Oxford: Basil Blackwell, 1957.

Zimmerli, W. *Erkenntnis Gottes nach dem Buche Ezechiel; eine theologische Studie. ATANT* XXVII; Zürich: Zwingli-Verlag, 1954.

Zimmerli, W. and Jeremias, J. *The Servant of God. SBT* XX; rev. ed. London: SCM Press, 1965.

C. *Commentaries*

Baentsch, B. *Exodus-Leviticus-Numeri. HKAT* I/2; Göttingen: Vandenhoeck & Ruprecht, 1903.

Baethgen, F. *Die Psalmen.* 3rd ed., rev., *HKAT* II/2; Göttingen: Vandenhoeck & Ruprecht, 1904.

Beer, G. *Exodus,* mit einem Beitrag von Kurt Galling. *HAT* III; Tübingen: J. C. B. Mohr (Paul Siebeck), 1939.

Briggs, Emilie. *The Book of Psalms.* 5th printing, *ICC;* Edinburgh: T and T Clark, 1952.

Cooke, G. A. *The Book of Ezekiel.* 2nd printing, *ICC;* Edinburgh: T and T Clark, 1951.

Driver, S. R. *Deuteronomy.* 3rd ed., *ICC;* Edinburgh: T and T Clark, 1902.

Duhm, B. *Die Psalmen.* 2nd ed., rev.; *KHAT* XIV; Tübingen: J. C. B. Mohr (Paul Siebeck), 1922.

Fohrer, G. *Ezechiel,* mit einem Beitrag von Kurt Galling. *HAT* XIII; Tübingen: J. C. B. Mohr (Paul Siebeck), 1955.

Galling, K. *Die Bücher der Chronik, Esra, Nehemia. ATD* XII; Göttingen: Vandenhoeck & Ruprecht, 1954.

Gray, G. B. *Numbers. ICC;* Edinburgh: T and T Clark, 1903.

Gray, J. *I and II Kings, a Commentary. OTL;* Philadelphia: The Westminster Press, 1963.

Gunkel, H. *Die Psalmen.* 4th ed., *HKAT* II/2; Göttingen: Vandenhoeck & Ruprecht, 1926.

Heinisch, P. *Das Buch Exodus. HSAT* I/2; Bonn: Peter Hanstein Verlagsbuchhandlung, 1934.

―――. *Das Buch Numeri. HSAT* II/1; Bonn: Peter Hanstein Verlagsbuchhandlung, 1936.

Holzinger, H. *Exodus. KHAT* II; Tübingen: J. C. B. Mohr (Paul Siebeck), 1900.

―――. *Numeri KHAT* IV; Tübingen: J. C. B. Mohr (Paul Siebeck), 1903.

Kittel, R. *Die Psalmen.* 2nd ed., *KAT* XIII; Leipzig: A. Deichertsche Verlagsbuchhandlung, 1914.

Kraus, H-J. *Psalmen.* 2 vols.; 2nd ed.; *BKAT* XV; Neukirchen, Kreis Moers: Neukirchener Verlag, 1961.

Noth, M. *Das Buch Josua. HAT* VII; Tübingen: J. C. B. Mohr (Paul Siebeck) , 1953.

———. *Exodus, a Commentary.* Tr. J. S. Bowden. *OTL;* Philadelphia: The Westminster Press, 1962.

———. *Das dritte Buch Mose: Leviticus. ATD* VI; Göttingen: Vandenhoeck & Ruprecht, 1962.

———. *Das vierte Buch Mose: Numeri. ATD* VII; Göttingen: Vandenhoeck & Ruprecht, 1966.

von Rad, G. *Das fünfte Buch Mose: Deuteronomium. ATD* VIII; Göttingen: Vandenhoeck & Ruprecht, 1964.

———. *Genesis, a Commentary.* Tr. John H. Marks. *OTL;* Philadelphia: The Westminster Press, 1961.

Rudolph, W. *Esra und Nehemia. HAT* XX; Tübingen: J. C. B. Mohr (Paul Siebeck) , 1949.

Schmidt, H. *Die grossen Propheten,* mit Einleitungen versehen von H. Gunkel. *SAT* II/2; Göttingen: Vandenhoeck & Ruprecht, 1915.

———. *Die Psalmen. HAT* XV; Tübingen: J. C. B. Mohr (Paul Siebeck) , 1934.

Steuernagel, C. *Das Deuteronomium.* 2nd ed., rev.; *HKAT* I/3; Göttingen: Vandenhoeck & Ruprecht, 1923.

Strack, H. *Die Bücher Genesis, Exodus, Leviticus, und Numeri. Kurzgefasster Kommentar zu den heiligen Schriften Alten und Neuen Testamentes,* I. München: C. H. Beck'sche Verlagsbuchhandlung, 1894.

Weiser, A. *The Psalms, a Commentary.* Tr. Herbert Hartwell. *OTL;* Philadelphia: The Westminster Press, 1962.

Wolff, H. W. *Hosea. BKAT* XIV/1; Neukirchen, Kreis Moers: Neukirchener Verlag, 1961.

Zimmerli, W. *Ezechiel. BKAT* XIII; Neukirchen, Kreis Moers: Neukirchener Verlag, 1956- .

D. Dissertations

Ahlemann, F. *Die Esra-Quelle, eine literarische Untersuchung.* Unpublished dissertation, Greifswald, 1941.

Bach, R. *Die Erwählung Israels in der Wüste.* Unpublished dissertation, Bonn, 1951.

Mallau, H.-H. *Die theologische Bedeutung der Wüste im Alten Testament.* Unpublished dissertation, Kiel, 1963.

Riemann, P. *Desert and Return to Desert in Pre-Exilic Prophets.* Unpublished dissertation, Harvard, 1964.

Schmid, H. *Jahwe und die Kulttraditionen von Jerusalem.* Unpublished dissertation, Mainz, 1955.

Schnutenhaus, F. *Die Entstehung der Mosetraditionen.* Unpublished dissertation, Heidelberg, 1958.

Tuck, R. *Election in the Old Testament.* Unpublished dissertation, Boston, 1939.

Wiebe, W. *Die Wüstenzeit als Typus der messianischen Heilszeit.* Unpublished dissertation, Göttingen, 1939.

E. Articles

Aberbach, M. and Smolar, L. "Aaron, Jeroboam, and the Golden Calves," *JBL* LXXXVI (1967), 129-40.

Albright, W. F. "Some Remarks on the Song of Moses in Dt. 32," *VT* IX (1959), 339-46.

Alt, A. "Das Königtum in den Reichen Israel und Juda," *VT* I (1951), 2-22.

Anderson, R. T. "The Role of the Desert in Israelite Thought," *Journal of Bible and Religion* XXVII (1959), 41-44.

Arden, E. "How Moses Failed God," *JBL* LXXVI (1957), 50-52.

Barth, Chr. "Zur Bedeutung der Wüstentradition," *Volume du Congrès Genève; VT Sup.* xv; Leiden: E. J. Brill, 1966, 14-23.

Bentzen, A. "Die Schwindsucht in Ps. 106:15," *ZAW* LVII (1939), 152.

Berry, G. "Priests and Levites," *JBL* XLII (1923), 227-38.

Coats, G. W. "The Traditio-Historical Character of the Reed Sea Motif," *VT* XVII (1967), 253-65.

Cross, F. M. and Freedman, D. N. "The Blessing of Moses," *JBL* LXVII (1948), 191-210.

Della Vida, G. L. "El 'Elyon in Genesis 14:18-20," *JBL* LXIII (1944), 1-9.

Eichrodt, W. "Der Sabbat bei Hesekiel. Ein Beitrag zur Nachgeschichte des Prophetentextes," *Lex Tua Veritas; Festschrift für Hubert Junker.* V. Heinrich Gross and F. Mussner, eds. Trier: Paulinus Verlag, 1961, pp. 65-74.

Eissfeldt, O. "El and Yahweh," *JSS* I (1956), 25-37.

Flight, J. W. "The Nomadic Idea and Ideal in the Old Testament," *JBL* XLII (1923), 158-226.

Fohrer, G. "Der Vertrag zwischen König und Volk in Israel," *ZAW* LXXI (1959), 1-22.

Funk, R. W. "The Wilderness," *JBL* LXXVIII (1959), 205-14.

Gemser, B. "The Rib- or Controversy-Pattern in Hebrew Mentality," *Wisdom in Israel and in the Ancient Near East.* M. Noth and D. W. Thomas, eds. *VT Sup.* iii; Leiden: E. J. Brill, 1960, 120-37.

Gillischewski, E. "Die Geschichte von der 'Rotte Korah,' Num. 16," *Archiv für Orientforschung* III (1926), 114-18.

Gordis, R. "Critical Notes on the Blessing of Moses," *JTS* XXXIV (1933), 390-92.

Gray, J. "The Desert Sojourn of the Hebrew and the Sinai-Horeb Tradition," *VT* IV (1954), 148-54.

Greenberg, M. "A New Approach to the History of the Israelite Priesthood," *JAOS* LXX (1950), 41-46.

Griffiths, J. "The 'Golden Calf,' Exod. 32," *Expository Times* LVI (1944-45), 110.

Gunneweg, A. H. J. "Sinaibund und Davidbund," *VT* X (1960), 335-41.

Haran, M. "The Nature of the ''ōhel mō'edh' in Pentateuchal Sources," *JSS* V (1960), 50-65.

Harrelson, W. "Guidance in the Wilderness," *Interpretation* XIII (1959), 24-36.

Herrmann, S. "Bemerkungen zur Inschrift des Königs Kilamuwa von Sengirli," *OLZ* VII (1953), 295-97.

Hertzberg, H. W. "Sind die Propheten Fürbitter?" *Tradition und Situation, Studien zur alttestamentlichen Prophetie.* Ernst Würthwein and Otto Kaiser, eds. Göttingen: Vandenhoeck & Ruprecht, 1963, pp. 63-74.

Hort, G. "The Death of Qorah," *Australian Biblical Review* VII (1959), 2-26.

Huffmon, H. B. "The Covenant Lawsuit in the Prophets," *JBL* LXXVIII (1959), 285-95.

Junker, H. "Die Entstehungszeit des Ps. 78 und des Deuteronomiums," *Bib* XXXIV (1953), 487-500.

————. "Traditionsgeschichtliche Untersuchung über die Erzählung von der Anbetung des Goldenen Kalbes (Ex. 32)," *Trierer Theologische Zeitschrift* LX (1951), 232-42.

Kapelrud, A. S. "How Tradition Failed Moses," *JBL* LXXVI (1957), 242.

Kennett, R. H. "The Origin of the Aaronite Priesthood," *JTS* VI (1905), 161-86.

Koch, K. "Zur Geschichte der Erwählungsvorstellung in Israel," *ZAW* LXVII (1955), 205-26.

Lauha, A. "Das Schilfmeermotiv im Alten Testament," *VT Sup.* IX; Leiden: E. J. Brill, 1963, 32-46.

Lehming, S. "Massa und Meriba," *ZAW* LXXIII (1961), 71-77.

————. "Versuch zu Ex. XXXII," *VT* X (1960), 16-50.

————. "Versuch zu Num. 16," *ZAW* LXXIV (1962), 291-321.

Lewy, I. "The Story of the Golden Calf Reanalysed," *VT* IX (1959), 318-32.

de Liagre-Böhl, F. M. T. "Missions- und Erwählungsgedanke in Alt-Israel," *Festschrift Alfred Bertholet zum 80 Geburtstag*. Ed., Walter Baumgartner, *et al.* Tübingen: J. C. B. Mohr (Paul Siebeck), 1950, pp. 77-96.

Linder, J. "Das Lied des Moses Dt. 32" *Zeitschrift für katholische Theologie* XLIX (1924), 374-406.

Liver, J. "Korah, Dathan and Abiram," *Studies in the Bible.* Ed., Chaim Rabin. *Scripta Hierosolymitana*, Vol. VIII; Jerusalem: The Magnes Press, The Hebrew University, 1961, 189-217.

Lohfink, N. "Darstellungskunst und Theologie in Dtn. 1, 6–3, 29," *Bib* XLI (1960), 105-34.

Marti, K. "Zu Dtn. 32:10," *ZAW* XXXIX (1921), 315-16.

Meek, T. J. "Aaronites and Zadokites," *AJSL* XLV (1929), 149-66.

————. "Moses and the Levites," *AJSL* LVI (1939), 113-20.

————. "Some Emendations in the Old Testament," *JBL* XLVIII (1929), 162-68.

Möhlenbrink, K. "Die levitischen Überlieferungen des Alten Testaments," *ZAW* LII (1934), 184-231.

Morgenstern, J. "A Chapter in the History of the High Priesthood," *AJSL* LV (1938), 1-24, 360-77.

————. "The Festival of Jeroboam I," *JBL* LXXXIII (1964), 109-18.

McCarthy, D. J. "Plagues and Sea of Reeds: Exodus 5–14," *JBL* LXXXV (1966), 137-58.

North, F. "Aaron's Rise in Prestige," *ZAW* LXVI (1954), 191-99.

Noth, M. "Israelitische Stämme zwischen Ammon und Moab," *ZAW* LX (1944), 11-57.

————. "Num. 21 als Glied der 'Hexateuch' Erzählung," *ZAW* LVIII (1940/41), 161-89.

————. "Zur Anfertigung des 'Goldenen Kalbes,'" *VT* IX (1959), 419-22.

von Rad, G. "Die falschen Propheten," *ZAW* LI (1933), 109-20.

————. "Die levitische Predigt in den Büchern der Chronik," *Festschrift Otto Procksch*. Ed., Albrecht Alt, *et al.* Leipzig: A. Deichert'sche Verlagsbuchhandlung, 1934, pp. 113-24.

Reventlow, H. "Die Völker als Zeugen Jahwes bei Ezechiel," *ZAW* LXXI (1959), 33-43.

Richter, G. "Die Einheitlichkeit der Geschichte von der Rotte Korah," *ZAW* XXXIX (1921), 123-37.

————. "Zum Text von Dtn. 32:10," *ZAW* LII (1934), 77-78.

Robinson, T. H. "Der Durchzug durch das Rote Meer," *ZAW* LI (1933), 170-73.

Rost, L. "Sinaibund und Davidsbund," *Theologische Literaturzeitung* LXXII (1947), 129-34.

Rothstein, J. W. "Psalm 78, ein Zeuge für die jahwistische Gestalt der Exodus-Tradition und seine Abfassung," *Zeitschrift für wissenschaftliche Theologie* XLIII (1900), 532-85.

Rowley, H. H. "Early Levite History and the Question of the Exodus," *JNES* III (1944), 73-78.

———. "Melchizedek and Zadok (Gen. 14. and Ps. 110)," *Festschrift Alfred Bertholet zum 80. Geburtstag*. Ed., Walter Baumgartner, *et al.* Tübingen: J. C. B. Mohr (Paul Siebeck), 1950, pp. 461-72.

———. "Zadok and Nehushtan," *JBL* LVIII (1939), 113-41.

Rudolph, W. "Der Aufbau von Ex. 19–34," *Werden und Wesen des Alten Testaments*. Ed., P. Volz, *et al. BZAW* LXVI; Berlin: Verlag Alfred Töpelmann, 1936, 41-48.

———. "Zum Texte des Buches Numeri," *ZAW* LII (1934), 113-20.

Schildenberger, J. "Psalm 78 (77) und die Pentateuchquellen," *Lex Tua Veritas; Festschrift für Hubert Junker*. V. Heinrich Gross and F. Mussner, eds. Trier: Paulinus Verlag, 1961, pp. 231-56.

Schmid, H. "Jahwe und die Kulttraditionen von Jerusalem," *ZAW* LXVII (1955), 168-97.

Sellin, E. "Wann wurde das Moselied Dtn. 32 gedichtet?" *ZAW* XLIII (1925), 161-73.

Skehan, P. W. "A Fragment of the 'Song of Moses' (Dt. 32) from Qumran," *BASOR* CXXXVI (1954), 12-15.

———. "The Structure of the Song of Moses in Dt.," *CBQ* XIII (1951), 153-63.

Stendahl, K. "Implications of Form-Criticism and Tradition-Criticism for Biblical Interpretation," *JBL* LXXVII (1958), 33-38.

Talmon, S. "The 'Desert Motif' in the Bible and in Qumran Literature," *Biblical Motifs, Origins and Transformations*. Ed., A. Altmann. Cambridge, Mass.: Harvard University Press, 1966, pp. 31-63.

Tunyogi, A. C. "The Rebellions of Israel," *JBL* LXXXI (1962), 385-90.

Wagner, S. "Die Kundschaftergeschichten im Alten Testament," *ZAW* LXXVI (1964), 255-69.

Waterman, L. "Some Determining Factors in the Northward Progress of Levi," *JAOS* LVII (1937), 375-80.

Watts, J. "The People of God, a Study of the Doctrine in the Pentateuch," *Evangelische Theologie* LXVII/8 (1956), 232-37.

Westphal, G. "Aaron und die Aaroniden," *ZAW* XXVI (1906), 201-30.

Westermann, C. "Arten der Erzählung in der Genesis," *Forschung am Alten Testament*. München: Chr. Kaiser Verlag, 1964, pp. 9-91.

Wijngaards, J. "הוצא and העלה, a Twofold Approach to the Exodus," *VT* XV (1965), 91-102.

Wolff, H. W. "Das Thema 'Umkehr' in der alttestamentlichen Prophetie," *ZThK* XLVIII (1951), 129-48.

Wright, G. E. "The Lawsuit of God: A Form-Critical Study of Dt. 32," *Israel's Prophetic Heritage*. B. Anderson and W. Harrelson, eds. New York: Harper & Row, 1962, pp. 26-67.

————. "The Levites in Deuteronomy," *VT* IV (1954), 325-30.

Würthwein, E. "Der Ursprung der prophetischen Gerichtsrede," *ZThK* XLIX (1952), 1-16.

Zimmerli, W. "Das Gotteswort des Ezechiel," *ZThK* XLVIII (1951), 249-62.

————. "Ich bin Jahwe," *Geschichte und Altes Testament*. Ed., M. Noth, *Beiträge zur historischen Theologie* XVI; Tübingen: J. C. B. Mohr (Paul Siebeck), 1953, 179-209.

————. "Das Wort des göttlichen Selbsterweises (Erweiswort), eine prophetische Gattung," *Mélanges Bibliques rédigés en l'honneur de André Robert. Travaux de l'institut catholique de Paris* IV; Paris: Bloud et Gay, 1957, 154-64.

index of scripture

*Numbers in italic are references
to footnotes*

index of persons and subjects

*Numbers in italic are references
to footnotes*